Fodor

Euro

Parts of this book appear in
Fodor's Paris

Fodor's Travel Publications, Inc.
New York • Toronto • London • Sydney • Auckland

ISBN 0-679-02290-2

Fodor's Euro Disney

Editor: Paula Consolo
Area Editors: Simon Hewitt, Kate Sekules
Editorial Contributors: Bob Blake, Karen Cure, Caroline Liou, Larry Peterson
Creative Director: Fabrizio La Rocca
Cartographer: David Lindroth
Illustrator: Karl Tanner
Cover Photograph: Jacques Cochin/Image Bank

Design: Vignelli Associates

Special Sales

Fodor's Travel Publications are available at special discounts for bulk purchases (100 copies or more) for sales promotions or premiums. Special editions, including personalized covers, excerpts of existing guides, and corporate imprints, can be created in large quantities for special needs. For more information, write to Special Marketing, Fodor's Travel Publications, 201 E. 50th Street, New York, NY 10022. Inquiries from Canada should be sent to Random House of Canada, Ltd., Marketing Department, 1265 Aerowood Drive, Mississauga, Ontario L4W 1B9. Inquiries from the United Kingdom should be sent to Fodor's Travel Publications, 20 Vauxhall Bridge Road, London, England SW1V 2SA.

Contents

Maps

Foreword

While every care has been taken to ensure the accuracy of the information in this guide, the passage of time will always bring change, and consequently the publisher cannot accept responsibility for errors that may occur.

All prices and opening times quoted here are based on information supplied to us at press time. Hours and admission fees may change, however, and the prudent traveler will avoid inconvenience by calling ahead.

Fodor's wants to hear about your travel experiences, both pleasant and unpleasant. When a hotel or restaurant fails to live up to its billing, let us know and we will investigate the complaint and revise our entries where the facts warrant it.

Send your letters to the editors of Fodor's Travel Publications, 201 E. 50th Street, New York, NY 10022.

Highlights and Fodor's Choice

Highlights

Before April 22, 1992, everyone was wondering how on earth wholesome, all-American, sentimental Disney would go down in cynical, sophisticated France. Would the staff gush sufficiently? Would cold and rain dampen spirits? Would there be enough smiling? Then the Euro Disneyland gates opened, and Europe discovered that nobody, but nobody, is immune to Disney magic.

Those who expected to watch the world's most famous mouse sailing back home again, tail between his legs, are still recovering from the shock of actually liking the place. For their part, the Imagineers, the Disney creative spirits, are holding off on further building to give curmudgeons time to get used to the whole idea; and the big event of 1993 will be the addition of another nine holes of golf to the 18-hole layout that opened in September 1992.

Further plans call for cloning of Epcot Center and Disney–MGM Studios, current features of the company's Florida property, Walt Disney World.

Fodor's Choice

No two people will agree on what makes a perfect vacation, but it's fun and helpful to know what others think. We hope you'll have a chance to experience some of Fodor's Choices yourself while visiting Euro Disneyland. For detailed information about each entry, refer to the appropriate chapters in this guidebook.

Lodging Newport Bay Club (*Expensive*)

Hotel Cheyenne (*Moderate/Expensive*)

Camp Davy Crockett (*Moderate*)

Dining California Grill, Disneyland Hotel (*Very Expensive*)

Auberge de Cendrillon, Fantasyland (*Expensive*)

Blue Lagoon, Adventureland (*Expensive*)

Key West Seafood, Festival Disney (*Expensive*)

Parkside Diner, Hotel New York (*Moderate*)

Carnegie's, Festival Disney (*Inexpensive*)

Euro Disney Attractions Big Thunder Mountain, Frontierland

CinéMagique, Discoveryland

Phantom Manor, Frontierland

Pirates of the Caribbean, Adventureland

Star Tours, Discoveryland

Buffalo Bill's Wild West Show, Festival Disney

Great Sights The view down Main Street towards Sleeping Beauty Castle during a parade

Mississippi Riverboats near Big Thunder Mountain at sunset

The Jolly Roger fluttering on the Adventureland horizon

The view across Lake Buena Vista from Festival Disney towards the Hotel New York, Sequoia Lodge and Newport Bay Club

Hotel Cheyenne's gravelly Desperado Street, preferably deserted at high noon

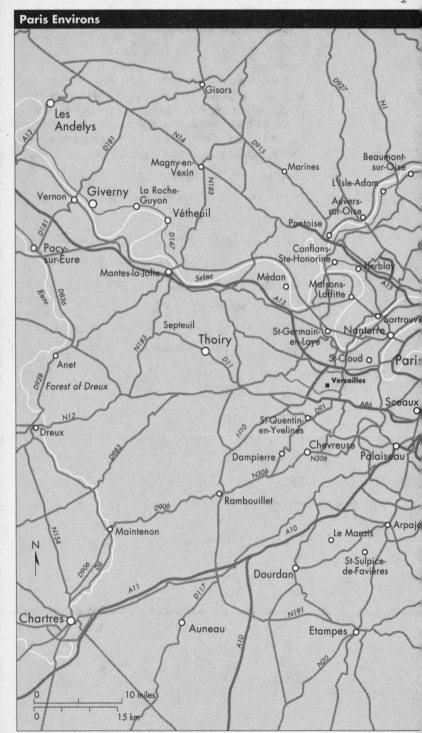

Paris Environs

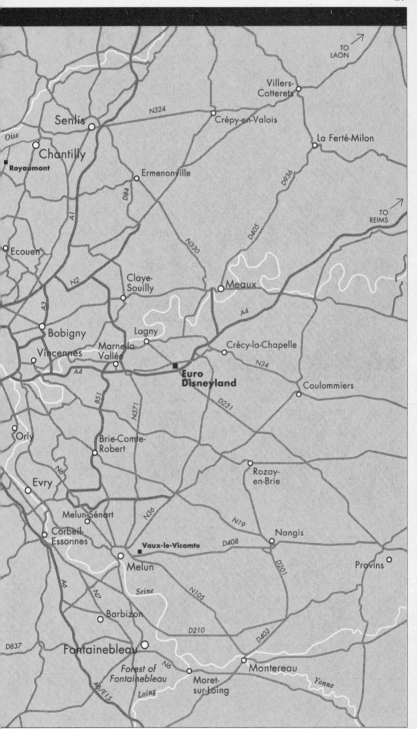

World Time Zones

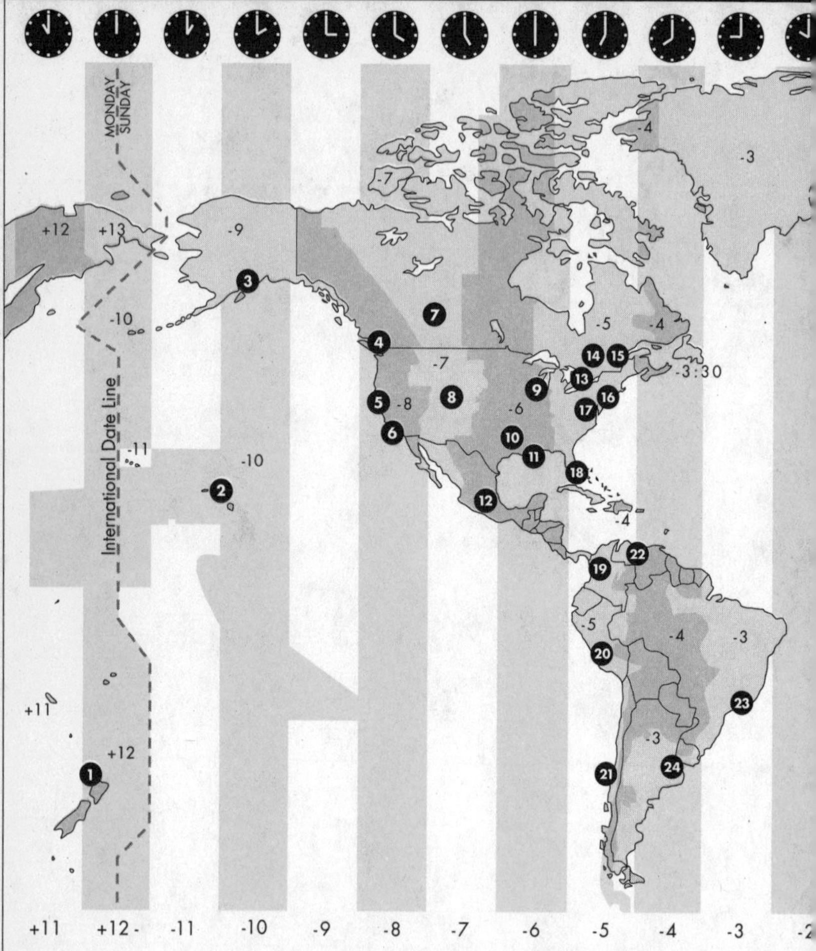

MONDAY
SUNDAY

International Date Line

+12 +13 -9

-4

-3

3

7

-5 -4

4 -7 14 15

-3:30

5 -8 8 9 13

-11 6 -6 16

-10 10 17

2 11 18

12 -4

+11

+12 19 22

1 20 -5 -4 -3

21 23

-3 24

+11 +12 - -11 -10 -9 -8 -7 -6 -5 -4 -3 -2

Numbers below vertical bands relate each zone to Greenwich Mean Time (0 hrs.).
Local times frequently differ from these general indications,
as indicated by light-face numbers on map.

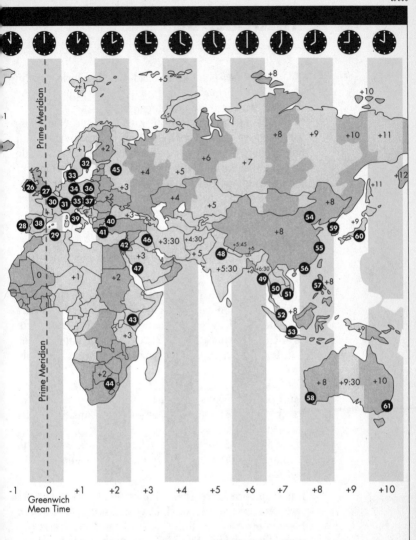

Introduction

By Simon Hewitt

Nowhere else in the world—not in Florida, not in California, not in Japan—is the impact of the Walt Disney Company quite as startling as it is in the Ile-de-France. Here in one of Europe's most historic regions, packed with châteaux and cathedrals, and only a short drive from Paris, rises a modern fairy-tale city showcasing the New World in all its 20th-century, high-tech glory: Euro Disney—a 1,945-acre recreational complex that includes Euro Disneyland, its 57-acre theme park and centerpiece; the Euro Disney Resort, a self-contained complex of hotels and recreational facilities; and Festival Disney, a mall-like affair full of shops, restaurants, and bars, with a post office and tourism office.

The whole ensemble is one of the most impressive architectural developments in modern Europe. Its hotels were designed by such renowned American architects as Michael Graves and Robert A. M. Stern, and each has a different and distinctly American style: the whole forms a picturesque grouping on the banks of the artificial Lake Buena Vista. It's a 20th-century, east-of-Paris equivalent of Versailles just 90 minutes away. Lake Buena Vista recalls Versailles's Grand Canal; both are flanked by manicured lawns and charming outbuildings—Disney hotels versus the Trianons and Marie Antoinette's hamlet, an example of make-believe architecture if there ever was one.

But step onto Euro Disneyland's Main Street U.S.A. and you might as well be light years away. No street in Europe ever looked like this (and did America really ever have such folksy charm? If so, probably not quite so much all along one street). For Americans, Main Street U.S.A. may be a trip down collective memory lane, but for Europeans, it's nothing short of culture shock.

The juxtaposition of American and European cultural elements provided at Euro Disneyland can be startling—in an enjoyable way, for the most part—and a lot of metaphors get cheerfully mixed along the way.

Some of Disney's best-known and most-loved stories and characters may have seeped into the European psyche as Disney originals, but are in fact European creations now come home to roost. Fantasyland is dominated by these prodigal superstars: Pinocchio, Peter Pan, Snow White, and Alice in Wonderland, to say nothing of Charles Perrault's 17th-century *Cendrillon* (Cinderella) and *Belle au Bois Dormant* (Sleeping Beauty).

Although it shouldn't be—this being France, and all—the use of the French language at Euro Disneyland can be jarring in certain contexts. Though Gallic children have long known that Dingo (Goofy) and Tigrou (Tigger) speak perfect French, it is something of a jolt, regardless of your national origin, to walk into the Lucky Nugget Saloon in Frontierland, one of Euro Disneyland's themed sections, and hear a cowboy crooning away in French.

It's also a surprise, to European visitors at least, that the Lucky Nugget Saloon does not sell beer or spirits. The ban on alcohol inside the theme park is a nuisance that has to be lived with, as are the forms you have to fill in before obtaining a lunch table, or the amateurish service you come to expect from ill-qualified young restaurant staff members. On the other hand, the compulsive ban on litter (the place is literally spic and span), and the mandatory cheerfulness of all Disney staff, largely compensate.

Despite ubiquitous reminders of the pioneering genius of the departed, deified, and ever-genial Uncle Walt, Disney Incorporated runs the show with a seamless, eerily Big Brotherish efficiency. There is even a form of Disneyspeak: staff are "Cast Members," paying customers are "Guests." The gray men in dark suits who read their boring speeches at Euro Disney's Grand Opening seemed closer in spirit to Scrooge McDuck than Mickey Mouse. Fun may be the product, but the profit is the motive, and the "Inc." part of the Disney equation displayed its business savvy, adherence to the bottom line, and negotiating skills in the deals they struck with the French government, which ranged from tax advantages and easier employment terms to a new expressway access road, a new TGV station (come 1994), and an extended suburban rail line that puts central Paris just 35 minutes away. Paris was chosen to host Euro Disney primarily for economic and geographic reasons: it's at the heart of Western Europe; it's easily accessible; and it allows for tour operators to promote "dream packages" that take in both the City of Light and the Magic of Disney. Paris is the world's leading conference venue, and Disney expects businessmen to fill its more expensive hotels, in the off-season especially.

Early teething problems may have left some thinking that Euro Disneyland operates like a stopped clock: One day within two months of the grand opening, most public telephones were out of order; the Visionarium cinema show had broken down; the trams meant to run around Lake Buena Vista every five minutes were nowhere to be seen; and you had to wait 30 minutes, not the advertised 10, for the shuttle bus from Camp Davy Crockett to the theme park.

Technical glitches such as these are to be expected in the early days of any such vast and complicated venture, but there is every reason to believe that they will be resolved. There are, however, a couple of missteps at Euro Disney that won't be so easily fixed. The most glaring blunder is the Hotel Santa Fe, which is meant to resemble a New Mexican Pueblo Indian Village but looks more like some dour postwar working-class housing project. The second is Festival Disney, designed by California architect Frank Gehry, which bears an uncanny resemblance to Main Street, Noisy-le-Grand, a grimy Paris suburb a few RER stops before Euro Disney. The third stumble—and not all visitors call it that—is Discoveryland, an assembly of warehouse-like hangars that remind some people, at least on the outside, of an airport freight-handling zone, despite a raucous paint job.

Skeptics made gloomy predictions for Euro Disney's success, citing the fickle French, high entrance prices, a weak dollar, and the failure of other French amusement parks. And, indeed, the French did stay away after press reports that the park's opening weeks would mean huge lines and massive traffic jams. London's *Daily Telegraph* envisioned Mickey Mouse slinking "back to America with his cute little tail between his dear little legs."

The minute Disney announced that attendance was lower than hoped, Parisians came charging up the expressway, attendance skyrocketed, and the gates had to be temporarily closed to avoid overcrowding.

When the Parisians finally got in, they found a theme park that is superbly designed, not too big, and easy to get around. They found magnificent landscaping—lush lawns, varied plants, flowers, trees, shrubs, lakes—not to mention architecture and ambience that's unique in Europe. The rides are fun and exhilarating, and many are new-and-improved versions of the American originals, rather than simply replicas. Future visitors to Euro Disneyland will have a great day out.

1 Essential Information

Before You Go

Euro Disney Information

To get information in English or make reservations, contact Euro Disney S.C.A., Central Reservations Office (B.P 105, F-77777 Marne-la-Vallée Cedex 4, France, tel. 01/49–41–49–10, fax 01/49–30–71–00). In the United Kingdom, call 071/753–2900. From the United States, you can contact Walt Disney World, Central Reservations (Box 10,100, Lake Buena Vista, FL 32830-0100, tel. 407/934–7639).

Government Tourist Offices

Contact the French Government Tourist Office for free information.

In the UK 178 Piccadilly, London W1V 0AL, tel. 071/629–1272.

In the USA 610 5th Ave., New York, NY 10020, tel. 212/315–0888 or 212/757–1125; 645 N. Michigan Ave., Chicago, IL 60611, tel. 312/337–6301; 2305 Cedar Springs Rd., Dallas, TX 75201, tel. 214/720–4010; 9401 Wilshire Blvd., Beverly Hills, CA 90212, tel. 213/271–6665; 1 Hallidie Plaza, Suite 250, San Francisco, CA 94102, tel. 415/986–4174.

In Canada 1981 McGill College Ave., Suite 490, Montreal, Quebec H3A 2W9, tel. 514/288–4264; 1 Dundas St. W, Suite 2405, Box 8, Toronto, Ontario M5G 1Z3, tel. 416/593–4723.

Tour Groups

When considering a tour, be sure to find out: (1) exactly what expenses are included (particularly tips, taxes, side trips, additional meals, and entertainment); (2) government ratings of all hotels on the itinerary and the facilities they offer; (3) cancellation policies for both you and for the tour operator; and (4) the single supplement, should you be traveling alone. Most tour operators request that bookings be made through a travel agent—there is no additional charge for doing so. Below is a selective sampling of the many tours available. Contact your travel agent and/or the French Government Tourist Office for additional resources.

In the UK, **Crystal Holidays** (The Courtyard, Arlington Rd., Serbison, Surrey, tel. 081/390–9900) sells holiday packages to Paris that can include excursions by train to

Euro Disney. Prices for these packages start at £134 for two nights, with a one-day excursion to Euro Disney costing an additional £35 per adult and a two-day excursion running £45. Both add-ons include train fare from Paris and entrance passes to the park.

American Express (tel. 071/930–4411, fax 071/930–9102) arranges individual tours from Britain to Euro Disney.

In the USA Multinight Euro Disney **American Express Vacations** (tel. 800/241–1700) include on-site accommodations, daily breakfast buffet, admission to the theme park and the Buffalo Bill Wild West dinner show, and all taxes. Rates range from $270 to $512 for two adults staying two nights; $347 to $702 for three nights; and $419 to $887 for four nights.

Walt Disney Travel (Box 22094, Lake Buena Vista, FL 32830, tel. 407/828–3232) packages to Euro Disney include train transportation from Paris, two nights' lodging in one of the six Disney hotels, and a three-day pass to the park. Prices range from $218 to $430 per adult, depending on which hotel you choose. Car rental to and from Paris can also be arranged at an additional fee.

When to Go

Paris has much to offer in every season, but the major tourist season stretches from Easter to mid-September, and Euro Disney is especially busy in July and August. Spring in this part of France can be disappointingly damp, but June brings good weather and plenty of cultural events in Paris and surrounding towns. Euro Disney visitors who want to sample Paris's many restaurants, theaters, and small shops should avoid summer, when many businesses close for at least four weeks.

Sunny weather usually continues through September and into the first half of October, making this an excellent time to visit Euro Disney. It is also the time when Paris's cultural life revives after its summer break, although the ballet and theater are not in full swing until November, when the weather is sometimes wet and cold, sometimes bright and sunny.

December is dominated by the *fêtes de fin d'année* (end-of-year festivities), with splendid displays in Parisian food shops and restaurants and a busy theater, ballet, and opera season continuing into January. February and March are the worst months, weatherwise, but with the coming of Easter, Paris and Euro Disney start looking beautiful again.

Climate What follow are the average daily maximum and minimum temperatures for Paris.

Jan.	43F	6C	May	68F	20C	Sept.	70F	21C
	34	1		49	10		53	12
Feb.	45F	7C	June	73F	23C	Oct.	60F	16C
	34	1		55	13		46	8
Mar.	54F	12C	July	76F	25C	Nov.	50F	10C
	39	4		58	14		40	5
Apr.	60F	16C	Aug.	75F	24C	Dec.	44F	7C
	43	6		58	14		36	2

Current weather information for foreign and domestic cities may be obtained by calling The Weather Channel Connection at 900/WEATHER from a touch-tone phone. In addition to supplying the weather report, The Weather Channel Connection will tell you the local time and give you travel tips as well as hurricane, foliage, and ski reports. The call costs 95¢ per minute.

National Holidays (1993) January 1 (New Year's Day); April 12 (Easter Monday); May 1 (Labor Day); May 8 (VE Day); May 20 (Ascension); May 31 (Pentecost Monday); July 14 (Bastille Day); August 15 (Assumption); November 1 (All Saints); November 11 (Armistice); December 25 (Christmas).

French Currency

The unit of currency in France is the franc, which is divided into 100 centimes. The bills are 500, 200, 100, 50, and 20 francs. Coins are 10, 5, 2, and 1 francs and 50, 20, 10, and 5 centimes. At press time (fall 1992), the exchange rate was 9.5 francs to the pound and 4.53 francs to the dollar.

Passports and Visas

Britons All British citizens need passports, applications for which are available from travel agencies or a main post office. Send the completed form to a regional Passport Office. The application must be countersigned by your bank manager or by a solicitor, barrister, doctor, clergyman, or justice of the peace who knows you personally. In addition, you'll need two photographs and the £15 fee. Alternatively, a British Visitor's Passport is good for entry to France. It is valid for one year, costs £7.50, and is nonrenewable. You'll need two passport photographs and identification. Apply at your local post office.

Visas are not required for British citizens entering France.

Americans All U.S. citizens need a passport to enter France. Applications for your first passport must be made in person; renewals can be obtained in person or by mail. First-time applicants should apply at least five weeks in advance of their departure date to one of the 13 U.S. Passport Agency offices. In addition, local county courthouses, many state and probate courts, and some post offices accept passport applications. Necessary documents include: (1) a completed passport application (Form DSP–11); (2) proof of citizenship (birth certificate with raised seal or naturalization papers); (3) proof of identity (valid driver's license, employee ID card, or any other document with your photograph and signature); (4) two recent, identical, two-inch square photographs (black-and-white or color head shot with a white or off-white background); (5) $65 application fee for a 10-year passport (those under 18 pay $40 for a 5-year passport). You must pay with a check, money order, or exact cash amount; no change is given. Passports should be mailed to you in 10 to 15 working days—but it can take longer in the early summer.

To renew your passport by mail, you'll need to complete Form DSP–82 and submit two recent, identical passport photographs, your current passport (if it is less than 12 years old and was issued after your 16th birthday), and a check or money order for $55. For further information, contact the Embassy of France (4101 Reservoir Rd., NW, Washington, DC 20007, tel. 202/944–6000).

Visas are no longer required of U.S. citizens entering France for under 90 days.

Canadians All Canadians need a passport to enter France. Send your completed application (available at any post office or passport office) to the Bureau of Passports (Suite 215, West Tower, Guy Favreau Complex, 200 René Lévesque Blvd. West, Montreal, Quebec H2Z 1X4). Include C$35, two photographs, a guarantor, and proof of Canadian citizenship. Applications can be made in person at the regional passport offices in many cities, including Edmonton, Halifax, Montreal, Toronto, Vancouver, and Winnipeg. Passports are valid for five years and are nonrenewable.

Visas are no longer required for Canadian citizens entering France.

Customs and Duties

On Arrival There are two levels of duty-free allowance for travelers entering France: one for those coming from a European Community (EC) country and one for those coming from anywhere else.

In the first category, you may import duty free: (1) 300 cigarettes or 150 cigarillos or 75 cigars or 400 grams of tobacco; (2) 5 liters of table wine and, in addition, (a) 1.5 liters of alcohol over 22% volume (most spirits) or (b) 3 liters of alcohol under 22% volume (fortified or sparkling wine) or (c) 3 more liters of table wine; (3) 90 milliliters of perfume and 375 milliliters of toilet water; and (4) other goods to the value of 2,000 francs (400 francs for those under 15).

In the second category, you may import duty free: (1) 200 cigarettes or 100 cigarillos or 50 cigars or 250 grams of tobacco (these allowances are doubled if you live outside of Europe); (2) 2 liters of wine and, in addition, (a) 1 liter of alcohol over 22% volume (most spirits) or (b) 2 liters of alcohol under 22% volume (fortified or sparkling wine) or (c) 2 more liters of table wine; (3) 60 milliliters of perfume and 250 milliliters of toilet water; and (4) other goods to the value of 2,400 francs (620 francs for those under 15).

Any amount of French or foreign currency may be brought into France, but foreign currencies converted into francs may be reconverted into a foreign currency only up to the equivalent of 5,000 francs.

On Departure
British Residents You have two different allowances: one for goods bought in a duty-free shop in France and the other for goods bought anywhere else in France. In the first category, you may import duty free: (1) 200 cigarettes or 100 cigarillos or 50 cigars or 250 grams of tobacco; (2) 2 liters of table wine and, in addition, (a) 1 liter of alcohol over 22% by volume (most spirits) or (b) 2 liters of alcohol under 22% by volume (fortified or sparkling wine) or (c) 2 more liters of table wine; (3) 60 milliliters of perfume and 250 milliliters of toilet water; and other goods up to a value of £32, but not more than 50 liters of beer and 25 cigarette lighters.

In the second category, you may import duty free: (1) 300 cigarettes or 150 cigarillos or 75 cigars or 400 grams of tobacco; (2) 5 liters of table wine and, in addition, (a) 1½ liters of alcohol over 22% volume (most spirits) or (b) 3 liters of alcohol under 22% volume (fortified or sparkling wine) or (c) 3 more liters of table wine; (3) 90 milliliters of perfume and 375 milliliters of toilet water; and (4) other goods to the value of £420, but not more than 50 liters of beer or 25 lighters.

No animals or pets of any kind may be brought into the United Kingdom without a lengthy quarantine; penalties are severe and strictly enforced.

U.S. Residents You may bring home duty free up to $400 worth of foreign goods, as long as you have been out of the country for at least 48 hours and haven't made an international trip in 30 days. Each member of the family is entitled to the same exemption, regardless of age, and exemptions may be pooled. For the next $1,000 worth of goods, a flat 10% rate is assessed; above $1,400, duties vary with the merchandise. Included for travelers 21 or older are 1 liter of alcohol, 100 cigars (non-Cuban), and 200 cigarettes. Only one bottle of perfume trademarked in the United States may be brought in. However, there is no duty on antiques or works of art over 100 years old. Anything exceeding these limits will be taxed at the port of entry and may be taxed additionally in the traveler's home state. Gifts valued at under $50 may be mailed to friends or relatives at home duty free, but you may not send more than one package per day to any one addressee, and packages may not include perfumes costing more than $5, tobacco, or liquor.

If you are bringing any foreign-made equipment from home, such as cameras, it's wise to carry the original receipt with you or register the item with U.S. Customs before you leave (Form 4457). Otherwise, you may end up paying duty on your return.

Before your trip, be sure to obtain "Know Before You Go," an invaluable brochure that carefully outlines what returning residents may and may not bring back to the United States and lists the amounts of duties charged. It is distributed free by the U.S. Customs Service (1301 Constitution Ave., Washington, DC 20229).

Canadian Residents Exemptions for returning Canadians range from $20 to $300, depending on length of stay out of the country. For the $300 exemption, you must have been out of the country for one week. For any given year, you are allowed one $300 exemption. You may bring in duty free up to 50 cigars, 200 cigarettes, 2.2 pounds of tobacco, and 40 ounces of liquor, provided these are declared in writing to customs on arrival and accompany the traveler in hand or checked-through baggage. Personal gifts should be mailed as "Unsolicited Gift—Value under $40." Request the Canadian Customs brochure *I Declare* for further details.

Renting and Leasing Cars

Renting It's best to arrange a car rental before you leave. You won't save money by waiting until you arrive in Paris, and you may find that the type of car you want is not available at the last minute. You'll have to weigh the added expense of renting a car from a major company with an airport office against the savings on a car from a budget company with offices in town. You could waste precious hours trying to locate the budget company in return for only small financial savings. If you're arriving and departing from different airports, look for a one-way car rental with no return fees. Be prepared to pay more for cars with automatic transmission, and since they are not as readily available as those with manual transmissions, be sure to reserve them well in advance.

Rental rates vary widely, depending on size and model, number of days you use the car, insurance coverage, and whether special drop-off fees are imposed. In most cases, rates quoted include unlimited free mileage and standard liability protection. Not included are Collision Damage Waiver (CDW), which eliminates your deductible payment should you have an accident; personal accident insurance; gasoline; and European value added taxes (VAT). The VAT in France is among the highest in Europe. Rental companies usually charge according to the exchange rate of the pound or dollar at the time the car is returned or when the credit card payment is processed.

Throughout the United Kingdom, there are offices of **Avis** (Hayes Gate House, Uxbridge Rd., Hayes, Middlesex UB4 ONJ, tel. 081/848–8733), **Hertz** (Radnor House, 1272 London Rd., London SW16 4XW, tel. 081/679–1799), and **Europcar** (Bushey House, High St., Bushey, WD2 1RE, tel. 081/950–4080).

Two companies with special programs that help Americans hedge against the falling dollar by guaranteeing advertised rates to those who pay in advance are **Budget Rent-a-Car** (3350 Boyington St., Carrollton, TX 75006, tel. 800/527–0700) and **Connex Travel International** (23

N. Division St., Peekskill, NY 10566, tel. 800/333–
3949). Other budget rental companies serving France
include **Europe by Car** (1 Rockefeller Plaza, New York,
NY 10020, tel. 800/223–1516 or 800/252–9401 in CA),
Foremost Euro-Car (5430 Van Nuys Blvd., Van Nuys,
CA 91401, tel. 800/272–3299), **Kemwel** (106 Calvert St.,
Harrison, NY 10528, tel. 800/678–0678). Other agencies
with offices in Paris include **Avis** (tel. 800/331–1212),
Hertz (tel. 800/654–3131), **National** or **Europcar** (tel.
800/CAR–RENT), and **Thrifty** (tel. 800/367–2277).

Driver's licenses issued in the United Kingdom, the
United States, and Canada are valid in France. It is recommended that you also obtain an International Driving
Permit before you leave, to smooth out difficulties if you
have an accident or as an additional piece of identification. Permits are available for a small fee through local
offices of the U.K.'s **Automobile Association,** the **American Automobile Association** (AAA), and the **Canadian
Automobile Association** (CAA), or from their main offices: AA, Sanum House, Basingstoke, Hants, England,
tel. 256/201–23; AAA, 1000 AAA Drive, Heathrow, FL
32746, tel. 800/336–4357; CAA, 2 Carlton Street, Toronto, Ontario M5B 1K4, tel. 416/964–3002.

Leasing For trips of 21 days or more, you may save money by
leasing a car. With the leasing arrangement, you are
technically buying a car and then selling it back to the
manufacturer after you've used it. You receive a factory-
new car, tax free, with international registration and
extensive insurance coverage. Rates vary with the make
and model of car and length of rental. Car leasing programs in France are offered by Renault, Citröen, and
Peugeot. Delivery is free to downtown Paris and to the
airports in Paris. There is a small fee for deliveries to
other parts of France. Before you go, compare long-
term rental rates with leasing rates. Remember to add
taxes and insurance costs to the car rentals, something
you don't have to worry about with leasing. Companies
that offer leasing arrangements include **Europe by Car**
and **Kemwel** (*see* Renting, *above*).

Rail Passes

British and American travelers under 26 who have not
invested in a rail pass should inquire about discount
travel fares under a **Billet International Jeune** (BIJ)
scheme. The special one-trip tariff is offered by
EuroTrain International (tel. 071/730–3402) with offices in London, Dublin, Paris, Madrid, Lisbon, Rome,

Zürich, Athens, Brussels, Budapest, Hannover, Leiden, Vienna, and Tangier. You can purchase a EuroTrain ticket at one of these offices or at travel agent networks, mainline rail stations, and specialist youth travel operators.

The **French Flexipass** (formerly the France-Vacances Rail Pass) is a good value for Americans and Canadians planning to do a lot of traveling by train. The pass allows you to stagger your train travel time instead of having to use it all at once. For example, the four-day pass ($175 in first class, $125 in second), may be used on any four days within a one-month period. Travelers may also add on up to five days of travel for $38 a day in first class and $27 in second class. You must buy the French Flexipass before you leave for France. It is obtainable through travel agents or through **Rail Europe** (226–230 Westchester Ave., White Plains, NY 10604, tel. 914/682–5172 or 800/345–1990).

The **EurailPass,** valid for unlimited first-class train travel through 20 countries, including France, is an excellent value if you plan on traveling around the Continent. The ticket is available for periods of 15 days ($430), 21 days ($550), one month ($680), two months ($920), and three months ($1,150). For those who will be 25 and under on the first day of travel there is the **Eurail Youthpass,** for one or two months' unlimited second-class train travel, at $470 and $640. The EurailPass is available only if you live outside Europe and North Africa. The pass must be bought from an authorized agent *before* you leave for Europe. Apply through a travel agent or through Rail Europe at the address above.

Travelers who want to spread out their journeys should consider the **Eurail Flexipass.** With this pass, you receive five days of unlimited first-class train travel within a 15-day period ($280), nine days of travel within 21 days ($450), or 14 days of travel within one month ($610).

Traveling with Children

Publications   *Family Travel Times* is an 8- to 12-page newsletter published 10 times a year by Travel with Your Children (45 W. 18th St., 7th Floor Tower, New York, NY 10011, tel. 212/206–0688). Subscription includes access to back issues and twice-weekly opportunities to call in for specific advice.

Traveling with Children—And Enjoying It (Globe Pequot Press, Box Q, Chester, CT 06412, $11.95). "Impossible!" you say? Maybe, but this book offers tips on how to cut costs, keep kids busy, eat out, reduce jet lag, and pack properly.

Family Travel **Families Welcome!** (21 W. Colony Pl., Suite 140, Dur-
Organizations ham, NC 27701, tel. 919/489–2555 or 800/326–0724) is a
travel agency that arranges tours to Paris and France
brimming with family-oriented activities, including
Euro Disney. Another travel arranger that understands
family needs (and can even set up short-term rentals) is
The French Experience (370 Lexington Ave., New York,
NY 10017, tel. 212/986–3800).

Getting There On international flights, children under age 2 not occupying a seat pay 10% of adult fare. Various discounts ap-
ply to children 2–12 years of age. Regulations about
infant travel on airplanes are changing. If you want to be
sure your infant is secure buy a separate ticket and
bring your own infant car seat. (Check with the airline
in advance; certain seats aren't allowed.) Some airlines
allow babies to travel in their own car seats at no charge
if the flight isn't full; sometimes safety seats will be
stored and the child must be held by a parent. (For the
booklet "Child/Infant Safety Seats Acceptable for Use
in Aircraft," write to the Federal Aviation Administration, APA–200 (800 Independence Ave., SW, Washington, DC 20591, tel. 202/267–3479.) If you opt to hold
your baby on your lap, do so with the infant outside the
seat belt so he or she won't be crushed in case of a sudden
stop.

Also inquire about special children's meals or snacks.
The February 1990 and 1992 *Family Travel Times* include a rundown of the children's services offered by 46
airlines.

Baby-sitting If you are staying in Paris, first check with the hotel
Services concierge for recommended child-care arrangements.
Paris Local agencies include: **American University of Paris,** 31
avenue Bosquet, 75007 Paris, tel. 45–55–91–73; **Baby
Sitting Express,** 22 rue de Picardie, 75003 Paris, tel. 42–
77–45–44; **Allo Service Maman,** 21 rue de Brey, 75017
Paris, tel. 42–67–99–37; **Baby Sitting Service,** 18 rue
Tronchet, 75008 Paris, tel. 46–37–51–24; and **Home
Service,** 5 rue Yvon-Villarceau, 75016 Paris, tel. 45–00–
82–51.

Euro Disney In Euro Disney, a baby-sitting service is provided at the
Neverland Club Children's Theater in Festival Disney between 5 PM and midnight. The cost is 120 francs for up to

three hours, then 40 francs for each additional hour (refreshments included).

In-room baby-sitting is also available in some hotels. However, there is no baby-sitting service in the theme park.

Baby-Care Center Changing facilities, bottle warmers, disposable diapers (nappies), and a small selection of baby food are available at **Relain Bébés,** at the far end of Main Street, next to the Plaza Gardens restaurant. There are also baby-changing tables in most women's rest rooms.

Stroller Rental Strollers (prams) can be rented just inside Euro Disneyland's Main Entrance, at Town Square Terrace, for 30 francs with a refundable 20-franc deposit. There are stroller "parking" areas at most attractions.

Lost Children Report them to any Disney cast member, at **City Hall,** or at the **Relain Bébé** booth at the far end of Main Street, next to the Plaza Gardens.

Special Activities A special treat for youngsters are the breakfasts at which Disney characters put in appearances, held daily at **Inventions** in the Disneyland Hotel (tel. 604–56583 for reservations, at least two days in advance).

Arriving and Departing

From the United Kingdom

Paris by Plane **Air France** (tel. 081/742–6600) and **British Airways** (tel. 081/897–4000) together offer service from London's Heathrow Airport to Paris every hour to two hours. Round-trip tickets are £98 if you purchase them 14 days in advance and stay over on a Saturday night. Otherwise, the price is £188.

There are three flights a day to Paris from London's newest and most central airport, London City, in the Docklands area, via **Brymon** (Plymouth City Airport, Crownhill, Plymouth, Devon PL6 8BW, tel. 0752/707023). Round-trip fares are the same as those of Air France and British Airways.

Paris Travel Service (115 Buckingham Palace Rd., London SW1 V9SJ, tel. 071/2337892) from Gatwick to Beauvais involves a 40-minute flight and a one-hour bus ride into central Paris, but there is only one departure a week (Friday), and passengers may not return until the following Monday. The cost is £89, and the package is called Paris Express.

From the Airports to Downtown
Charles de Gaulle (Roissy)

The easiest way to get into Paris is on the **RER-B** line, the suburban express train. A free shuttle bus—look for the word *navette*—runs between the two terminal buildings and the train station; it takes about 10 minutes. Trains to central Paris (Les Halles, St-Michel, Luxembourg) leave every 15 minutes. The fare (including Métro connection) is 31 francs, and journey time is about 30 minutes. **Buses** run every 15 minutes between Charles de Gaulle airport and the Arc de Triomphe, with a stop at the Air France air terminal at Porte Maillot. The fare is 38 francs, and journey time is about 40 minutes. Rush-hour traffic often makes this a slow and frustrating trip. **Taxis** are readily available. Journey time is around 30 minutes, depending on the traffic, and the fare is around 200 francs.

Orly Airport

The easiest way to get into Paris is on the **RER-C** line, the suburban express train. Again, there's a free shuttle bus from the terminal building to the train station. Trains to Paris leave every 15 minutes. The fare is 24 francs, and journey time is about 25 minutes. **Buses** run every 12 minutes between Orly airport and the Air France air terminal at Les Invalides on the Left Bank. The fare is 31 francs, and journey time is between 30 and 60 minutes, depending on traffic. **Taxis** take around 25 minutes in light traffic; the fare will be about 160 francs.

A relatively new shuttle-train service, **Orlyval,** runs between the RER-B station at Antony and Orly airport every 7 minutes. The fare from downtown Paris, however, is steep: 55 francs.

Paris by Car

There are a number of different driving routes to Paris. The Dover–Calais route includes the shortest Channel crossing; the Newhaven–Dieppe route requires a longer Channel crossing but a shorter drive through France.

Dover–Calais

Ticket prices for ferries vary widely depending on the number of passengers in a group, the size of the car, the season and time of day, and the length of your trip. Call one of the ferry service reservation offices for more exact information. **P&O European Ferries** (Channel House, Channel View Rd., Dover, Kent CT17 9TJ, tel. 081/575–8555) has up to 15 sailings a day; the crossing takes about 75 minutes. The driver's fare is £24. **Sealink British Ferries** (Charter House, Park St., Ashford, Kent TN24 8EX, tel. 0233/646801) operates up to 18 sailings a day; the crossing takes about 90 minutes. The driver's fare is £26. **Hoverspeed** (Maybrook House, Queens Gardens, Dover, Kent CT17 9UQ, tel. 0304/240241) operates up to 23 crossings a day, and the crossing (by Hovercraft) takes 35 minutes.

Dover–Boulogne **P&O European Ferries** has up to six sailings a day with a crossing time of 100 minutes. Fares are the same as for the Dover–Calais crossing. **Hoverspeed** also operates on this route, with six 40-minute crossings a day. The fares are the same as for the Dover–Calais route.

Ramsgate– **Sally Line** (Argyle Centre, York St., Ramsgate, Kent
Dunkerque CT11 9DS, tel. 0843/595522) has up to five crossings a day; each takes 2½ hours. Motorists' fees are £26.

Newhaven–Dieppe **Sealink Dieppe Ferries** has up to four sailings a day; the crossing takes four hours. The motorist's fare is £26.

Portsmouth– **P&O European Ferries** has up to three sailings a day,
Le Havre and the crossing takes 5¾ hours by day, 7 by night. The motorist's fare is £46.

Driving distances from the French ports to Paris are as follows: **from Calais,** 290 kilometers (180 miles); **from Boulogne,** 243 kilometers (151 miles); **from Dieppe,** 193 kilometers (120 miles); **from Dunkerque,** 257 kilometers (160 miles). The fastest routes to Paris from each port are via the N43, A26, and A1 from Calais; via the N1 from Boulogne; via the N15 from Le Havre; via the D915 and N1 from Dieppe; and via the A25 and A1 from Dunkerque.

Paris by Train **British Rail** has four departures a day from London's Victoria Station, all linking with the Dover–Calais/Boulogne ferry services through to Paris. There is also an overnight service using the Newhaven–Dieppe ferry. Journey time is about eight hours. Round-trip fare is £65 (five-day excursion). Credit card bookings are accepted by phone (tel. 071/834–2345) or in person at a British Rail Travel Centre.

The Channel Tunnel, destined for trains only (with cars taken on board), should be operational in fall 1993, and will slash the Paris–London journey time to under four hours.

Train Stations Paris has six international rail stations, each serving trains from a different region: **Gare du Nord** (northern France, northern Europe, and England via Calais or Boulogne); **Gare St-Lazare** (Normandy, England via Dieppe); **Gare de l'Est** (Strasbourg, Luxembourg, Basle, and central Europe); **Gare de Lyon** (Lyon, Marseille, the Riviera, Geneva, Italy); and **Gare d'Austerlitz** (Loire Valley, southwest France, Spain). Note that **Gare Montparnasse** has taken over as the main terminus for trains bound for southwest France since the introduction of the new TGV-Atlantique service.

For train information from any station, call 45–82–50–50. You can reserve tickets in any Paris station, irrespective of destination. Go to the **Grandes Lignes** counter for travel within France and to the **Billets Internationaux** desk if you're heading out of France.

Paris by Bus **Eurolines** (52 Grosvenor Gardens, London SW1W 0AU, tel. 071/730–0202) operates a service from London's Victoria Coach Station, via the Dover–Calais ferry, to Paris. Departures are at 9 AM, arriving at 6:15 PM; 12 noon, arriving at 9:45 PM; and 9 PM, arriving at 7:15 AM. Fares are £52 round-trip (under 25 youth pass £49), £31 one-way.

Hoverspeed (Maybrook House, Queen's Gardens, Dover, Kent CT17 9UQ, tel. 0304/240241) offers a faster journey time with up to five daily departures from Victoria Coach Station. The fare is £25 one-way, £43 round-trip.

Both the Eurolines and Hoverspeed services are bookable in person at any **National Express** office or at the **Coach Travel Centre,** 13 Regent Street, London SW1 4LR. Credit card reservations can be made by calling 071/824–8657.

From North America

By Plane Be certain to distinguish among (1) nonstop flights—no changes, no stops; (2) direct flights—no changes but one or more stops; and (3) connecting flights—two or more planes, one or more stops.

Airlines Paris is served by **Air France,** tel. 800/237–2747; **TWA,** tel. 800/892–4141; **American Airlines,** tel. 800/433–7300; and **Delta,** tel. 800/241–4141. **United** (tel. 800/538–2929) flies from Chicago and Washington, D.C., only; **Continental** (tel. 800/231–0856) flies into Orly airport.

Flying Time From New York: 7 hours. From Chicago: 9½ hours. From Los Angeles: 11 hours.

Getting to Euro Disney

By Train from The **RER A** line runs from **Charles-de-Gualle-Etoile, Au-**
Paris **ber, Châtelet-les-Halles, Gare de Lyon, La Défense,** and **Nation** directly to the **Marne-la-Vallée-Chessy** station, 150 yards from the Euro Disney Resort. Trains depart central Paris every 10 to 20 minutes, and the journey takes about 35 minutes. The first train of the day pulls

out of Charles-de-Gaulle–Etoile at 5:20 AM and the last
train leaves Marne-la-Vallée–Chessy at approximately
12:20 AM. The round-trip fare is 62 francs, including a
Métro ticket.

By Bus from the Airports In summer, shuttle buses link Euro Disney to the airports at **Roissy** (56 km/35 mi) and **Orly** (50 km/31 mi) every 45 minutes; tickets cost 65 francs, and journey time varies between 50 minutes and 1½ hours, depending on traffic.

By Car from Paris Euro Disney is 37 kilometers (23 mi) east of Paris. Take the **A4** expressway from Porte de Bercy towards Strasbourg, Metz, and Nancy, and follow signs to Marne-la-Vallée until you see Euro Disney exit signs. The park is 5 kilometers (3 miles) from the expressway. The drive from Paris can take as little as 35 minutes, but it's safer to allow at least an hour. Be prepared for a grinding, bumper-to-bumper approach on sunny Sundays and any day in July and August.

As you arrive, head for the *Parking Visiteurs* (30 francs per car). If you're staying in a Disney hotel, follow signs to the hotel and use its parking lot. Depending on where you park, you will be anywhere between 550 and 1190 meters (600 and 1,300 yards) from the entrance to the theme park. A moving walkway will take you there from the parking lot.

Staying in Paris

Important Addresses and Numbers

Tourist Information The main **Paris Tourist Office** (127 av. des Champs-Elysées, 75008 Paris, tel. 47–23–61–72) is open daily 9–8. There are also offices at all main train stations, except Gare St-Lazare. Dial 47–20–88–98 for recorded information in English.

Embassies **British Embassy** (35 rue du Faubourg St-Honoré, 8e, tel. 42–66–91–42). **U.S. Embassy** (2 av. Gabriel, 8e, tel. 42–96–12–02). **Canadian Embassy** (35 av. Montaigne, 8e, tel. 47–23–01–01).

Emergencies **Police** (tel. 17). **Ambulance** (tel. 15 or 45–67–50–50). **Doctor** (tel. 47–07–77–77). **Dentist** (tel. 43–37–51–00).

Hospitals **The Hertford British Hospital** (3 rue Barbès, Levallois-Perret, tel. 47–58–13–12) offers 24-hour emergency service. **The American Hospital** (63 blvd. Victor Hugo, Neuilly, tel. 46–41–25–25) also has a 24-hour service.

Pharmacies **Dhéry** (Galerie des Champs, 84 av. des Champs-Elysées, 8e, tel. 45–62–02–41) is open 24 hours. **Drugstore Publicis** (corner of blvd. St-Germain and rue de Rennes, 6e) is open daily till 2 AM. **Pharmacie des Arts** (106 blvd. Montparnasse, 14e) is open daily till midnight.

English–Language Bookstores **W. H. Smith** (248 rue de Rivoli, 1er, tel. 47–60–37–97). **Galignani** (224 rue de Rivoli, 1er, tel. 42–60–76–07). **Brentano's** (37 av. de l'Opéra, 2e, tel. 42–61–52–50). **Shakespeare and Co.** (rue de la Bûcherie, 5e, no phone).

Tour Operators **American Express** (11 rue Scribe, 9e, tel. 47–77–70–00). **Air France** (119 av. des Champs-Elysées, 8e, tel. 42–99–23–64). **Wagons-Lits** (32 rue du Quatre-Septembre, 2e, tel. 42–68–15–80).

Telephones

To call Paris from the United Kingdom, dial 01–33 and the the local eight-digit number; to call from the United States, dial 011–33–1 and then the local number.

Local Calls The French telephone system is modern and efficient. A local call costs 73 centimes plus 12 centimes per minute. Call-boxes are plentiful; they're found at post offices and often in cafés.

Pay phones operate with 50-centime, 1-, 2-, and 5-franc coins (1 franc minimum). Lift the receiver, place your coin(s) in the appropriate slots, and dial. Unused coins are returned when you hang up. Many French pay phones are now operated by cards *(télécartes)*, which you can buy from post offices and some *tabacs* (cost is 40 francs for 50 units; 96 francs for 120). These cards will save you money and hassle.

All French phone numbers have eight digits; a code is required only when calling Paris from outside the city (add 16–1 for Paris) and when calling outside the city from Paris (add 16, then the number). Note that the number system was changed in 1985, so you may come across some seven-figure numbers in Paris and some six-figure ones elsewhere. Add 4 to the start of such Paris numbers, and add the former two-figure area code to the provincial numbers.

International Calls Dial 19 and wait for the tone, then dial the country code (44 for the United Kingdom; 1 for the United States and Canada) and the area code (minus any initial 0) and number. Expect to be overcharged if you make calls from your hotel. Approximate daytime rates, per minute, are

4.50 francs to the United Kingdom; 7.70 francs to the United States and Canada; reduced rates, per minute, are 3 francs to the United Kingdom (9:30 PM–8 AM, 2 AM–8 PM Sat., all day Sun., and public holidays); and 5.60 francs (2 AM–noon) to the United States and Canada or 6.30 francs (8 PM–2 AM weekdays, noon–2 AM Sun. and public holidays). AT&T's USA Direct program allows callers to take advantage of AT&T rates by connecting directly with the AT&T system. To do so from France dial 19–0011. You can then either dial the number (1 + area code + number) and bill the call to your AT&T calling card, or call collect. There is a $2.50 surcharge for calls billed to a calling card and a $5.75 surcharge for those dialed collect.

Operators and Information To find a number within France or to request information, dial 12. For international inquiries, dial 19–33 plus the country code.

Mail

Postal Rates Letters to the United Kingdom cost 2.50 francs for up to 20 grams, as they do within France. Airmail letters to the United States and Canada cost 4.00 francs for 20 grams, 6.90 francs for 30 grams, 7.20 francs for 40 grams, and 7.50 francs for 50 grams. Postcards cost 2.30 francs within France and to the United Kingdom, Canada, the United States, and EC countries; 3.70 francs if sent to North America by airmail. Stamps can be bought in post offices and cafés sporting a red TABAC sign.

Getting Around Paris

Paris is relatively small as capital cities go, and most of its prize monuments and museums are within easy walking distance of one another. The most convenient form of public transportation is the Métro, with stops every few hundred yards. Buses are a slower alternative, though you do see more of the city. Taxis are relatively inexpensive and convenient, but not always easy to hail. Private car travel within Paris is best avoided; parking is extremely difficult.

Maps of the Métro/RER network are available free from any Métro station and in many hotels. They are also posted on every platform, as are maps of the bus network. Bus routes are also marked at bus stops and on buses. To help you find your way around Paris, we suggest you buy a *Plan de Paris par arrondissement* (about 20 frs), a city guide with separate maps of each district, including the whereabouts of Métro stations and an index of street names. They're on sale in newsstands, bookstores, stationers, and drugstores.

By Métro Métro stations are recognizable either by a large yellow M within a circle or by the distinctive curly green Art Nouveau railings and archway bearing the full title (Métropolitain). The Métro is the most efficient way to get around Paris and is so clearly marked at all points that it's easy to find your way around without having to ask directions.

There are 13 Métro lines crisscrossing Paris and the suburbs, and you are seldom more than 500 yards from the nearest station. It is essential to know the name of the last station on the line you take, as this name appears on all signs. A connection (you can make as many as you like on one ticket) is called a *correspondance*. At junction stations, illuminated orange signs bearing the name of the line terminus appear over the correct corridors for each *correspondance*. Illuminated blue signs marked *sortie* indicate the station exit.

The Métro service starts at 5:30 AM and continues until 1:15 AM, when the last train on each line reaches its terminus. You can calculate the time of the last train from a particular station by counting the number of stops to the terminus and allowing 90 seconds for each stop.

Some lines and stations in the less salubrious parts of Paris are a bit risky at night; in particular Lines 2 and 13. But in general, the Métro is relatively safe throughout, providing you don't walk around with your wallet hanging out of your back pocket or (especially women) travel alone late at night. The biggest nuisances you're likely to come across will be the wine-swigging *clochards* (tramps) blurting out drunken songs as they bed down on platform benches.

The Métro network connects at several points in Paris with the **RER** network. RER trains, which race across Paris from suburb to suburb, are a sort of supersonic Métro and can be great time-savers.

First class no longer exists in the Métro. All Métro tickets and passes are valid for RER *and* bus travel within Paris. Métro tickets cost 5.50 francs each, though a carnet (10 tickets for 34.50 francs) is better value. Alternatively, you can buy a weekly *(coupon jaune)* or monthly *(carte orange)* ticket, sold according to zone. Zones 1 and 2 cover the entire Métro network; tickets cost 54 francs a week or 190 francs a month. If you plan to take

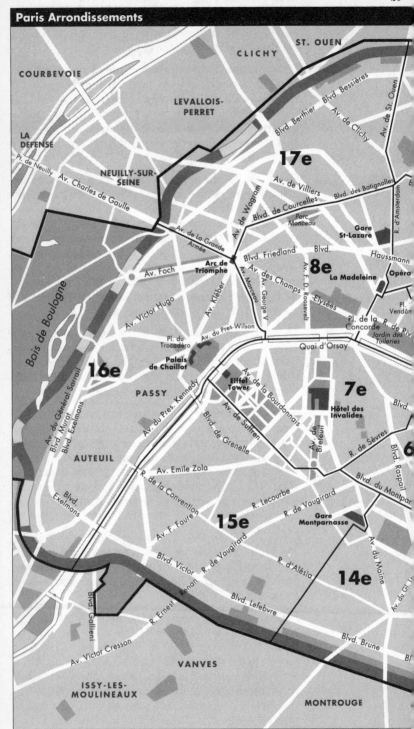

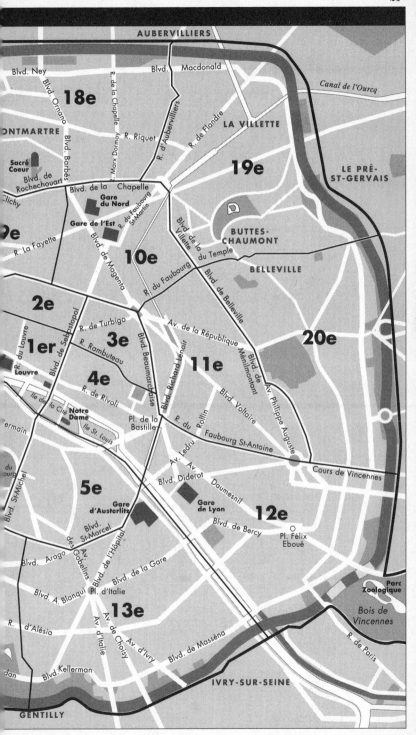

AUBERVILLIERS

Blvd. Ney

18e

Blvd. Macdonald

Canal de l'Ourcq

Blvd. Ornano

R. de la Chapelle

Blvd. Barbès

ONTMARTRE

Sacré Coeur

Blvd. de Rochechouart

Clichy

Blvd. de la Chapelle

LA VILLETTE

R. de Flandre

R. d'Aubervilliers

19e

LE PRÉ-ST-GERVAIS

Gare du Nord

R. du Faubourg St-Martin

9e

R. La Fayette

Gare de l'Est

Blvd. de Magenta

10e

Blvd. de la Villette

BUTTES-CHAUMONT

du Temple

BELLEVILLE

R. du Faubourg

Blvd. de Belleville

2e

R. de Turbigo

Blvd. de Sebastopol

3e

Av. de la République

Blvd. de Ménilmontant

20e

1er

R. du Louvre

R. Rambuteau

Blvd. Beaumarchaise

Richard Lenoir

Av. Philippe Auguste

Louvre

4e

R. de Rivoli

11e

Blvd. Voltaire

Ile de la Cité

Notre Dame

Ile St. Louis

Pl. de la Bastille

R. du Rollin

Faubourg St-Antoine

ermain

du ourg

Blvd. St-Michel

Av. Ledru

Av. Daumesnil

Cours de Vincennes

5e

Blvd. Diderot

Gare d'Austerlitz

Gare de Lyon

12e

Blvd. St-Marcel

Blvd. de Bercy

Pl. Félix Eboué

Blvd. Arago

Av. des Gobelins

Blvd. de l'Hôpital

Blvd. de la Gare

Parc Zoologique

Blvd. A. Blanqui

Pl. d'Italie

Bois de Vincennes

R. d'Alésia

13e

Av. d'Italie

Av. de Choisy

Av. d'Ivry

Blvd. de Masséna

R. de Paris

dan

Blvd. Kellerman

IVRY-SUR-SEINE

GENTILLY

Paris Métro

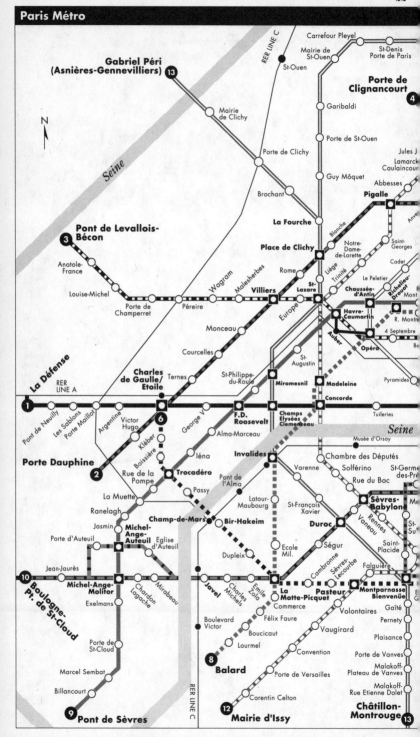

Gabriel Péri
(Asnières-Gennevilliers) 13

Carrefour Pleyel

St-Denis
Porte de Paris

Mairie de
St-Ouen

St-Ouen

RER LINE C

Porte de
Clignancourt 4

Garibaldi

Mairie
de Clichy

Porte de St-Ouen

Jules J
Lamarck
Caulaincour

Porte de Clichy

Guy Môquet

Abbesses

Brochant

Pigalle

N

Seine

Pont de Levallois-
Bécon 3

La Fourche

Blanche

Notre-
Dame-
de-Lorette

Anve

Saint-
Georges

Anatole-
France

Place de Clichy

Liège

Cadet

Rome

Louise-Michel

Wagram

Malesherbes

Villiers

St-
Lazare

Trinité

Le Peletier

Richelieu-
Drouot

Mont

Porte de
Champerret

Péreire

Europe

Chaussée-
d'Antin

Monceau

Havre-
Caumartin

R. Montm

4 Septembre

Courcelles

Auber

Opéra

Be

La Défense

RER
LINE A

Charles
de Gaulle/
Etoile

Ternes

St-Philippe-
du-Roule

St-
Augustin

Pyramides

1

Pont de Neuilly   Les Sablons
Porte Maillot

Argentine

6

Victor
Hugo

George V

Miromesnil

Madeleine

Concorde

Tuileries

Kléber

F.D.
Roosevelt

Champs
Elysées
Clemenceau

Seine

2

Porte Dauphine

Boissière

Rue de la
Pompe

Iéna

Alma-Marceau

Musée d'Orsay

Trocadéro

Passy

Pont
de l'Alma

Invalides

Varenne

Chambre des Députés

Solférino

St-Germ
des-Pré

La Muette

Ranelagh

Champ-de-Mars

Latour-
Maubourg

Rue du Bac

Jasmin

Michel-
Ange-
Auteuil

Eglise
d'Auteuil

Bir-Hakeim

St-François
Xavier

Duroc

Sèvres-
Babylone

Me

Rennes

Vaneau

St-
Su

Porte d'Auteuil

Dupleix

Ecole
Mil.

Ségur

Saint-
Placide

Jean-Jaurès

10

Michel-Ange-
Molitor

Chardon
Lagache

Mirabeau

Javel

Charles
Michels

Emile
Zola

Cambronne

Sèvres-
Lecourbe

Falguière

Exelmans

La Motte-
Picquet

Pasteur

Montparnasse
Bienvenüe

E

Boulogne-
Pt. de St-Cloud

Commerce

Volontaires

Gaîté

Boulevard
Victor

Félix Faure

Vaugirard

Pernety

Porte de
St-Cloud

Boucicaut

Plaisance

Marcel Sembat

Lourmel

Convention

Porte de Vanves

8

Balard

Porte de Versailles

Malakoff-
Plateau de Vanves

Billancourt

Malakoff-
Rue Etienne Dolet

9 **Pont de Sèvres**

RER LINE C

12

Mairie d'Issy

Corentin Celton

Châtillon-
Montrouge

13

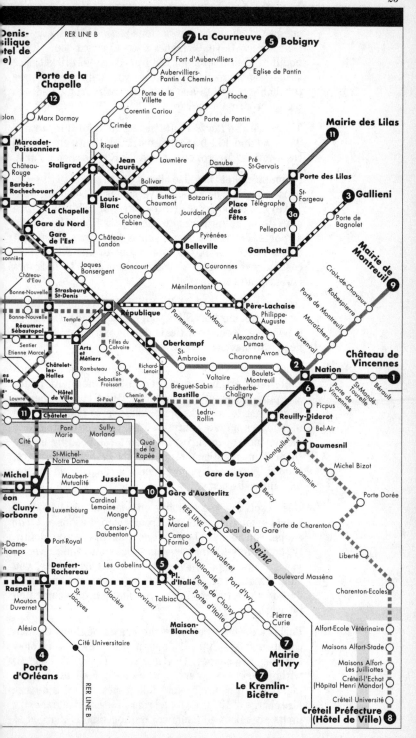

suburban trains to visit places in the Ile-de-France, we suggest you consider a four-zone (Versailles, St-Germain-en-Laye; 98 francs a week) or six-zone (Rambouillet, Fontainebleau; 123 francs a week) ticket. For these weekly/monthly tickets, you will need a pass (available from rail and major Métro stations) and two passport-size photographs.

There are also *Paris-Visite* tickets valid for three or five days (80 and 130 francs, respectively) entitling you to travel on the Métro, buses, and RER lines within Paris.

A similar ticket that also allows you to travel in the suburbs around Paris (e.g., Versailles, St-Germain-en-Laye) costs 150 francs (three days) or 185 francs (five days)—including access to and from Roissy and Orly airports. For travel over a single day, buy a *Formule 1* ticket for travel on the Métro, buses, and RER. This costs anywhere from 23 francs (Paris only) to 70 francs (suburbs and airports).

Access to Métro and RER platforms is through an automatic ticket barrier. Slide your ticket in and pick it up as it pops out. Keep your ticket during your journey; you'll need it to leave the RER system.

By Bus Paris buses are green single-deckers, marked with route number and destination in front and with major stopping-places along the sides. Most routes operate from 6 AM to 8:30 PM; some continue to midnight. Ten night buses operate hourly (1–6 AM) between Châtelet and various nearby suburbs; they can be stopped by hailing them at any point on their route. The brown bus shelters, topped by red and yellow circular signs, contain timetables and route maps.

Bus tickets are *not* available on buses themselves; they must be bought in advance from Métro stations or *tabac* shops. You need to show (but not punch) weekly, monthly, and *Paris-Visite/Formule 1* tickets to the driver as you get on. If you have individual yellow tickets, you should state your destination and be prepared to punch one or more tickets in the red and gray machines on board the bus.

By Taxi Paris taxis may not have the charm of their London counterparts—there is no standard vehicle or color—but they're cheaper. Daytime rates (7 AM till 7:30 PM) within Paris are around 2.80 francs per kilometer, and nighttime rates are around 4.20 francs. There is a basic hire charge of 10 francs for all rides. Rates outside the city limits are about 40% higher. Waiting time is charged at roughly 80 francs per hour. You are best off asking your hotel or restaurant to ring for a taxi; cruising cabs with their signs lit can be hailed, but are annoyingly difficult to spot. Taxi ranks are a better bet, providing you know where to look. Note that taxis seldom take more than three people at a time.

By Bike You can hire bikes in the Bois de Boulogne (Jardin d'Acclimatation), Bois de Vincennes, some RER stations, and from the Bateaux-Mouches embarkation point by place de l'Alma. Or try **Paris-Vélo** (2 rue du Fer à Moulin, 5e, tel. 43–37–59–22). Rental rates vary from about 80 to 140 francs per day, 140 to 220 francs per weekend, and 350 to 500 francs per week, depending on the type of bike.

Guided Tours of Paris

Orientation Tours Bus tours of Paris offer a good introduction to the city. The two largest operators are **Cityrama** (3 pl. des Pyramides, 1er, tel. 42–60–30–14) and **Paris Vision** (214 rue de Rivoli, 1er, tel. 42–60–31–25). Their tours start from the place des Pyramides, across from the Louvre end of the Tuileries Gardens. **American Express** (11 rue Scribe, 9e, tel. 47–77–70–00) also organizes tours from its headquarters near Opéra.

Tours are generally in double-decker buses with either a live or tape-recorded commentary (English, of course, is available) and last three hours. Expect to pay about 150 francs.

The **RATP** (Paris Transport Authority, tel. 40–46–42–17) has many guide-accompanied excursions in and around Paris. Inquire at its Tourist Service on the place de la Madeleine, 8e (to the right of the church as you face it) or at the office at 53 bis quai des Grands-Augustins, 6e. Both are open daily 9–4:30.

Special-Interest Tours **Cityrama, Paris Vision,** and **American Express** (*see* Orientation Tours, *above*) offer a variety of thematic tours ("Historic Paris," "Modern Paris," "Paris-by-Night") lasting from 2½ hours to all day and costing between 150 and 300 francs (more if admission to a cabaret show is included).

Boat Trips Boat trips along the Seine, usually lasting about an hour, are a must for the first-time visitor. Many boats have powerful floodlights to illuminate riverbank buildings; on some, you can also lunch or wine and dine—

book ahead. The following services operate regularly throughout the day and in the evening.

Bateaux-Mouches has departures from Pont de l'Alma (Right Bank), 8e, tel. 42–25–96–10. Boats depart 10–noon, 2–7, and 8:30–10:30. The price is 30 francs (15 francs children under 14). Lunch is served on the 1 o'clock boat and costs 300 francs (150 francs children under 14). Dinner on the 8:30 service costs 500 francs (no children). Wine and service are included in the lunch and dinner prices.

Vedettes du Pont Neuf has departures from Square du Vert Galant (Ile de la Cité), 1er, tel. 46–33–98–38. Boats depart 10–noon, 1:30–6:30, and 9–10:30 every half hour. The price is 35 francs during the day (20 francs children under 10 and 40 francs at night).

Bateaux Parisiens–Tour Eiffel has departures from Pont d'Iéna (Left Bank), 15e, tel. 47–05–50–00. Boats depart at 10 and 11 AM and 12, 2, 3, 4, 5, and 6 PM. The price is 40 francs during the day (20 francs children under 12). Lunch cruises cost 300 francs (200 francs children under 12). Dinner cruises on the 8:30 departure cost 550 francs (no children). Wine and service are included in the lunch and dinner prices.

Canauxrama (tel. 42–39–15–00) organizes leisurely half-day canal tours in flat-bottom barges along the picturesque but relatively unknown St-Martin and Ourcq Canals in East Paris. Departures are from 5 bis quai de la Loire, 19e (9:15 and 2:45), or from Bassin de l'Arsenal, 12e (9:45 and 2:30), opposite 50 boulevard de la Bastille. The price is 70 francs (60 francs on weekend afternoons).

Walking Tours There are plenty of guided tours of specific areas of Paris, often concentrating on a historical or architectural topic—"Restored Mansions of the Marais," "Private Walled Gardens in St-Germain," or "Secret Parts of the Invalides." Tours are often restricted to 30 people and are popular with Parisians as well as tourists. They are accompanied by guides whose enthusiasm and dedication is invariably exemplary, though most are French and may not be able to communicate their enthusiasm to you in English. These potential linguistic problems are more than outweighed by the chance to see Paris in a new light and to visit buildings and monuments that are not usually open to the public. Charges vary between 35 and 50 francs, depending on fees that may be assessed to visit certain buildings. Tours last around two hours and generally start at 2:30 or 3. Details are published in the weekly magazines *Pariscope* and *L'Officiel des Spectacles* under the heading "Conférences." In most cases, you must simply turn up at the meeting point (usually listed as "RV" or "rendezvous"), but it's best to get there early in case of restriction on numbers.

You can sometimes make advance reservations for walking tours organized by the **Caisse Nationale des Monuments Historiques** (Bureau des Visites/Conférences, Hôtel de Sully, 62 rue St-Antoine, 4e, tel. 44–61–20–00), which publishes a small booklet every two months listing all upcoming tours.

For visits to some private mansions, you may be asked to show identification, so be sure to have your passport with you.

Personal Guides **Espaces Limousine** (18 rue Vignon, 9e, tel. 42–65–63–16) and **Executive Car** (25 rue d'Astorg, 8e, tel. 42–65–54–20) have limousines and minibuses (taking up to seven passengers) that will take you around Paris and environs for a minimum of three hours. Reservations are required. The cost is about 250 francs per hour.

Opening and Closing Times in Paris

Banks Banks are open weekdays, but there's no strict pattern to their hours of business. Generally, they're open from 9:30 to 4:30 or 5. Some banks close for lunch between 12:30 and 2.

Museums Again, there is no strict pattern to when museums are open. Most Paris museums close one day a week—usually either Monday or Tuesday—and on national holidays. Usually, they're open from 10 to 5 or 6. Many museums close for lunch (12 to 2) and are open Sundays only in the afternoon.

Shops Large stores are open from 9 or 9:30 to 6 or 7 and don't close at lunchtime. Smaller shops often open earlier (8 AM) but take a lengthy lunch break (1 to 4); small food shops are often open Sunday mornings, 9 to 1. Some corner grocery stores will stay open until about 10 PM. Most shops close all day Monday.

Staying in Euro Disney

Opening and Closing Times

Euro Disneyland is open daily year-round. Opening times vary according to the season and the day of the week: April–mid-June, weekdays 9 AM–7 PM, weekends 9 AM–midnight; mid-June–August, daily 9 AM–midnight; September–October, weekdays 9 AM–7 PM, weekends 9–9; November–March, weekdays 10 AM–6 PM, weekends 10–7.

Admission

One-, two-, or three-day "Passports" give unlimited access to all attractions except the Rustler Roundup Shooting Gallery. Passports need not be used on consecutive days, and holders may leave and return on the same day provided they have their hand stamped at the exit and retain the valid passport. Ticket windows are on the ground floor of the Disneyland Hotel, just outside the entrance gates; re-admission gates are on the far right. Children under 7 must be accompanied by an adult. Costs are:

One-day Passport: 225 francs adults, 150 francs children 3–11, under 3 free.
Two-day Passport: 425 francs adults, 285 francs children.
Three-day Passport: 565 francs adults, 375 francs children.

Information

There are several information centers in Euro Disneyland. City Hall, on the west (left) side of Town Square as you enter the park, can answer questions about all aspects of Euro Disney, including the hotels. Other Disney Information Centers within the park are located at the Ticket Office, upstairs in Main Street Station; at the Frontierland Depot and Cottonwood Creek Ranch in Frontierland; in Fantasyland, west of March Hare Refreshments; in Adventureland, near the Explorer's Club and Trader Sam's.

At Festival Disney, there is a large, informative **Maison de Tourism** (Tourist Office, tel. 60–43–33–33) with a wealth of documentation on Paris and the Ile-de-France, plus a slick audiovisual presentation of local sites, with earphones providing commentary in English.

Special Services

Lost and Found **City Hall,** Town Square (tel. 64–74–25–00).

Lost Adults Report them and rendezvous at City Hall. If your party splits up, arrange to meet again at a specific site known to all of you; crowds may make it difficult to find each other in a larger area.

Currency Exchange There are currency-exchange booths at the Main Entrance and at any of the park information centers.

First Aid The first aid station (tel. 64–74–23–00) is next to Plaza Gardens on Central Plaza.

Storage Coin-operated lockers (10 francs) are outside main entrance and underneath Main Street Station.

Barbershop Main Street's Harmony Barber Shop isn't just for show—it's a for-real place to get a haircut and a shave.

Disabled Guests A **Guest Special Service Guide** is available at the Main Entrance, City Hall, and all information booths. Cast members (Disneyspeak for employees) are not available to accompany guests in wheelchairs.

Vision-Impaired Guests Portable tape recorders and guide tapes are available free at City Hall. Guide dogs are allowed in most locations.

Camera Rentals Still and video cameras can be hired from **Town Square Photography** on Main Street. Same-day film processing is also available.

Guided Tours Guided tours through the park are good for giving you an overview (but not for avoiding lines). Tickets are available at the Main Entrance and at City Hall for 30 francs to those with valid Euro Disneyland Passports. Reservations are required for groups of 15 or more (tel. 64–74–30–00).

Car Care There is a **gas station,** with automatic car wash, near the entry to the visitors' parking lot.

2   **Euro Disney**

Disney's Imagineers have big plans for Euro Disney's future. But for the moment the main event is the theme park, Euro Disneyland, with its five sections ("lands" in Disneyspeak), and to a lesser extent the restaurants, hotels, nightspots, and sports facilities built to amuse and accommodate theme park guests. So the key question in planning a Euro Disneyland visit is how you plan a visit through Euro Disneyland.

Americans, for whom a trip to a Disney theme park is almost a birthright, have the right techniques: (1) Arrive as early as possible and leave as late as possible, and tackle the biggest attractions at each end of the day. Or: (2) Save lining up at the three-star attractions for times when everyone else is watching the big daily parade of Disney characters. (3) Eat early or late, before or after everyone else. (4) Shop before the evening rush hour. (5) Allow plenty of time to get where you want to go. Like something from Alice in Wonderland, the park appears compact one moment, only to grow to enormous size the next—say, when you're at Phantom Manor with a rendezvous at Café Hyperion in five minutes. (6) Wear running shoes and comfortable clothes. If the forecast is grim, bring cold-weather gear or umbrellas (or invest 25 francs in a canary yellow Mickey rain poncho), because some lines are in the open and a certain amount of strolling is inevitable. (7) Figure out what rides you want to hit, and map out your route. (*See* Orientation, *below*, for a few tips.)

Opinion is divided as to whether it's better to cram all the best rides into the morning before you get tired to appreciate them or spread them over the day in a series of highlights. Opinion, for that matter, is divided as to which the best rides are, except for the handful of blockbusters (*see* Highlights for First-time Visitors, *below*). There will always be a perverse someone who insists the Visionarium was the best thing they've ever seen in France. For the very young, that honor might go to It's a Small World and Dumbo, the Flying Elephant; older visitors might prefer the gently scenic Riverboats and the trip around the park on the Euro Disneyland Railroad.

Whatever the maturity of your party, agreeing which land to explore first should never be left until you see the pink gates, by which time you (yes, even you) will be too excited to tell left from right. Ultimately, it doesn't matter one bit where you go first, as long as you see every land, and Euro Disney is small enough for you to do

Euro Disney Overview

EURO DISNEYLAND

EURO DISNEY RESORT COMPLEX

FESTIVAL DISNEY

(Planned Theme Park)

Entrance

First Aid Station

Golf Course

Boulevard Circulaire

Boulevard du Parc

Avenue de l'Europe

N34

D54

D54

D93

D344

RER A

TO LAGNY

TO IF50

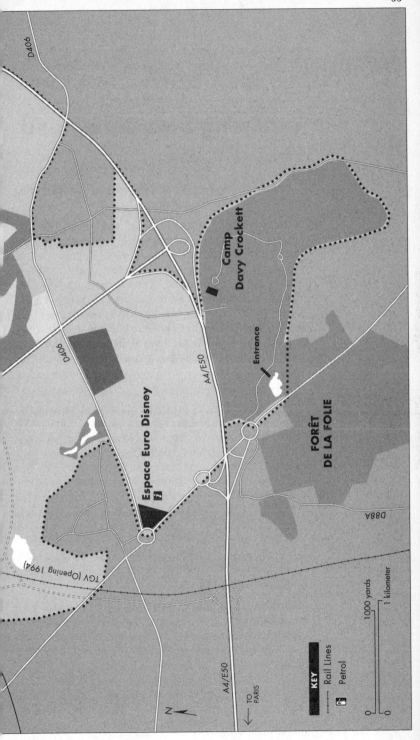

D406

Camp
Davy Crockett

D406

Espace Euro Disney
i

A4/E50

Entrance

FORÊT
DE LA FOLIE

D88A

TGV (Opening 1994)

A4/E50

TO
PARIS

N

KEY

Rail Lines

Petrol

1000 yards

1 kilometer

that easily in just one day. Neither need you bother to kill yourself lining up for absolutely everything if you don't have much time, since the atmosphere, sights, and sideshows are at least half the fun. As the phrase goes, "what you lose on the swings, you gain on the roundabouts."

Exploring Euro Disneyland

Orientation

Numbers in the margin correspond to points of interest on the Euro Disneyland map.

You enter Euro Disneyland from underneath the Disneyland Hotel and are immediately greeted by Main Street Station and the Euro Disneyland Railroad, which are raised above ground level like sections of the Paris Métro. Beyond the station is Town Square, home to City Hall, a major information center, and the start of Main Street U.S.A., lined with shops and restaurants, that leads straight down to the Central Plaza and, just beyond it, the **Le Château de la Belle au Bois Dormant** (Sleeping Beauty's Castle), a dramatic and whimsical pastiche of turrets, fretwork, and steep roofs visible for miles around.

Main Street U.S.A. is one of the theme park's five lands. The Central Plaza is also known as the Hub, because the other lands radiate from it: Frontierland, Adventureland, Fantasyland, and Discoveryland (as you encounter them moving clockwise around the park). Attractions, as theme park rides are called here, are distributed fairly evenly throughout these lands and interspersed with shops and restaurants. Each land has a theme, which carries through in everything from the food and decor in the restaurants and the merchandise in the shops to the architecture, to the design of the trash bins and the uniforms of employees (Disney calls them "cast members").

Maps are handed out when you pay your admission to enter the park, and the park is just 686 meters (750 yards) across at its widest, with no part of the park more than a 10-minute stroll from the Central Plaza. So, if you have a good sense of direction, it's hard to get lost at Euro Disneyland. In practice, however, it's fairly easy to get temporarily turned around, since all the walkways curve this way and that, buildings are placed at odd angles, and have several entrances.

The tour below moves from the end of Main Street into Frontierland, where, if you arrive in the park early enough, you can try to be ahead of the throngs streaming toward Big Thunder Mountain, whose queue area, unlike many in the park, is not equipped with exhibits and other entertaining features that make a long wait pass quickly. Get there quickly, bypassing the Main Street shops for the moment—save them for late afternoon or day's end. From Frontierland, move counterclockwise into Adventureland, pass through the Central Plaza to Discoveryland, and wind up in Fantasyland. By that time, you may be too weary for more queuing—but all the attractions there except It's A Small World are easily skippable the first time around. (If you have a small child in tow, you will definitely want to do the trip in reverse.)

Note that French, as well as English, is used for signs and directions, and that a number of attractions are designated by their French, rather than their English, name.

Entertainment Live entertainment adds texture to a Euro Disneyland visit. While the jokes may be silly, the humor broad, and the themes sometimes excessively wholesome, the level of professionalism is high and the energy of the performers unquestionable. Performance schedules are available at City Hall; stop by to pick one up as soon as you enter the park.

Disney characters are the main event, especially if you're traveling with children (but even if you're not). They put in appearances to sign autographs and pose for snapshots throughout the park—Town Square in the morning is a good bet. If you miss them then, you can get the requisite eyeful at the big **daily parade,** which begins in Fantasyland and proceeds down Main Street to Town Hall at least once a day. Along with the characters, this includes singers and dancers aplenty—the singers usually lip-syncing to music played over the PA system.

If the park is open at night when you visit, don't miss the **Main Street Electrical Parade,** an extravaganza of toe-tapping music and floats themed on scenes from Disney classics, aglitter with hundreds of thousands of tiny lights; it's staged twice an evening in busy seasons.

Whenever you go, you'll come upon all kinds of short shows and happenings themed to the various lands—on Main Street, brass bands, barbershop quartets, and Dixieland; in Adventureland, pirates doing stunts, steel

Euro Disneyland

FANTASYLAND

Fantasyland Station

Fantasy Festival Stage

Toad Hall

Blue Lagoon

Au Chalet de la Marionnette

ADVENTURELAND

Explorer's Club

Fuente del Oro

Cowboy Cookout

Pueblo Trading Post

Frontierland Depot

Big Thunder Mountain

FRONTIERLAND

Wilderness Island

Rivers of the Far West

0   100 yards

0   100 meters

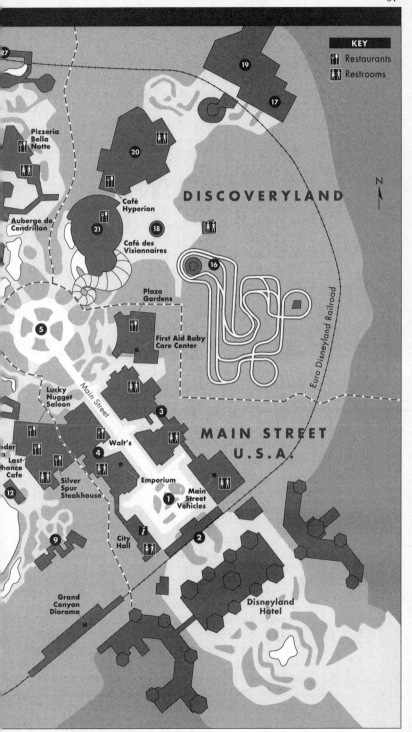

KEY
🚻 Restaurants
🚻 Restrooms

Pizzeria
Bella
Notte

20

DISCOVERYLAND

Auberge de
Cendrillon

Café Hyperion

21   18

Café des
Visionnaires

16

Plaza
Gardens

5

First Aid Baby
Care Center

Euro Disneyland Railroad

N

Lucky
Nugget
Saloon

Main Street

3

Walt's

4

MAIN STREET
U.S.A.

Last
hance
Cafe

Silver
Spur
Steakhouse

Emporium

1

Main
Street
Vehicles

12

9

7

City
Hall

2

Grand
Canyon
Diorama

Disneyland
Hotel

drummers, and African singers and dancers; in Discoveryland, a pair of friendly robots; in Fantasyland, troubadors, jesters, and strolling actors who tap audience members for impromptu reenactments of favorite fairy tales, plus big singing-and-dancing shows on the Castle Stage in front of the Castle and the Fantasy Festival Stage at the Fantasyland Railroad Station. Exactly what you find depends on when you visit.

Highlights for First-time Visitors

Big Thunder Mountain, Frontierland
Phantom Manor, Frontierland
Pirates of the Caribbean, Adventureland
CinéMagique, for the film *Captain EO*, Discoveryland
Star Tours, Discoveryland
It's a Small World, Fantasyland
Dumbo the Flying Elephant, Fantasyland (but only if you have small children)

Main Street, U.S.A.

This street is where you first pick up the contagious Disney atmosphere of almost hysterical joy. On either side are prettified versions of the buildings that might have been found on the main streets of American small towns at the turn of the century. Dixieland jazz, barbershop quartet songs, and honky-tonk piano music beam out onto streets so clean-scrubbed and sweet you could almost lick them.

Any cynicism you may have had about the whole idea of Euro Disneyland will probably melt after only a few steps into the park, in **Town Square,** where the **Main Street Vehicles** clop and rumble, crowds mill and swarm, and you catch sight of the excruciatingly lovable Disney characters—actually park employees wearing the costumes of the heroes and heroines of classic Disney films (check at the hat shop or the Camera Shop).

The four Main Street Vehicles are perfect, shiny vintage autos: a police van, a fire engine, a limo, and a double-decker omnibus. There are also streetcars drawn by heavy Percheron horses, who look bored (as will you if you wait around too long; you can get down the avenue much faster on foot). On the ground floor of the gingerbread-trimmed Main Street buildings are a multitude of shops, among them **Main Street Motors,** which displays and sells real vintage cars such as the 1908 EMF Gentleman's Roadster Model 30 tagged at 470,000 francs, and the mahogany-and-marble **Harmony Barber Shop,** where French youths in decidedly 20th-century spandex cycling shorts get a shave, anachronistically enough, from Disney cast members in 19th-century costumes wielding 19th-century straight-edge razors.

2 At **Main Street Station,** which you pass almost immediately upon entering the park, an announcer who sounds as smooth as Cary Grant attempts to amuse people queuing in the first of many Disney lines by asking the passenger who "lost a roll of bills wrapped in a red rubber band" to "come claim the red rubber band." The main thing with the **Euro Disneyland Railroad,** which is what they're all waiting for, is whether to bother waiting at all. The three narrow-gauge steam trains, downsized versions of U.S. trains of the 1880s complete with whistle bells and cow catchers, are gorgeous, and they make a pleasant, informative 20-minute trip around the park's perimeter that could be a good way to get oriented. However, many people board at other stops along the way (in Frontierland and Fantasyland), and they tend to stay put for the entire circuit, leaving you often watching in envy and frustration as carriage after carriage pulls out of the station full, for as much as an hour. Either skip it or board at one of the other stations, where lines are usually shorter; or go in the middle of the afternoon or at night, when the wait may be less and you'll welcome the chance to rest your feet as much as to take in the one attraction in the park that can only be seen from the train, the **Grand Canyon Diorama,** a somewhat tired 80-meter (262-foot) evocation of the Arizona countryside with stuffed animals and painted backdrops.

Two covered, gaslit walks provide rainy-day access to **3** Main Street stores: **Discovery Arcade,** behind the shops on the east side of Main Street and lined with display cabinets containing sketches, models, and plans of cars, cities, and trains of the future, and its counterpart on **4** the other side of the street, the **Liberty Arcade,** which also leads to **Liberty Court,** where you can step through a red-velvet curtain to see a swagged nighttime diorama of the Statue of Liberty's 1886 inauguration, complete with speechmaking, crowd noise and other sound effects, and merrymakers silhouetted against a vivid cobalt-blue sky. The famous statue was made in France on the designs of French sculptor Frédéric-Auguste Bartholdi.

⑤ Central Plaza, at the top of Main Street, gives access to the other four "Lands" of Disney (or Dees-nay, as they say around here).

Located just beyond, nominally in Fantasyland but dominating Euro Disneyland's skyline is **Le Château de la Belle au Bois Dormant** (Sleeping Beauty's Castle). This 43-meter (140-foot) monument to make-believe has everything: the patterned roof from St. Stephen's in Vienna, turrets and spires from Bavaria, Loire château gables, and Moorish battlements. It's a pink, blue, and gold wedding cake—bemoated, enough to make the spectator giddy, all apparently larger than life thanks to the use of forced perspective (a set-maker's technique, which designers have drawn upon throughout Euro Disneyland, whereby architectural features are scaled progressively smaller from the bottom of the building to the top, in order to exaggerate what the eye actually sees and make the building appear larger than it actually is).

Frontierland

This Wild West playground is the stuff of everyone's childhood cowboy fantasies, including those young enough still to be having them. Here, on the Rivers of the Far West—a man-made body of water that's really a 300-yard-wide lake—are the red rocks, lonesome pines, and cacti, the streets lined with wooden corrals, barns, and shacks, the sun-baked pueblo houses. If dining with Cinderella didn't put you in a Disney frame of mind, the gunshots, cicadas, whooping prairie birds, and cowboy strumming will soon git to ya. Not to mention all the western tunes you can hum, played over the PA system. From Wilderness Island south to the Thunder Mesa area, Davy Crocketts—but no buffalo—roam along with Mexican banditi and cowboys in 10-gallon hats and ⑥ leather-look weskits; dominating the scene is **Big Thunder Mountain,** looking like something out of Monument Valley.

Thrilling it surely is, but the scariest thing about this famous big dipper ride on what's supposed to be a runaway mine train is the long line—if it starts from the sign at the foot of the hill, then what you see is only half what you get. Try the absolute first thing in the morning or as late in the evening as possible, and get in the right-hand lane after the line splits in two, as you approach the boarding area, for the best views over Frontierland as you wait. Once you're finally ready to climb aboard, everyone is in a carnival mood and shouting a French-accented "Here we go!" (which comes out something like "ere we go . . . "); you're ready to scream your head off and extract every ounce of fun from the next three minutes. Suffice it to say that on this roller-coaster (this is Disney, after all), the pace is not extreme, the corners none too sharp, and the drops not the sheerest; the showmanship, however, is fantastic. The sometimes schmaltzy Disney sense of humor really works here: Glowing rats' and bats' eyes line the tunnels, and there are floods, broken tracks, explosions, falling timbers, collapsing mine shafts, and jokey scenery in the slow stretches, such as a goat eating a pair of jeans off a washing line. Big Thunder Mountain is practically compulsory. Under-threes are not allowed, but sturdy four-year-olds will love it. *All ages.*★★★

If you're worried the kids now believe that all ducks wear sailor suits and pigs walk on two legs, show them
7 **Cottonwood Creek Ranch Critter Corral,** home of the only animals in Euro Disneyland who behave like animals, right down to providing a mighty challenge for the white-suited clean-up gang. Here are ducks, kids, lambs, piglets, bunnies, chickens, and calves, all picked for their perfect baby-ness and high Disney aaaah-rating and all wandering freely around a gravel-covered yard past which the Euro Disneyland Railroad steams picturesquely. Uniquely, it is possible to get filthy dirty in the Corral (there's a "wash yer hands here" pump at the exit), or get bits of clothing chewed, and as a reality check it's essential viewing. *Children.* ★★

8 At **Indian Canoes,** 20 Euro Disney guests are given paddles with ends like baseball bats and launched, slave-galley style, into the Rivers of the Far West. Boy instructors in Davy Crockett outfits, complete with coonskin caps, make a show of the warm-up and paddling lesson; then you're off as fast as your collective skill allows. The canoes appeal predominantly to adults and ply the same route as the steamboats and the River Rogue Keelboats (which often look like they're on collision course). The trip takes about 10 minutes whether or not you're any good at rowing. This ride closes down at dusk and is not open in winter; then, only the steamboats ply the Rivers of the Far West. *Adults and older children.*★★

9 You know that **Phantom Manor** is going to be good as soon as the door opens onto the cobwebby, elegantly decayed entrance hall and you shuffle through into the gallery for the first of many horrible surprises. Once you've caught up with the continuous line of funereal chariots, the cocoon-like black ride vehicles, you're twisted this way and that at the mercy of your ghostly hosts, and you're always feeling that you must be missing something in the other direction. Not to give too much away, the best bits consist of the most lifelike—or should we say deathlike—AudioAnimatronic creations in the park: the soon-to-be-jilted bride, left to get older and older (and older and older) alone in her haunted mansion; the decapitated green talking head; the ghostly banquet, where revelers appear to vanish before your eyes; the barbershop quartet of marble busts in the cemetery; the nasty polyglot spooks on the descent into the hellish cellar; and the surprise in the mirrors at the end. Phantom Manor is billed as too scary for the very young and it is probably best to leave them upstairs lest their terrified wails distress you, but melodic phantom choruses and the usual Disney jokery completely dissipate any frissons of true terror, so older children should be fine and adults may want to repeat the journey. On your way out, don't miss the pint-size bride begging you to return, and listen at the unmarked green marble tomb on Boothill graveyard—someone's trying to get out. Go first thing in the morning or in the evening; lines are almost nonexistent then. *Adults and older children.* ★★★

🔟 The **River Rogue Keelboats** travel the same waters as the Indian Canoes and the steamboats; the difference is the speed (much faster than the canoes and somewhat faster than the riverboats), the music (twangy), the commentary from the cowboy at the rudder (boring or funny depending on the individual), and the viewpoint (closer to water level than from aboard the steamboats, higher up than from the canoes). There is only one of the two 32-seater boats in service at a time and the line is viewless, seatless, and tedious, and if you miss the boat, you're looking at another 15-odd-minute wait for a 7-minute ride. If you've cruised aboard the riverboats, skip this. However, if you go, remember that these close down at dusk, like the Indian Canoes, and the line is shorter just before then. *All ages.* ★

⓫ At the **Rustler Roundup Shooting Gallery,** 10 francs buys a lease on a rifle that makes a ricochet sound as if it's shooting bullets, but actually works by laser. Little targets scattered all over a 3-D cartoon Wild West landscape do funny things when hit: Jailbird Del struggles to escape his coffin, a vulture's neck rotates, tin cans leap and spin, and something in the mine explodes—all amid satisfyingly bleeps, pings, pongs, dings, screeches, and whees. Optional for all except firearm freaks. *Adults and older children.*★

⑫ **Thunder Mesa Riverboat Landing** is where you begin a leisurely cruise on the Rivers of the Far West aboard one of the two beautiful steamboats, the stern-wheeler *Mark Twain*, which has a huge red paddle wheel and towering, smoke-belching chimney stacks, or the side-wheeler *Molly Brown*, patterned on boats that plied the Sacramento River during the California Gold Rush. Go at dusk when the atmosphere along the river is so peaceful that you can easily forget where you are—at least until the Keelboat captains start whooping out and calling to your fellow passengers and the Thunder Mountain runaway mine train screams and whooshes around its red-rock mountain. It's a wonderfully relaxing ride, with a gentle cowboy music soundtrack, white bent-wood chairs on deck, and soothing scenery—an Audio-Animatronic Old Joe rocking on his veranda near the beginning of the ride while his dog barks, glimpses of illuminated Main Street in the distance, and the steam train chugging past. A geyser blows, a coyote is silhouetted against the sky, and there goes that screaming train again. It may all be too slow for hyped-up children. There is always plenty of room aboard, and your wait shouldn't exceed 15 or 20 minutes, although late morning and mid-afternoon are not the optimal time. *All ages.*★

Adventureland

The soundtrack to this lightning dash through the world's wild places segues from sea shanties to African speaking drums, Arabic wailing, marimba, didgeridoo, sitar, and tabla, according to which sun-soaked continent you've wandered into. Cast members wear voluminous harem pants and turbans, pretend to hammer copper dishes in a splendid bazaar, and greet you at the Explorer's Club in safari suits, or swash and buckle in pirate garb; faded adobe buildings, lush vegetation, tropical lagoons, and craggy island rocks provide the holiday high. The Explorer's Club restaurant is great for romantic, child-free dinners.

⑬ **Adventure Isle,** a pair of close-together islands linked by a pair of bridges in the middle of an unnamed, man-made waterway caters to the Robinson Crusoe and Captain Hook in all of us—and by no means just children. Adults can be seen attempting to overturn the floating barrel bridge or upset the swinging suspension bridge, trying out a few rock-climbing moves, and playing hide-and-seek with their kids in the amazing cave networks. Whether you go in at Davy Jones's Locker, Dead Men's Maze, the Keelhaul Caverns, or Hook's Hideout, you never seem to come out where you intended, having lost your way amid blinking "bats'" eyes and wet-look stalactites in the flickering gloom with moans and distant voices calling (tourists or ghosts?); with paths emerging behind waterfalls and plunging back down again, it feels like the real thing. Above ground, teens scamper around like drunkards, and youngsters clamber over on Captain Hook's handsome scarlet pirate ship and the *Rocher-Qui-Bascule* (Teetering Rock). A skull-shaped boulder known as Skull Rock holds more caverns, and there's a lookout point with telescopes, a peaceful bamboo grove with its own jungle noises, and a stone-rimmed aerie overlooking a perfect baby beach. As you may well imagine, it's best to explore all this with your energy levels at maximum. The isle is stunningly pretty at twilight when the lights go on in the Swiss Family Robinson's neighboring banyan tree house and pools of light dapple the lapping "sea." *All ages.*★★

In the middle of the more southerly of the two Adventure Isle landfalls, a sign explains to anyone who hasn't seen the 1960 Disney movie, *The Swiss Family Robinson*, how papa Franz Robinson and his brood were shipwrecked in 1805 and built a new life in an amazing tree house from the wreckage. You can view the remains of their ship, the *Swallow*, near the floating bridge, and at **⑭ La Cabane des Robinson** (Swiss Family Treehouse), climb the house they built in a concrete-and-fiberglass fig tree that climbs 89 feet (27 meters) above ground level. In their new home, waterfalls power the family's ingenious plumbing; the kitchen is filled with apparently real papayas, melons, and bananas; and the livingrooms and bedrooms are furnished with ship's furniture and home-made accessories (decorating ideas galore for anyone with access to a shipwreck). Because nobody ever really grows out of his childhood tree-house fantasy, all this is charming and well worth tackling the stairs; even vertigo sufferers can handle it since there are no sheer drops or open sides. There are telescopes for distance viewing, and lines are sometimes nonexistent, particularly in early morning or later afternoon. *All ages.*★★

⑮ The adventurous romp known as **Pirates of the Caribbean** is practically everybody's favorite Euro Disneyland ride, as you can tell from the size of the waiting crowd.

Luckily, the march through the line area—past ever-more-sinister corridors punctuated by occasional skeletons in dungeons and on to some jungly paths down to the water—is entertaining in itself. Once aboard your ride vehicles, simple 23-passenger john boats, you cruise through a serene moonlit night, past a shipwreck and Adventureland's Blue Lagoon restaurant, up a steep ramp, and on through 22 incredibly lifelike scenes in which high-tech and therefore incredibly lifelike AudioAnimatronic pirates fight, carouse, burn, rape, and pillage their way through a West Indies town. (Rape? This being Disney, what you see is a "wife auction," with some pirate on the opposite shore yelling for the redhead.) Everything's in French, so the kids shouldn't understand, and it's all utterly tame, if not exactly as politically correct to a '90s audience as it might have been back in the '60s, when an almost identical Pirates debuted at Disneyland. After the AudioAnimatronic buccaneers have sacked the town, drained the rum barrels, and sung a few rounds of "It's a Pirate's Life for Me," they get their come-uppance: You see them rotting with their booty as your boat returns to shore, down a splashy ramp that may mean a brief shower for those in the boat's front seats—a good spot to avoid when it's chilly outside. All in all, an incredible feat of Imagineering. The line is not only entertaining but also fairly fast-moving. *All ages.*★★★

Discoveryland

This is not called "Tomorrowland" as it is in Euro Disneyland's American cousins, where the Disney "Imagineers" who planned all the parks have seen how today persists in overtaking tomorrow. So they threw out their crystal ball and instead designed a Jules Verne–H. G. Wells vision of the distant future—that is, circa 1950. It is dominated by the Orbitron, a tower ringed by odd-looking "planets" and Flash Gordon–style rockets, and its entrance is guarded by a stair-stepped waterfall-fountain. Done in sophisticated shades of turquoise, bronze, peach, and purple, and neon-lit at nightfall, Discoveryland is indeed beautiful. But despite its looks and its soundtrack, which ranges from *Star Wars* anthems to bleepy stuff that sounds as if it must have been written by some '50s computers, this is the least atmospheric of the Lands.

16 At **Autopia,** Bugatti-Thunderbird hybrids painted in tasteful red, purple, yellow, and turquoise and aflash with tail fins, chrome detailing, and big black bumpers roar around a leafy course. The cars are patently on tracks, they can't run into one another, and they move at a mere 7 mph. Yet children and even adults who take the wheel invariably display expressions of sheer fear as they approach a corner and appear ready to collide with another vehicle. The scene resembles *Wacky Races* without Muttley or Penelope Pitstop, but with plenty of underage Dick Dastardlies striking cool poses behind the wheel, and bumping other cars ("accidentally" because bumping is not allowed). The waiting area is a tiered space ship with open sides, so you can see the whole line. Great fun for kids, who must be over 1 meter 32 (4⅓ feet) high. *Children.*★

⓱ Don't go to see *Captain EO*, the 16-minute 3-D film that plays at 700-seat **CinéMagique,** expecting some dull feature with lame effects. Technology for 3-D has improved dramatically since the days of white cardboard spectacles with one green and one red lens, and the film you see here, a good-guys-win morality tale about the power of music, has got the lot: not only a coherent storyline (parts of which are frightening to adults as well as kids, such as the fingernail-knives that jab at you), but also suspense, thrills, music, dancing, inventive detail, direction by Francis Ford Coppola, powerful special effects by George Lucas, and, oh yes, Michael Jackson. Although you remain static, parts of the experience are not dissimilar to moments in *Star Tours*, and the sensation of movement seems more real than movement itself; often the action seems to be taking place just feet, or even inches, in front of you. Taking center stage in all this is a cast that includes Anjelica Huston as the evil queen, and a batch of peculiar aliens, among them a cute little creature named Hooter (a fuzzy orange cross between a moth and one of *Star Wars'* Ewoks). Jackson has the white-knight rôle he must have been born to play, and his fans will love having him feel close enough to kiss (even though there's no eye contact). Meanwhile, the jaded can amuse themselves by removing the 3-D glasses handed out free at the film's entrance and watching the audience, all 694 of them, simultaneously grabbing at thin air. The line is static but more or less disappears every 15 minutes or so as the waiting hordes disappear into the auditorium; there are three "magic lanterns" featuring Hooter to amuse kids in the interim. *Adults and older children.*★★★

⓲ No doubt **Orbitron** occupies center stage in Discoveryland for aesthetic reasons—it's the "weenie" that Walt knew would draw people where you wanted them to go. It's lovely when lit up at night, and it's intriguing by daylight with its "planets," which are like sputniks or old-fashioned spherical vacuum cleaners, rotating around a tall tower, in the opposite direction from a ring of hissing rocket ships straight out of Flash Gordon, the vehicles for this ride. The retrograde motion of these planets makes it seem as if the rockets move very fast; but this is actually Fantasyland's Dumbo ride in another costume, a short, gentle, rising-and-dipping ride around a central spire with your flight height left in your own control. Don't bother to queue unless you're trailing a small, space-mad child. *Young children.*★

19 The most entertaining line in Discoveryland is at **Star Tours.** It snakes around space-station corridors (natural habitat of Luke Skywalker), and passes, at various moments, a video wall advertising new tour packages to the Intergalactic Zoo and the Moon of Endor, windows overlooking engineer aliens at work and R2D2 and C3PO repairing one of the StarSpeeder 3000s you're about to ride, and an illustrated map of the Tion Hegemony, Cron Drift, Bala Trix Nebula, et al. Rousing *Star Wars* music, two binocular-faced beasties, flight stewards in Thierry Mugleresque uniforms, and what may be the world's only watchable safety film raise the anticipation to fever pitch. Finally you strap yourself in (do it), stow your bags under your feet, and brace yourself while robot RX24, inept first-time pilot, takes your craft lurching through space, wisecracking in French all the way. The state-of-the-art flight simulator that provides the effects gives you the bumpiest ride in the park bar none. For a short 6 minutes, you whiz through a gorgeous ice-crystal tunnel and into something that looks like the Death Planet canyon at the end of *Star Wars*, then narrowly avoids assorted missiles and asteroids, shoots into hyperspace, and swerves back into the landing bay for a surprise ending. The French will tell you that it's *vaut le détour* (worth the detour), and even veterans of similar simulators may have trouble maintaining their disbelief. No children under three are allowed, and the ride could unsettle sensitive four- to six-year-olds. *All but young children.*★★★

A scarlet and yellow "replica" of Jules Verne's *Hyperion* airship, 35 meters (115 feet) long, protrudes from the facade of **Videopolis,** a warehouse-size fast-food court **20** with tier upon tier of tables, armadas of jade- and tangerine-colored space-ship miniatures stuck to the ceiling, and natural light streaming through the window-walls. As guests line up for fast food, rock videos play on giant screens; these are interrupted five times a day by the song-and-dance "Rock Choc" show, a sort of a cross between a cruise-ship cabaret act and the Eurovision Song Contest or U.S. television's Star Search, with a French emcee, tinny Europop music, and cosmic special effects (look out for the setting moon). It appeals mainly to preteen girls, who want to *be* Videopolis dancers and, at night, to older kids; then, it's like a school hop, with parents standing in for teachers (though it can be dead if the dance floor isn't full). Under the same roof are a relaxing video wall showing travelogues and a Compact Disc Interactive gallery, full of televisions with attached modems that allow you to determine what image you'll see next. *Older children.* ★

The wait is seldom more than 10 minutes for the two-part show at **Le Visionarium,** a short film introduction and a 15-minute movie-in-the-round. It begins in one carpeted stand-up movie theater with pretty models of the *Hyperion* and Montgolfier's pioneer balloons dangling from the ceiling and the voice of a character known as "the Timekeeper" introducing the great visionaries of our time and his assistant "9-Eye," a 360° camera. Then the audience herds into the circular main auditorium to stand for an enveloping CircleVision movie, *From Time to Time,* made with a special camera rig—actually nine 35mm cameras mounted on a pole—and shown high on the walls all around you. In it, the Timekeeper throws 9-Eye back in time, accidentally abducts Jules Verne, and sets you racing around the space-time continuum. The historical tableaux and epic European scenery are spectacular for anyone, and there are stellar jokes for grown-ups—Gérard Dépardieu as an airport security man, for instance, confirming the widely held belief that he does, in fact, appear in every French movie ever made. "Go quickly now and begin *your* future," advises the Timekeeper after a quick spin through outer space at journey's end, and you really do feel exhilarated, if a bit stiff from all that standing. The film is in French, and the number of translation phones—you'll find them in the last three rows of the theater—not always adequate, so when you enter the first theater, position yourself near the doors into the main auditorium so you can be first in. At this attraction, Disney folk have considerately positioned an LCD timer outside to tell you how long it will be until the next show begins. The show is hopeless for small to medium children—because everybody stands they can't see unless you can hold them up for the duration, a wearing prospect for most parents. *Adults and older children.* ★★

Fantasyland

Fantasyland is a jolly, happy fairy-tale-a-rama of higgledy-piggledy Hansel and Gretel houses in nursery colors, with artfully gnarled trees, pillars, and chimney stacks. The air is alive with organ-grinder renditions of "Give a Little Whistle" and Strauss 'n' Disney tunes spliced with chirping birds, amid a multitude of merrily strolling Princes Charming in brocade frock coats and von Trapps in Tyrolean loden jackets and dirndls. It's as if the cartoon backdrop of Disney's family favorites has come to life—Fantasyland in the rain is a contradiction in terms. In general lines here are longest in late morning and all afternoon up to 6 PM, with a slight slackening between 1 and 2.

❷❷ The most striking feature of Fantasyland is the **Sleeping Beauty Castle.** Inside are La Galerie (the Gallery) and La Tanieíre du Dragon (the Dragon's Lair). The former displays tapestries and stained-glass scenes, exact as stills, from the $6 million 1959 Disney film *Sleeping Beauty*; the whole thing seems pointless, and is boring. The Dragon's Lair, a dingy dungeon, shows exactly how to house a dragon, should you find one. Disney's is a magnificent, highest-tech AudioAnimatronic creature with flaming red eyes and giant claws. He breathes smoke and roars most satisfyingly. Don't miss him—but don't bother to queue if there's a line; just go back later, since you can often walk straight in. *All ages.* ★★

❷❸ Some of the ivy at the entrance of **Alice's Curious Labyrinth** is real, some of it isn't; some of this low-hedged maze is fabulous, some of it isn't. In fact, it isn't a maze at all, since there's only one route through, with many false trails and niches and a series of encounters with Cheshire cats and caterpillars and—everyone's favorite—square columns that spit out little squirts of water. You enter through little doors that look like rabbit holes, usually with a crowd whose pace is unfortunately dictated by a dawdler; after that it's full steam ahead to the Queen of Hearts' castle, the ultimate objective of your trip through the labyrinth, dodging overexcited 12-year-olds and pausing for a photo opportunity where you stick your head on a playing card soldier. The queen herself hides in a bush ordering heads to be chopped off—"coupe la tête!"—to the grisly sound of a head falling into a basket. While her pink-and-blue castle offers good views of the park, this isn't an attraction to visit when you're footsore, since it seems an awfully long way through, and there is only one abort-mission route (it's signposted "To the Un-birthday Party," just before the queen's section). Lines are not under cover and their length is directly affected by the weather. Imagery is courtesy the Disney studios' 1951 version of Lewis Carroll's *Alice in Wonderland*. *Children.*★

24 At **Blanche-Neige et les Sept Nains** (Snow White and the Seven Dwarfs), you take a train for a two-minute ride through the famous tale, from the dwarves' bright, cozy cottage into the dark forest, where the queen turns from the Mirror on the Wall and becomes the horrid wicked witch, and sinister trees reach down to grab you in underwhelming feats of very low-tech animation. Everything is styled exactly as in the 1959 film, but those great songs are barely audible—no "Whistle While You Work" whatsoever. At the end, as you leave the ride, be sure to direct your small child's attention to the shelf on top of the exit door, where Snow White and the prince have materialized. Blanche Neige is one of Euro Disneyland's three "dark rides"—so called because there's no illumination but black light, which makes the phosphorescent paints used to create the sets glow vividly; the other two are Peter Pan's Flight and Pinocchio's Travels (*see below*). *Small children.*★

25 At **Le Carrousel de Lancelot** (Lancelot's Merry-go-round), 86 hand-carved horses and a couple of chariots whirl quaintly round and round and up and down to a calliope rendition of "Chim Chim Cheree" from Disney's 1964 *Mary Poppins*. Horses at the outside are garishly dressed in gold, bronze, silver, purple, and blue scaly armor encrusted with jewels, while smaller inside ones are plainer and more traditional. This is one of the gentlest rides here and one of the shortest, so you should hardly have to wait. *All ages.*★

26 At **Dumbo the Flying Elephant,** kids climb into little cars—small Dumbos in saddlecloths and matching hats—attached to long arms that circle around a central post topped by a hot-air balloon and Timothy Mouse, the pachyderm's friend. These, together with the ring of gilt-framed storks on sticks and a marching circus band, are cute as a button and not frightening at all. Nervous parents can ride with their offspring and control the up-and-down movement of the Dumbos as they play ring around the mouse. Disney's 1941 64-minute ani-

mated feature, *Dumbo,* inspired the imagery. *Young children.*★★★

27 At first glimpse **It's a Small World,** a boat glide through a world of musical moppets dressed in the national costumes of every land, comes across as mildly chlorine-scented, unbearably cutesy, a bit dated (as you'd expect from a creation of the 1964–65 World's Fair). But by the time you've seen Europe with the Dutch babies in clogs, the Spanish flamenco dancers, and the German oompah band, and passed the Russian balalaikas and reached the more exotic continents, the music has filled out, the spectacle kicked in, and you've been won over. The clever soundtrack shoots out temple bells as you pass Himalayan dolls and sitar music as you pass the sloe-eyed Indians, and tugs at the heartstrings in classic Disney fashion in the rousing, glittering, Busby Berkeley Hollywood finale—by which time you've decided you'd like to pack the whole thing up and take it home to cheer you up after run-ins with the surly bank manager or the IRS. Just beyond, in the World Chorus section at the ride exit area, powder blue models of famous monuments of the world house screens where you watch cartoons of grinning kids from around the world communicating The Song to each other via the technology of the ride's sponsor, France Telecom. Warning to the musically sensitive: The Song will never leave you. (For the record, its name is the same as the ride's, and it was penned by the very Richard M. and Robert B. Sherman who won an Academy Award for Disney's *Mary Poppins* score.) *Young children.*★★

28 The **Mad Hatter's Tea Cups,** a familiar sight at California Disneyland, is exactly the same as European fairground waltzers and American Tubs-O-Fun, except here riders control the speed of vehicle rotation via a central silver disc; the vehicles are, of course, giant cups and saucers that seat up to four; and there's scenery—Chinese lanterns suspended from the roof; a sugar bowl and milk jug along the edge, which match the teapot outside the ride next to the March Hare's thatched hut (a refreshment stand with a real thatched roof out of which a goofy dormouse periodically pops). The variable speed makes this okay for little ones and offers thrills and spills for speed fiends. The ride is less than two minutes long, so turnover is fast. *All ages.*★

29 At **Peter Pan's Flight,** you board miniature pirate galleons, which move on tracks suspended from the roof, and fly through a series of black-lighted sets—through a

very authentic London nursery and then over the
Houses of Parliament into a night sky full of glittery
stars, which you circle several times in full view of two
other galleons—distracting because anyone wearing
white glows like a ghost under the UV illumination.
Neverland is a missable hill with a freestanding rain-
bow, but the scenes of piracy that follow are better, and
Wendy's chattering teeth as she walks the gangplank
are one of those Disney details you have to doff your hat
to. Since the story's set in London, there might have
been a case for these characters to make their comments
in English but everything's in French. Peter Pan attracts the longest line in Fantasyland (with nothing
much to look at as you queue), and it's not worth the usually interminable wait. If you must, try to catch it at an
off-time, such as first thing in the morning or later on in
the evening. The characters and images here come
straight from the Disney studios' 1953 animated feature, based on a Sir James M. Barrie play. *Young children.*★

30 The best of the three children's dark rides, **Les Voyages
de Pinocchio** (Pinocchio's Travels)—based on Disney's
1940 Pinocchio, the company's second animated feature—has you board little six-person trains for a ride
along twisty tracks through scenes from the puppet
boy's life, from toymaker Geppetto's workshop through
morally menacing Pleasure Island to Pinocchio's trials
in the Rough House and a surprisingly affecting finale,
in which the hero of the tale becomes human. The famous growing-nose scene is missing, but Monstro the
whale makes an appearance, rearing up nightmarishly
like the shark in *Jaws*. Children will like the ride better
if they're familiar with the story. The line is under the
cover of a Swiss ski lodge affair, and entertainers are occasionally on hand to amuse the waiting throngs. *Young
children.*★

Shopping

Shopping is an integral part of the entertainment of
Euro Disneyland, and all the lands are peppered with
stores offering something in every price range—and not
just Disney souvenirs. Each store has a theme (related
to its location), the merchandise is presented amid enticing decor, and the salesclerks are costumed appropriately: You'll find cowboy hats and sturdy boots in
Frontierland, say, or South Sea shells and Oriental jew-

elry in Adventureland. All of the shops accept American Express, and most stores accept traveler's checks.

Euro Disneyland

Main Street U.S.A. **Plaza West** and **Plaza East Boutiques,** to the left and right of the main entrance, sell souvenirs and practical goods (films, sunglasses, hats, sunscreen). The **Storybook Store,** on Town Square, carries stationery, books, and cassettes of the Disney versions of Perrault's and Grimms' fairy tales in various languages; a well-behaved, unbouncy Tigger is happy to stamp books with the park logo and date of your visit. Across the square is the **Ribbons & Bows Shop,** the primary outlet for Mickey Mouse Ears—they cost a mere 25 francs and can be customized. Donald Duck and Goofy headgear is also available here, plus a choice of Victorian-style hats; peek into the back room, where there's an array of old-time sewing machines, and ask for your name to be embroidered on the hat of your choice. **Town Square Photography** contains a display of old cameras; stop off to hire a still or video camera, or buy film or have it developed (same-day service). A silhouette artist is on hand to snip out your portrait in profile.

On Main Street itself is the **Emporium** (the park's largest store), which stocks a huge variety of souvenirs ranging from Mickey Mouse earrings to clothes, toys, dolls, and video cassettes. In the glassed-in kitchen at **Boardwalk Candy Palace,** aproned lasses stir huge vats of Disneyfudge, available in 25-franc cartons and three flavors; huge Mickey *sucettes* (lollipops) are the essential souvenir at 12.50 francs. For a haircut or shave, pop into **Harmony Barber Shop,** full of large mirrors and old-fashioned instruments (on display, not in use). **Disney Clothiers Ltd.** offers some upmarket garments; even if you don't need a new shirt or jacket, step through to the back of the shop to admire the tailor's dummy and mechanical piano. The most elegant store on the street is **Harrington's Fine China & Porcelains,** adorned with a stained-glass cupola, marble statues, and a crystal chandelier. Disney souvenirs can be had at **Disneyana Collectibles,** which also stocks rare books and lithographs, or **Disney & Co.,** where you can watch a glassblower at work. The **Newsstand,** half-way down the street, sells newspapers and magazines of long ago.

Frontierland The Western-style, wood-fronted **Thunder Mesa Mercantile Building** houses three stores: **Tobias Norton & Sons–Frontier Traders** (leather goods); **Bonanza**

Outfitters (men and women's clothing, boots, belts, hats); and **Eureka Mining Supplies & Assay Office** (children's cowboy outfits, sheriff's badges, miniature rifles, and such foodstuffs as bison pâté and New Mexico red-hot beans). Tiny, quiet **Pueblo's Trading Post** is full of unusual gifts: traditional Indian pottery, rugs, flutes, and statuettes (most with a cactus theme). At the **Woodcarver's Workshop,** you can watch as a craftsman carves animals or hews your name out of a piece of wood.

Adventureland **Merlin L'Enchanteur** (Merlin the Magician), a boutique hewn out of the Faux rock on the left side of the castle as you approach from the Central Plaza, stocks knights, wizards, and dragons in pewter or wood, plus chess sets and kaleidoscopes. Christmas trees glitter in the stone-vaulted **Boutique du Château** (Castle Shop), in the other wing of the castle, and filled with toy soldiers, dolls, Santa statuettes, and Disney Christmas decorations. **La Confiserie des Trios Fées** (the Three Fairies Sweets Shop) is handy for candy; **La Petite Maison des Jouets** (the Little House of Toys), roofed in bright colors and topped by a weathervane, is a big noise in toys. Tortoises, squirrels, and rabbits bathe in the stream that tumbles past **La Chaumière des Sept Nains** (the Cottage of the Seven Dwarfs), which contains cuddly toys representing the seven dwarfs. **La Bottega di Geppetto** (Gepetto's Shop) resembles a carpenter's workshop and sells toys, puppets, music boxes, jigsaw puzzles, and cuckoo clocks. Donald Duck, implausibly clad as a medieval tailor and surrounded by scissors, ribbons, and reels of thread, lords over **Le Brave Petit Tailleur** (the Brave Little Tailor), which stocks clothes and hats. **Sir Mickey's** has a thatched roof, a giant beanstalk, and what looks like pods full of Disney toys and games. Minnie Mouse and Goofy (here clad as an armored knight) market souvenirs and cuddly toys at **La Ménagerie du Royaume** (the Menagerie of the Realm).

Discoveryland There are only two stores here. Amid trite galactic motifs and star-spangled walls, **Constellations** offloads souvenir toys, ties, key rings, tea sets, and candy. **Star Traders,** a cheap-looking glass and metal structure with a radar dish on the roof, sells *Star Wars*–type memorabilia, space-age toys, glittery pens, and high-tech whatnots; it's easy to find: you are gently directed there upon exiting the Star Tours ride.

Festival Disney

Day visitors to Euro Disney will not wish to "waste" precious theme-park time at Festival Disney. But if you're staying at a Disney hotel, or have time in the evening before leaving Euro Disney, you can spend a cheer-filled hour or so wandering around the stores at Festival Disney. Many of the souvenirs are the same as those sold inside the theme park, but some specialty items here are not available elsewhere. If, for instance, you crave a surfboard or a bottle of California wine, Festival Disney is the place to come.

Disney Store, Festival Disney's largest shop, purveys a welter of Disney clothes, books, watches, jewelry, limited-edition collector's items, and other souvenirs in a large vaulted room inspired by New York's Grand Central Station. **Team Mickey** offers sportswear bearing the Disney logo or the name of American baseball teams. The **Surf Shop** caters to water babies with its stock of summer clothing, swimwear, sunglasses, caps, towels, and surfboards. **Hollywood Pictures** re-creates a movie-studio atmosphere with its scattering of movie cameras and directors' chairs, and sells posters, postcards, and books about and inspired by the American film industry. You can buy cowboy hats, jeans, boots, buffalo horns, and Indian headdresses from the **Buffalo Trading Company.** The decor at **Streets of America** evokes New York (gewgaws shaped like skyscrapers and yellow taxis), New Orleans (books and souvenirs with a jazz theme), and San Francisco (clothing suspended from a model of the Golden Gate Bridge). Come here for American food and wines.

Dining

Every day at Euro Disney, no fewer than 528 cooks prepare to serve up to 32,000 meals. Over the course of a week they'll use 3,750 chickens, 300,000 rolls of bread, and 7 tons of tomatoes. But apart from impressive numbers, what can you expect from the food at Euro Disney? For starters: to pay more than you would elsewhere for comparable fare. Then: a chance to eat in a setting you won't experience anywhere else—a world of Disney cartoon magic or nostalgic Americana, for instance—and an opportunity to sample dishes that are unfamiliar in Europe. But while the culinary options here are wide, the quality is inconsistent.

In Euro Disneyland, you can eat on the run (food carts are almost as numerous as fast-food outlets) or spend two hours lingering over a multicourse meal. You cannot bring food and drink into the theme park, but there is a picnic area between the entrance and the parking lot, and you can reenter the park at no charge if you have your hand stamped before you leave. To be sure of getting a table at any Euro Disneyland restaurant, you must make reservations in person; arrive at the restaurant early—either to eat immediately or make a same-day reservation. Be prompt; your table will be held for only 15 minutes. Casual dress is entirely appropriate everywhere in the park.

In restaurants in Euro Disney hotels, casual dress is also appropriate, though guests do dress up a bit more, as noted below, and things are generally a shade dressier than in the theme park. Oddly, reservations must be made in person here, too, even if you're staying in one of the Disney resorts.

Credit cards and traveler's checks are accepted in all Euro Disney restaurants, both sit-down and counter service.

Waiter service is decidedly casual—rather a jolt to those accustomed to the proud professional waiters of France—at best (and always) cheerful, at worst not quite competent. Except in the top hotel restaurants, most Disney waiters are young, inexperienced, and unable to offer worthwhile advice.

Euro Disneyland

If you're spending only a day in Euro Disney, it's probably not a good idea to leave Euro Disneyland at lunchtime to eat at a hotel restaurant. On the other hand, if you're staying on the property and Euro Disneyland is open late, it can be refreshing to leave the park for a meal, a drink, and a snooze or swim. In any event, there are plenty of choices within the park—everything from snack bars and cafeterias to full-fledged restaurants with waitress service. The decor at nearly all venues is superbly atmospheric. It's probably a good idea to stick with more casual spots at lunchtime: Food in the more ambitious restaurants tends to be fussy and overpriced, and no alcoholic beverages of any kind—even beer or wine—are served in any Euro Disneyland restaurant within the park. On the whole, it makes sense to take your main evening meal at Festival Disney or one of the hotel restaurants.

The theme park's opening and closing hours apply to all restaurants and snack bars within it.

Main Street U.S.A.
Full-Service

Plaza Gardens Restaurant. Behind the bay-windowed facade and a veranda overlooking Central Plaza and Sleeping Beauty's Castle are two large dining rooms separated by a colonnade and adorned with a mural depicting a Victorian park. To the strains of chamber music played by the Plaza Gardens Trio, you can choose from a hot and cold buffet, or order stuffed breast of veal, crab in pastry, or grilled items. There is also an extensive dessert counter. *Expensive.*

Walt's—An American Restaurant. From the bistro on the ground floor where you can order from an abbreviated American menu, a staircase lined with pictures of Walt Disney throughout his career leads up to the main dining area, a series of rooms, each containing about 15 tables and each decorated to evoke one of the theme park's lands: Here gothic arches suggest Fantasyland or old wooden bookcases recall Frontierland; there, Moroccan wall-hangings exude the exoticism of Adventureland or a brass model of Captain Nemo's *Nautilus* conjures up Discoveryland. The cuisine is American (lamb with goat cheese, veal with crab and asparagus, steak with corn and a tomato-based sauce, or salad with shrimp, orange sections, nuts, and Missouri bread). *Expensive.*

Snacks and Fast Food

Main Street could also be called Snackland. Baseball bats, trophies, and posters line the walls at **Casey's Corner,** and a pianist tickles the ivories, redeeming an otherwise unremarkable hotdog-and-hamburger joint. **Victoria's Home-Style Cooking** means chicken and beef potpies in a 19th-century-style town house, with cozy alcoves and sturdy wooden tables. Salami and sausages dangle from the ceiling inside the bustling **Market House Deli,** which serves hot and cold sandwiches.

Cookies, muffins, and cinnamon cakes can be had at the **Cookie Kitchen,** while next door the **Cable Car Bake Shop,** hung with old photos of San Francisco, serves up freshly made brownies, cheesecake, and chocolate cookies. Ice-cream fans can choose between the tiled-counter **Ice-Cream Company** and the more lavish **Gibson Girl Ice Cream Parlor,** which has a soda fountain, music box, and chairs with heart-shaped backs; both serve sundaes, banana splits, and milkshakes. Coffee and pastries await at the **Coffee Grinder.**

Frontierland *Full Service*	**Silver Spur Steakhouse.** Reaching your table here can be arduous. First, you're met outside by a hostess who fills in your name, number, language, and your preference for smoking or no-smoking section; then you step inside to be greeted by a second hostess, who examines your form and passes you on to yet a third hostess, who finally ushers you to your table. (It's the same rigamarole at the Lucky Nugget Saloon.) Is the experience worth the trouble? Yes and no. Yes, for both the handsome wood and leather decor, and the American steak house fare: juicy, good-size T-bone steaks, chicken wings, grilled lamb and pork, and elaborate salads. No for the excessive prices and somewhat lackluster service. *Expensive*.

Lucky Nugget Saloon. Several times daily, Diamond Lil leads a corny, campy, good-humored 35-minute song-and-dance routine, in the company of a cowboy crooning in French(!) and a giggling gaggle of high-kicking gals in petticoats and frilly skirts. Check in when you arrive at Frontierland, the earlier in the day the better, to reserve your table. The saloon is horseshoe-shaped, and a balcony is pressed into service when demand warrants. Young waitresses, dolled up in antebellum satin ball gowns, serve a limited selection of smallish dishes such as prawn salad, beef sandwiches, and the ubiquitous (at Euro Disneyland) chili con carne. Make the most of the potato chips and dips that are laid out for free while you mull over the menu choices. The costumes and presentation almost make up for the occasionally inept service and the high prices. *Moderate*.

Cafeteria	**Cowboy Cookout Barbecue.** This huge wooden barn complete with silo and hay loft, and a scattering of cowboy gear, wagon wheels, and other American antiques, is an unpretentious setting for down-home American fare such as hamburgers, spare ribs, salads, and apple pies. Waiters wear jeans and lumberjack shirts, and the Cowhand Band belts out country music. Cast members say the chili con carne here, made in the restaurant's own kitchen, is the best in Euro Disney. *Inexpensive*.

Fuente del Oro Restaurante. Mariachi musicians stroll around the gaily flowered patio of this Mexican hacienda, where you line up for guacamole, tacos, chili con carne, enchiladas, tortillas, and a "Mexican Club Sandwich" of red-bean purée, tomatoes, and cheese. *Inexpensive*.

Snacks and *Fast Food*	The **Last Chance Café,** festooned with Wanted posters, is next to the Lucky Nugget Saloon. Grab your Texas-style barbecue sandwich and eat outside at one of the handful of tables with a view of Big Thunder Mountain.

Adventureland
Full-Service

Blue Lagoon. Palm trees and bamboo recall the tropics at this three-level restaurant overlooking the stream of boats floating off for their encounter with the Pirates of the Caribbean. Perhaps because of the boats and the sense of being in a cavern, children seem to enjoy this restaurant, and, luckily for the adults with them, this is perhaps the finest restaurant in the theme park, with a varied menu of well-prepared fare. Try the spicy Blue Lagoon Platter, laden with swordfish, grilled prawns, and chicken curry. Starters are included in the price of a main course. For dessert, sample the Jamaica nougat with coconut ice, or the rum cake with pineapple sauce. *Expensive.*

Explorers Club. This green-and-white African colonial–style house, which has murals of landscapes from around the world on the walls, woos visitors with its coconut chicken, cold seafood platters, and roast mutton. A tropical tree sprouts in the middle of the dining room, and Audio Animatronic parrots flutter in its branches. A Disney cast member in the guise of African explorer Dr. Stanley Livingston plays the ukelele and regales diners with tales of his trek across the Dark Continent. On a warm day the veranda, on the edge of the Adventureland lagoon, makes an ideal lunch spot. Children like the place—it's casual and fun, and there's a lot to look at. *Expensive.*

Cafeteria

Aux Epices Enchantées. Paintings of animals on whitewashed walls create a jungle-safari ambience here. The food attempts similar exoticism, but the kebabs and fried vegetables—even the spicy "African" stews—won't fool anyone. *Inexpensive.*

Snacks and Fast Food

For swift refreshment, make for either **Café de la Brousse** (chicken wings and fruit juice), opposite Adventure Isle, or **Captain Hook's Galley** (sandwiches, macaroons, and fruit punch), anchored alongside Adventure Isle's Skull Rock.

Fantasyland
Full-Service

Auberge de Cendrillon. Cinderella's sumptuous inn, full of stone arches and plush alcoves with Cinderella's glass coach in the center of it all, is the only Euro Disneyland restaurant to make a big deal of French cuisine, and it manages creditable versions of such dishes as suckling pig in cider, lamb with shallots, and salad with dried magret (duck breast); the white-chocolate dessert in the shape of a slipper is justly popular. A lute-strumming troubadour turns up occasionally to warble medieval ballads, and it's pleasant to eat on the pretty patio with a view of the Tea Cups and the Queen of Hearts Castle in Alice's Curious Labyrinth. *Expensive*.

Cafeteria **Au Chalet de la Marionnette.** Geraniums spill from window boxes at this large Tyrolian inn. Behind the restaurant's facade is a re-creation of a street from *Pinocchio*, and each house holds one of this restaurant's dining rooms—all but a few done up in the vaguely Tyrolean styles of the movie's sets. The others, the ones that overlook Adventureland, exhibit a shipwreck motif— canvas curtains, plank floors and paneling, and tables with legs shaped like anchors. Grilled chicken and meats predominate on the menu. *Moderate*.

Pizzeria Bella Notte. Hams, salamis, braided heads of garlic, and bunches of grapes dangle from the walls and ceiling of this pizza joint inspired by the famous spaghetti scene from Disney's 1955 *Lady and the Tramp*. The pasta is shaped like Mickey Mouse, and the pizzas themselves, though served in cardboard boxes with plastic cutlery, are circles with two ears. Pasta, lasagna, and garlic bread are alternatives. *Moderate*.

Toad Hall Restaurant. This Elizabethan-style manor (wood and stone flooring, leather chairs) is a temple to both English gastronomy and the vainglorious Mr. Toad, a character from Disney's October 1949 *The Adventures of Ichabod and Mr. Toad* (in turn based on novelist Kenneth Grahame's childhood classic *The Wind and the Willows*). On the walls here are paintings of the conceited but lovable buffoon in action, or posing (as, say, Mona Lisa). On your plate are British specialties like fish-and-chips ploughman's lunches with Scotch eggs, roast-beef sandwiches, trifle, and apple pie. We'll leave it to you to appreciate the juxtaposition of decor and cuisine. *Moderate*.

Snacks and **Fantasia Gelati** is home to fresh fruit dishes and Italian
Fast Food ice cream; the walls are painted with scenes from *Fantasia*, and the pretty terrace is shared with neighboring Pizzeria Bella Notte. If you're thirsty after trekking around Alice's Labyrinth, wend your way to **March Hare Refreshments,** a thatched cottage (with real thatch), which serves fruit punch and unbirthday cakes. The sails at the **Old Mill** still turn; inside you'll find yogurt and marzipan figurines based on the musical moppets of It's a Small World.

Discoveryland Salads, couscous, and *paella* are mainstays at the **Café**
Snacks and **des Visionnaires;** a vast sci-fi fresco illustrating scenes
Fast Food from *20,000 Leagues Under the Sea*, a Jules Verne novel that the Walt Disney Company released as a film in 1954,

dominates the futuristic bronze, brass, and granite decor, and a skylight lends airiness. The outdoor terrace overlooks Sleeping Beauty's Castle and the start of the daily Disney parade. At the score of take-out counters in **Café Hyperion,** you can get spaghetti, hamburgers, pizza, and yogurt for consumption in an adjoining hall overlooking the Videopolis stage.

Euro Disney Resort

Disneyland Hotel
Full-Service

California Grill. This is the only Euro Disneyland restaurant to have won enthusiastic plaudits from the exacting French food critics, which is reassuring given that your check won't be much under 600 francs per head. Service is classy and professional, and the parquet floor, white columns, and pastel wallpaper exude chic; there is a superb view of the theme park and of the gleaming kitchens where meals are prepared. The menu offers American specialties ranging from warm goat cheese and beef carpaccio with basil to veal cutlet with olives and a scrumptious walnut-and-honey millefeuille dessert. An extensive selection of French and American wines is served by the bottle or by the glass. *Open noon–3 PM and 6 PM–midnight. Very Expensive.*

Cafeteria

Inventions. Here, for a flat 220 francs, you can help yourself to whatever you fancy from the immense buffet—four tables laden with hot and cold appetizers, fish, meats, and sweets—and experiment with American dishes such as New England clam chowder, New Orleans jambalaya, Florida Key-lime pie, or California cioppino (the West Coast's answer to bouillabaisse). Scale models of pioneer planes, automobiles, and airships hang from the ceiling. *Open daily 7 AM–11 PM. Expensive.*

Café Fantasia. Of the characters from Disney's 1940 *Fantasia* who make up the decor here, perhaps the most amusing are the four dancing alligators that show up as the legs of a table whose top bears the image of the film's hippopotamus ballerina. Breakfast is served until 11 AM, and sandwiches, salads, and ices are offered into the evening. *Open 7 AM–11 PM. Moderate.*

Hotel New York
Full-Service

Club Manhattan. This is the most luxurious restaurant in the Disney complex, as a quick look at the menu reveals: smoked salmon, oysters Rockefeller, foie gras with truffles, caviar, lobster thermidor. Expect to pay more than 800 francs if you indulge in even a few of these delicacies. Grilled duck and veal Oscar are less pricey alternatives. In any case, the real sense of occasion is provided by the 1930s New York nightclub decor and the big band, whose members, wearing white tie and tails, play throughout the evening. Be sure to take a turn on the dance floor before you round off your meal with a flaming meringue-based omelet norvégienne. There's no dress requirement, but you may want to put on the ritz for this one. *Open 6 PM–1 AM. Very Expensive.*

Cafeteria **Parkside Diner.** This elegant diner has real style with its black-and-white checkered floor, gleaming bar, and tinkling piano. Young chefs in tall caps prepare dishes that are sometimes straightforward (chicken-noodle soup, white-chocolate tart) but never mundane (grilled salmon with bacon and lettuce, veal meat loaf with wild mushrooms). The 195-franc menu is a good value, and the milk shakes are good and thick. *Open 7 AM–midnight. Moderate.*

Newport Bay Club
Full Service

Yacht Club. Of the two full-service restaurants in the Newport Bay Club, the Yacht Club is the more luxurious and spacious, and it is open only for dinner—presumably to ensure that guests have several hours to appreciate what it offers, most notably a New England clambake chowder unknown in Europe (chunky with clams, mussels, chicken, potatoes, corn, and sausage). Rounding out the menu are all-American dishes like crab cakes with mustard and chives, and an elaborate soup chunky with lobster and scallops. You can order fresh oysters at the oyster bar; maritime prints, model ships, and an aquarium lend a nautical air. Ginger soufflé with hot lemon sauce makes a tart, tasty finale. Like the Cape Cod restaurant, this one is on the hotel's ground floor overlooking Lake Buena Vista. *Open 6 PM–midnight. Expensive–Very Expensive.*

Cape Cod. Every evening, while serious food lovers are across the corridor at the Yacht Club, the Cape Cod offers a 180-franc buffet loaded with salads, meat cuts, and desserts; this spread is reasonably copious and affordable as meals here go. But if you can, come at lunchtime instead. While you wait for your entrée—perhaps scallops with bacon or grilled swordfish with herbs—you can munch on complimentary hunks of bread spread with garlic and olive oil. And all entrées are served with a selection of cooked vegetables (corn, tomatoes, peppers, potatoes, mushrooms). A generous watercress-and-chicory salad or grilled breast of chicken are other options. Waiters wearing striped shirts look thoroughly at home in the cool blue decor, which you can survey beforehand from the upstairs corridor off the reception area. *Open 7 AM–11 PM. Moderate–Expensive.*

Sequoia Lodge **Hunter's Grill.** Leg of lamb with garlic and rosemary,
Full Service marinated pork ribs, and chicken kebabs are among the
hearty dishes served in this ground-floor restaurant
overlooking Lake Buena Vista. At the center of the
chunky wooden tables, large revolving platters are piled
with breads, salads, and crudités. While not worth a
special visit if you're not staying in the hotel, it's all
good, honest fare. *Open 11 AM–11 PM. Moderate.*

Cafeteria **Beaver Creek Tavern.** A maître d' in the guise of a forest
ranger greets you in this rustic cafeteria, where you can
enjoy a quick, sturdy meal of meat cuts, roast meats,
spare ribs, hamburgers, and salads. *Open 11 AM–11 PM.
Moderate.*

Hotel Cheyenne **Chuckwagon Café.** Despite a long wooden bar and some
Cafeteria cute fittings (flameproof fake straw and barrel-shape tables), this huge dining hall has a utilitarian, institutional
feel. The food is pretty institutional, too: The soups,
beef sandwiches, cattleman's stew, and pork pâté might
fill your stomach, but definitely without tickling your
taste buds. Opt for a salad if you're not too hungry, and
by all means avoid the poor house wine. *Open weekdays
5–11 PM, weekends noon–11 PM. Inexpensive–Moderate.*

Hotel Santa Fe **La Cantina.** Chili con carne is virtually inescapable at
Cafeteria Euro Disney, but if you haven't had a surfeit of it and
don't mind the fact that your barbecued chicken sandwich is filled mostly with barbecue sauce, this is the
place for a quick meal in the Hotel Santa Fe. There are
nine different serving tables (salads, soups, grilled
meats, tortillas, etc.), and a band of Mexican musicians
in fine form. *Open 7 AM–11 PM. Inexpensive–Moderate.*

Camp Davy **Crockett's Tavern.** This *L*-shape wooden dining room
Crockett lacks character despite its location inside an immense
Cafeteria log building, and its perch overlooking the splendid
camp swimming pool. It is good for breakfast, when you
can get buckwheat pancakes, sausage, and scrambled
eggs; for lunch and dinner, the choice is uninspired:
mostly sausages, roast beef, baked potatoes, and the
like. *Open 7 AM–11 PM. Inexpensive–Moderate.*

Festival Disney

Full Service **Los Angeles Bar & Grill.** Charcoal-grilled pizzas are
the official "house specialty" in this roomy, large-
windowed, pastel-toned restaurant overlooking Lake
Buena Vista. The pies come with a wide variety of top-
pings. But the restaurant also provides an imaginative
range of other dishes. If you're feeling adventurous, you

can opt instead for corn gazpacho, warm goat cheese
with garlic, grilled chicken with tomatilla sauce, or
fresh pasta with smoked salmon. The upstairs cocktail
bar has a fine view of the lake and surrounding hotels,
and serves minipizzas and other snacks. There is a wide
range of relatively inexpensive young French and California wines (some by the glass), both upstairs and
down. The pizzas are on the pricey side. *Open noon–3 PM
and 6 PM–midnight. Expensive.*

The Steakhouse. This redbrick lakeside restaurant,
built to resemble an archetypal Chicago steak house,
boasts a jazz pianist, waitresses in flapper outfits
straight from the 1920s, and sumptuous mahogany furnishings. After an appetizer of onion soup or spinach salad, a succulent T-bone steak is an obvious main course.
Finish your meal off with a rich dessert of cheesecake or
chocolate mousse. Grilled lamb and chicken and walnut-
smoked pork are also available. *Open noon–3 PM and 6
PM–midnight. Expensive.*

Key West Seafood. In this vast restaurant next to Lake
Buena Vista, beachfront Southern Florida is the theme.
A copy of the Key West newspaper serves as a table-
cloth, and seafood is the specialty: oysters on the half
shell, garlicky blue crab, spicy giant prawns, and fish
stew regally infused with shrimps, mussels, clams, and
crab claws. Try the sweet-tart Key-lime pie. Good service and excellent fresh fish (probably caught in neither
Lake Buena Vista nor Florida) make this one of the best
dining options in Festival Disney. *Open noon–3 PM and 6
PM–midnight. Expensive.*

Cafeteria **Annette's Diner.** Nostalgic automobile mementoes and
miniature tabletop jukeboxes playing golden oldies by
Elvis Presley, Chuck Berry, and Buddy Holly lend a
"Happy Days" air to this '50s-inspired American snack
bar. Waitresses on rollerskates serve the obvious fare:
hamburgers, Coca-Colas, milk shakes, and brownies.
Open 8 AM–1 PM. Inexpensive.

Snacks and French fries and chili con carne are among the snacks
Fast Food served at the **Champions Sports Bar;** it's also Euro Disney's cheapest place for a beer and pours a huge selec-
tion of American imports. Oversized New York–style
deli sandwiches can be enjoyed next door at **Carnegie's.**
Try the pastrami or salmon and cream cheese.

Lodging

Six hotels, with more than 5,500 rooms and more than 12,000 beds, have been built alongside the theme park at the Euro Disney Resort. Shuttle buses run from all hotels to the park every 10 minutes, and a small tram (a brightly colored vintage 1920s bus), circulates around Lake Buena Vista every five minutes, linking the New York Hotel, Sequoia Lodge, and Newport Bay Club to Festival Disney.

The Disney Imagineers set out to create hotels with a distinctly non-European look, and they succeeded: Especially in the context of the Ile-de-France, these buildings are, to say the least, unconventional. They vary in style—each evokes a specific region or period of American history—and range from deluxe resort properties to woodsy cabin complexes. All rooms come with private bath and can accommodate up to four.

Prices, here by the room rather than per person as is common in Europe, reflect the level of comfort and luxury. Out of season (that is, from early November through March), they drop by about 15% on weekends and 30% weekdays. Each hotel takes all major credit cards and is open year-round. To book, contact the Central Reservations Office (BP 105, 7777 Marne-la Vallée Cedex 4, tel. 1/49–41–49–10).

Very Expensive **Disneyland Hotel.** The silhouette of this pink extravaganza at the entrance to the theme park 150 yards from the RER station is spiky with gables, steep red roofs, and giant mock-Tudor brick chimneys. The mood indoors, along the plush-carpeted, white-walled corridors, is less whimsical and more elegant and refined, even a bit formal. Many rooms overlook the park; all are decorated in subdued tones, and there are floral quilts on the beds and Disney characters on the doorknobs. Created by Disney's own architects in conjunction with the American firm of Wimberly, Allison, Tong & Goo, the hotel's design was inspired by San Francisco's Victorian architecture, and recalls that of a turn-of-the-century American resort. *79 rooms and 21 suites (some nonsmoking). Facilities: 3 restaurants, bar, fitness center, sauna, massage, indoor pool, video game room, room service, in-room babysitting, Information Desk.*
Hotel New York. Architect Michael Graves's nine-story, postmodern evocation of the Manhattan skyline has a blocky, geometric facade that makes it seem more appropriate to businessmen than holidaymakers, and,

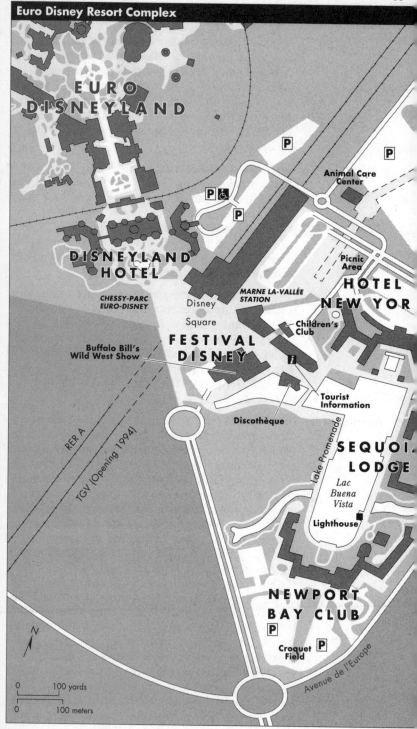

Euro Disney Resort Complex

EURO DISNEYLAND

DISNEYLAND HOTEL

CHESSY-PARC EURO-DISNEY

Disney Square

FESTIVAL DISNEY

Buffalo Bill's Wild West Show

Discothèque

Animal Care Center

Picnic Area

MARNE LA-VALLÉE STATION

Children's Club

HOTEL NEW YORK

Tourist Information

RER A

TGV (Opening 1994)

SEQUOIA LODGE

Lac Buena Vista

Lighthouse

Lake Promenade

NEWPORT BAY CLUB

Croquet Field

Avenue de l'Europe

N

0   100 yards

0   100 meters

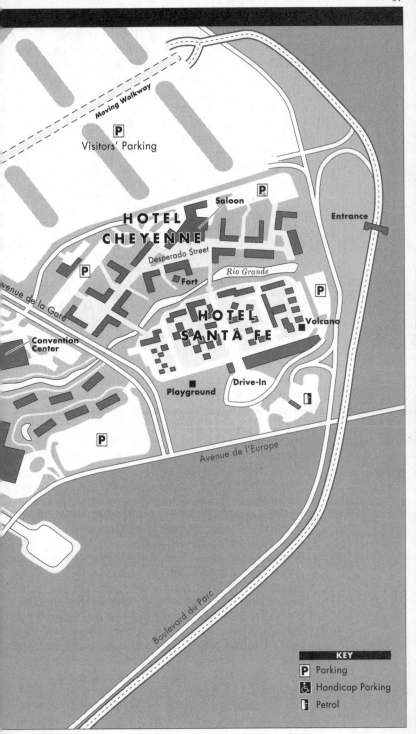

Moving Walkway

P Visitors' Parking

P

Saloon

**HOTEL
CHEYENNE**

Entrance

P

Desperado Street

Rio Grande

venue de la Gare

P

Fort

P

**HOTEL
SANTA FE**

Volcano

Convention
Center

Drive-In

P Playground

P

Avenue de l'Europe

Boulevard du Parc

KEY
P Parking
Handicap Parking
Petrol

sure enough, the Hotel New York is also a conference center. But it has great style: It's fronted by a tree-lined skating rink that becomes an ornamental swimming pool in summer (with Lake Buena Vista beyond), and there's a marble-paved foyer, framed photographs of Manhattan in the guest rooms, and mahogany chairs and sleek art deco flourishes throughout. Adults may feel more at home here than children, though youngsters will like some of the whimsical room fittings—the bedside lamps in the shape of skyscrapers, for instance, or the carvings of apples on the chair frames. *539 rooms, 36 suites (some nonsmoking). Facilities: 2 restaurants, 2 bars, 2 lighted tennis courts, fitness center, sauna, Jacuzzi, steam room, video game room, beauty salon, indoor and outdoor pools, skating rink (winter only), barbershop, room service, in-room babysitting, 2 auditoriums, private meeting rooms, secretarial and translation services, telecommunications.*

Expensive **Newport Bay Club.** You half expect to see the Great Gatsby strolling under the colonnaded portico into the spacious lobby at this re-creation of a chic 1920s seaside resort. Architect Robert A. M. Stern's design is elegantly restrained; the pale yellow shingle-style facade is punctuated by dormer windows and striped awnings, and topped by a sea-green roof. A manicured croquet lawn extends from the front of the hotel; at the rear, a promenade lined with deck chairs overlooks Lake Buena Vista, and a squat, gleaming red-and-white lighthouse adds a yacht-harbor touch. Inside, maps, prints, and barometers in lobby, restaurants, and corridors continue the nautical theme; and in the guest rooms, a ship's wheel is carved into the beds' headboards and the drapery fabric is patterned with sailing motifs. *1,083 rooms, 15 suites. Facilities: 2 restaurants, bar, fitness center, indoor and outdoor pools, sauna, Jacuzzi, steam room, video game room, croquet, playground.*

Sequoia Lodge. Pines, cedars, and 500 sequoia trees imported from British Columbia are scattered around the grounds of this hotel complex facing Lake Buena Vista. The building was designed by French architect Antoine Grumbach as Frank Lloyd Wright might have done it during his Prairie-style days: It's uncluttered and austere, with determinedly horizontal lines and a palette of colors and materials that conjures up images of the Rocky Mountains—rugged gray stone at ground level, dark wood beams above, and low, pale-green roofs on top. The flagstone-paved reception area is at its most inviting in winter, when there's a log ablaze in the stone fireplace. Five smaller lodges in the same style are clustered behind the main building, in a wooded area along the banks of the Rio Grande, a shallow man-made river that flows into Lake Buena Vista; they're named for scenic areas of the American West (Yellowstone, Yosemite, Monterey, Sierra, and Big Sur). In these and in the main building, guest rooms are done in elegantly rustic style, with wood-frame beds covered with patchwork quilts and Mission-style oak chairs and tables. The lodges are a little quieter, the main building more convenient. *997 rooms, 14 suites. Facilities: 2 restaurants, bar, playground, fitness center, sauna, Jacuzzi, steam room, indoor pool with outdoor terrace, video game room.*

Moderate–Expensive **Hotel Cheyenne.** Robert A. M. Stern has cleverly disguised the exterior of this complex on the north bank of the Rio Grande as an entire Wild West town, like some set from the movie *High Noon.* Gravel-surfaced Desperado Street is lined with the hotel's 14 two-story buildings, each with a colorful, painted wooden facade and named for a Wild West notable such as Doc Holliday or Jesse James; wooden barrels are scattered around the street, and there's a covered wagon near the Chuckwagon Cafe. Guest rooms have overhead paddle fans, lamps made from cowboy boots with buffalo-skin shades, and bunk beds for youngsters—cowhands, as they're styled here. The Fort Apache play area has swings, a slide, a lookout tower, and a child-size tepee village. *1,000 rooms. Facilities: restaurant, bar, video game room, 2 playgrounds, country music bar (summer only).*

Hotel Santa Fe. A giant portrait of Clint Eastwood glowers down from a drive-in-movie-style screen towering above the parking lot that fronts this hotel complex. Eastwood's dour expression is unintentionally appropriate: Beyond said parking lot, you are confronted with architect Antoine Predoc's 42 dull gray and brown concrete prefabs masquerading as pueblos; the giant fake cacti, the 8-meter (25-foot) lump of concrete intended to look like a volcano, and the rusted automobiles here called sculpture create a mood about as cheerful as a post-war Paris suburb. The "volcano" and Eastwood's visage are the landmarks, but there's no other central focus. Luckily, the oppressive atmosphere doesn't extend into the guest rooms, and the faux Navajo patterned quilts on the beds and bright, multicolored mirrors on the walls add a warm touch. The main appeal here is, of course, the low price, but the Hotel Cheyenne costs only a bit more, and is far more atmospheric. *1,000* *rooms. Facilities: restaurant, bar, video game room, playground.*

Inexpensive– **Camp Davy Crockett.** An alternative to hotel accommo-
Moderate dation, Camp Davy Crockett gives you the option of setting up camp at a tent site (270 francs per night) or
renting a wood-shuttered "log cabin" (a boxy prefab log-
look structure that sleeps four to six). Tucked away in a
heavily forested setting well to the south of Euro Disneyland on the other side of the expressway, the camp
feels like the wilderness retreat it was intended to be.
The dense foliage serves not only to create a convincingly woodsy atmosphere, but also to effectively muffle the
noise from the road. It makes sense to arrive with your
own car, because the shuttle buses that make the 15-
minute run to the theme park are notoriously unrelia-
ble—at least as of press time. If you're camping, you
need your own tent; there are none are for hire. The cab-
ins come with maid service, microwave, television, dish-
washer, patios, picnic tables, and barbecue grill; all
have private bath. The camp village, a half-dozen log
buildings at the far end of a snaking drive, has a food
store, bike-rental service, and facilities for volleyball,
basketball, and tennis. Also in the village is one of
Europe's largest timber buildings—a log cabin on a
grand scale—containing a restaurant that overlooks the
immensely impressive Blue Springs swimming pool,
complete with a waterfall, slide, and Jacuzzi. *414 cab-
ins, 181 campsites. Facilities: restaurant, bar, outdoor
pool, 2 lighted tennis courts, sports fields, playgrounds, video game room, jogging path, pony rides,
nature trails.*

Nightlife

The options range from dinner shows to discos and bars,
with and without music. The bars in the Euro Disney
Resort hotels tend to be quieter and more upscale, pouring genteel cocktails; those in Festival Disney, where
nightlife is concentrated, are noisier and attract crowds
whose idea of a good time begins at least partly with a
large glass of beer.

Bars and Discos **Champions Sports Bar** (*see* Festival Disney Dining,
Festival Disney *above*), where you can choose from a huge selection of
American brews and watch sporting events on oversized
TVs, is one of the two principal watering holes at Festival Disney. The other is **Billy Bob's Country Western Saloon,** where you can feast on chicken wings or Mexican
nachos with cheese and hot peppers. Waiters in Stetsons

serve up imported and domestic beers, along with spirits and soft drinks from the four bars adorned with hunting trophies. Country-and-western singers are on stage from 5 PM through 2 AM. *Inexpensive.*

You can also dance the night away—at least till 3 AM—at **Hurricane's,** a disco upstairs from Key West Seafood. There are four bars on different levels (one on an outside terrace), a dance floor, and conversation areas; 20 video screens show music videos. The beachfront-theme of the restaurant downstairs prevails, with the addition of flashing disco lights. Drinks tend to be pricey, but guests of any Euro Disney hotel are admitted for free. *Admission to the general public: 120 francs (includes first drink).*

Euro Disney Resort Every hotel has its complement of bars and lounges; most serve specialty cocktails in addition to wine and beer, and some have live music. In the **Disneyland Hotel** is the Main Street Lounge, overlooking the theme park. In the **Hotel New York** you can drink at the smallish Club Manhattan Lounge, next to the dressy restaurant of the same name, and at the 57th Street Bar overlooking Lake Buena Vista. Singers entertain in the Rio Grande Bar in the **Hotel Santa Fe,** and there are pianists in Fisherman's Wharf in the **Newport Bay Club** and in the Redwood Bar and Lounge in **Sequoia Lodge.** The **Hotel Cheyenne** has the Red Garter, with appropriately Wild West live music. Crockett's Tavern in Camp Davy Crockett is open until 11 PM; most others usually stay open until 1 AM.

Dinner Shows Festival Disney Chow time at **Buffalo Bill's Wild West Show** means sausages, spareribs, chili con carne (of course), and a rodeo. The two-hour dinner-show staged here twice nightly at 5:30 and 8:30 PM features performances by a huge cast of stunt riders, bronco busters, Native American tribal dancers, and musicians, plus some 50 horses, a dozen buffalo, a bull, and Annie Oakley, Princess of the Winchester Rifle, with a silver-maned Buffalo Bill as emcee. A re-creation of a show that dazzled Parisians 100 years ago, it's corny but great fun for those who can manage the appropriate suspension of disbelief. *Tel. 60–45–71–00 for reservations. Admission (includes dinner): 300 francs adults, 150 francs children under 12.*

Sports

The Disney organization has big plans to make Euro Disney a complete resort destination. Even now, provided you're staying on property, you can take a break from Euro Disneyland for any number of sporting activities.

Golf To see the Euro Disneyland golf course today, you would never guess that this verdant, 18-hole, par-72, 6,200-meter (6,900-yard) layout was once flat-as-a-French-pancake farmland devoid of all trees. It's open to the public as well as to guests (though guests have an edge in reserving tee times; tel. 6045–6804); greens fees are about 400 francs during the week, about 550 on weekends. An additional nine holes are scheduled to open in mid-1993.

Tennis French clay has yielded to a more practical hard surface here, but there are four lighted courts—two each at the Hotel New York and Camp Davy Crockett. Reserve at the hotels' Information Desks.

Toobies These little boats, which look like inner tubes, can accommodate up to three. Cost is about 50 francs per half hour, 30 francs per 15 minutes. Rentals are available at the Festival Disney Marina on Lake Buena Vista.

Ice Skating From November through March, Disney hotel guests can take a turn on the ice at this Disney version of the scenic rink in New York City's Rockefeller Center. Two-hour sessions cost about 55 francs with skate rental, 40 francs without.

Other Sports There are **swimming pools** and **fitness centers** in all hotels but the Santa Fe and Cheyenne; guests there can use facilities at other properties (the pools at no charge, the fitness centers for a small fee). Camp Davy Crockett has trails for **jogging** and **bicycling** and rents two-wheelers for about 150 francs per day; there are also **pony rides** as well as **soccer** fields and **basketball** and **volleyball** courts. Newport Bay Club has a lawn for **croquet** and provides balls and mallets at no charge.

3 Paris

Paris is a city of vast, noble perspectives and winding, hidden streets. This combination of the pompous and the intimate is a particularly striking and alluring feature of Paris. The French capital is also, for the tourist, a practical city: It is relatively small as capitals go, with many of its major sites and museums within walking distance of one another.

In fact, the best method of getting to know Paris is on foot, although public transportation—particularly the Métro subway system—is excellent. Buy a *Plan de Paris* booklet: a city map-guide with a street-name index that also shows Métro stations. Note that all Métro stations have a detailed neighborhood map just inside the entrance.

Paris owes both its development and much of its visual appeal to the river Seine, which weaves through its heart. Each bank of the Seine has its own personality; the Rive Droite (Right Bank), with its spacious boulevards and haughty buildings, generally has a more sober and genteel feeling to it than the more carefree and bohemian Rive Gauche (Left Bank) to the south.

Paris's historical and geographical heart is Notre Dame Cathedral on the Ile de la Cité, the larger of the Seine's two islands (the other is the Ile St-Louis). The city's principal tourist axis is less than 4 miles long, running parallel to the north bank of the Seine from the Arc de Triomphe to the Bastille.

Monuments and museums are sometimes closed for lunch, usually between 12 and 2, and one day a week, usually Monday or Tuesday. Check before you set off. And don't forget that cafés in Paris are open all day long. They are a great boon to foot-weary tourists in need of a coffee, a beer, or a sandwich. *Boulangeries* (bakeries) are another reliable source of sustenance.

We've divided our coverage of Paris into six tours, but there are several "musts" that any first-time visitor to Paris is loath to miss: the Eiffel Tower, the Champs-Elysées, the Louvre, and Notre Dame. It would be a shame, however, not to explore the various *quartiers*, or districts, each with its own personality and charm.

The Historic Heart

Numbers in the margin correspond to points of interest on the Historic Heart map.

Of the two islands in the Seine—the Ile St-Louis (*see* The Marais and Ile St-Louis, *below*) and Ile de la Cité—it is the Ile de la Cité that forms the historic heart of Paris. It was here, for obvious reasons of defense, and in the hope of controlling the trade that passed along the Seine, that the earliest inhabitants of Paris, the Gaulish tribe of the Parisii, settled in about 250 BC. They called their little home Lutetia, meaning "settlement surrounded by water." Whereas the Ile St-Louis is today largely residential, the Ile de la Cité remains deeply historic, the result not just of more than 2,000 years of habitation, but of the fact that this is the site of the most important and one of the most beautiful churches in France—the great brooding cathedral of Notre Dame. Few of the island's other medieval buildings have survived to the present, most having fallen victim to Baron Haussmann's ambitious rebuilding of the city in the mid-19th century. But among the rare survivors are the jewel-like Sainte Chapelle, a vision of shimmering stained glass, and the Conciergerie, the grim former city prison.

Another major attraction on this tour—the Louvre—came into existence in the mid-13th century, when Philippe-Auguste built it as a fortress to protect the city's western flank. It was not until pleasure-loving François I began a partial rebuilding of this original rude fortress in the early 16th century that today's Louvre began gradually to take shape. A succession of French rulers was responsible for this immense, symmetrical structure, now the largest museum in the world, as well as the easiest to get lost in.

Toward the Louvre

The tour begins at the western tip of the Ile de la Cité, at ❶ the sedate **Square du Vert Galant.** Nothing is controversial here, not even the statue of the Vert Galant himself, literally the vigorous—by which was really meant the amorous—adventurer, Henri IV, sitting foursquare on his horse. Henri, King of France from 1589 until his assassination in 1610, was something of a dashing figure, by turns ruthless and charming, a stern upholder of the absolute rights of monarchy, and a notorious womanizer. He is probably best remembered for his cynical re-

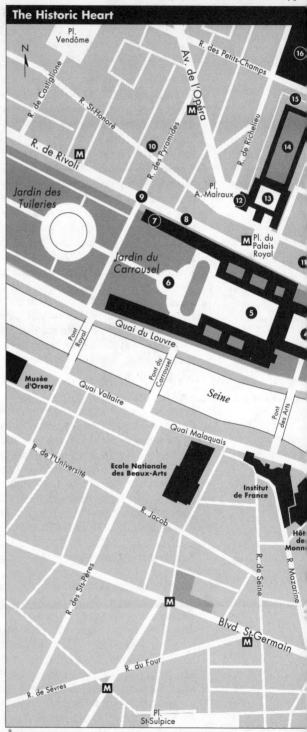

The Historic Heart

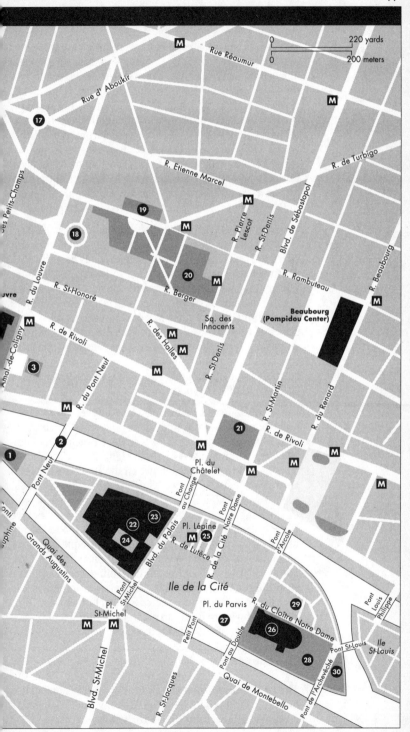

Rue Réaumur

0 ——— 220 yards
0 ——— 200 meters

Rue d' Aboukir

17

R. Etienne Marcel

R. de Turbigo

19

R. Pierre Lescot

R. St-Denis

Blvd. de Sébastopol

18

R. du Louvre

R. St-Honoré

20

R. Berger

R. Rambuteau

R. Beaubourg

uvre

Amal.-de-Coligny

R. de Rivoli

Sq. des
Innocents

**Beaubourg
(Pompidou Center)**

3

R. des Halles

R. du Pont Neuf

R. St-Denis

R. St-Martin

R. du Renard

21

R. de Rivoli

2

1

Pont Neuf

Pl. du
Châtelet

oni.

Dauphine

Quai des
Grands Augustins

Pont au Change

Pont Notre Dame

Pont d'Arcole

23

22

Blvd. du Palais

Pl. Lépine

25

R. de Lutèce

R. de la Cité

24

Ile de la Cité

Pl.
St-Michel

Pont St-Michel

Petit Pont

Pl. du Parvis

R. du Cloître Notre Dame

29

Pont Louis Philippe

27

26

Pont St-Louis

*Ile
St-Louis*

Blvd. St-Michel

R. St-Jacques

Pont au Double

28

30

Pont de l'Archevêché

Quai de Montebello

mark that *Paris vaut bien une messe* ("Paris is worth a mass"), a reference to his readiness to renounce his Protestantism as a condition of gaining the throne of predominantly Catholic France, and indeed of being allowed to enter the city. A measure of his canny statesmanship was provided by his enactment of the Edict of Nantes in 1598, by which French Protestants were accorded (almost) equal rights with their Catholic counterparts. It was Louis XIV's renunciation of the Edict nearly 100 years later that led to the massive Huguenot exodus from France, greatly to the economic disadvantage of the country. The square itself is a fine spot to linger on a sunny afternoon. It is also the departure point for the glass-topped *vedette* tour boats on the Seine.

Crossing the Ile de la Cité, just behind the Vert Galant, ❷ is the oldest bridge in Paris, confusingly called the **Pont Neuf,** or New Bridge. It was completed in the early 17th century and was the first bridge in the city to be built without houses lining either side. Turn left onto it. Visible to the north of the river is the large-windowed **Samaritaine** department store. Once across the river, turn left again and walk down to rue Amiral-de-Coligny. Opposite you is the massive eastern facade of the Louvre. It is Baroque dignity and coherence with no frills, a suitably imposing entrance to the rigorous classicism of the Cour Carrée beyond.

However, before heading for the Louvre, stay on the right-hand sidewalk and duck into the church of ❸ **St-Germain l'Auxerrois.** This was the French royal family's Paris church, used by them right up to 1789, in the days before the Revolution, when the Louvre was a palace rather than a museum. The fluid stonework of the facade reveals the influence of 15th-century Flamboyant Gothic, the final, exuberant fling of the Gothic before the classical takeover of the Renaissance. Notice the unusually wide windows in the nave and the equally unusual double aisles. The triumph of classicism is evident, however, in the fluted columns around the choir, the area surrounding the altar. These were added in the 18th century and are characteristic of the desire of 18th-century clerics to dress up medieval buildings in the architectural raiment of their day.

The Louvre

The best times to visit the Louvre are during lunchtime between 12:30 and 2:30 or on Monday and Wednesday evenings, when it stays open till 9:45.

The Louvre colonnade across the road from St-Germain l'Auxerrois screens one of Europe's most dazzling court-

4 yards, the **Cour Carrée**, a monumental, harmonious, and superbly rhythmical ensemble. It has something of the assured feel of an Oxford or Cambridge quadrangle, though on a much grander scale. In the **crypt** under it, excavated in 1984, sections of the defensive towers of the original, 13th-century fortress can be seen.

If you enter the museum via the quai du Louvre entrance, saunter through the courtyard and pass under the **Pavillon de l'Horloge**—the Clock Tower—and you come face to face with the Louvre's latest and most con-

5 troversial development, I. M. Pei's notorious **glass pyramid**, surrounded by three smaller pyramids. It's more than just a grandiloquent gesture, a desire on the part of French President François Mitterrand, who commissioned it, to make his mark on the city. First, the pyramid marks the new, and much needed, entrance to the Louvre; it also houses a large museum shop, café, and restaurant. Second, it acts as the terminal point for the most celebrated city view in Europe, a majestic vista stretching through the Arc du Carrousel, the Tuileries Gardens, across place de la Concorde, up the Champs-Elysées to the towering Arc de Triomphe, and ending at the giant modern arch at La Tête Défense, 4 kilometers (2½ miles) more to the east. Needless to say, the architectural collision between classical stone blocks and pseudo-Egyptian glass panels has caused a furor. Adding insult to injury, at least as far as many Parisians are concerned, is the shocking fact that Pei isn't even a Frenchman! Before making up your mind, however, it may help to remember that the surrounding buildings in this part of the Louvre, although thoroughly cleaned in 1991–92, are mainly earnest 19th-century pastiche, whose pompous solemnity neither jars nor excites.

Paintings, drawings, antiquities, sculpture, furniture, coins, jewelry—the quality and the sheer variety are intimidating. The number-one attraction for most is Leonardo da Vinci's enigmatic *Mona Lisa*, "La Joconde" to the French. But there are numerous other works of equal quality. The collections are divided into seven sections: Oriental antiquities; Egyptian antiquities; Greek and Roman antiquities; sculpture; paintings, prints, and drawings; furniture; and objets d'art. What follows is no more than a selection of favorites, chosen to act as key points for your exploration. If you have time for only one visit, they will give some idea of the riches of the museum. But try to make repeat visits—the Louvre is half-price on Sundays. With the rearrangement of the museum far from complete—the rue de Rivoli wing, which used to house the French Finance Ministry, is to become part of the museum in the mid-1990s—it's not possible to say with certainty just what works will be on display where. Study the plans at the entrance to get your bearings, and pick up a map to take with you.

Palais du Louvre. Admission: 31 frs adults, 16 frs 18–25 years and Sun. Open Thurs.–Sun. 9–6, Mon. and Wed. 9 AM–9:45 PM. Some sections open some days only.

North of the Louvre

Stretching westward from the main entrance to the Louvre and the glass pyramid is an expanse of stately, formal gardens. These are the **Tuileries Gardens** (*see* From the Arc de Triomphe to the Opéra, *below*). Leading to them is the **Arc du Carrousel,** a small relation of the distant Arc de Triomphe and, like its big brother, put up by Napoleon. To the north, in the Pavillon de Marsan, the northernmost wing of the Louvre, is the **Musée des Arts Décoratifs,** which houses over 50,000 objects charting the course of French furniture and applied arts through the centuries. The museum also stages excellent temporary exhibits. *107 rue de Rivoli. Admission: 23 frs. Open Wed.–Sat. 12:30–6, Sun. 12–6.*

Running the length of the Louvre's northern side is Napoleon's elegant, arcaded **rue de Rivoli,** a street whose generally dull tourist shops add little to their surroundings. Cross it and you're in **place des Pyramides** and face-to-face with its gilded statue of Joan of Arc on horseback. The square is a focal point for city tour buses.

Walk up rue des Pyramides and take the first left, rue St-Honoré, to the Baroque church of **St-Roch.** The church was begun in 1653 but completed only in the 1730s, the decade of the coolly classical facade. Classical playwright Corneille (1606–1684) is buried here; a commemorative plaque honoring him is located at the left of the entrance. It's worth having a look inside the church to see the bombastically baroque altarpiece in the circular Lady Chapel at the far end.

Double back along rue St-Honoré to place du Palais-Royal. On the far side of the square, opposite the Louvre, is the **Louvre des Antiquaires,** a chic shopping mall housing upscale antiques shops. It's a minimuseum in itself. Its stylish, glass-walled corridors deserve a browse whether you intend to buy or not.

You've Let Your Imagination Go, Now Get Up And Follow Your Dreams.

For The Vacation You're Dreaming Of, Call American Express® Travel Agency At 1-800-YES-AMEX.*

American Express will send more than your imagination soaring. We'll fly you, sail you, drive you to any Fodor's destination and beyond. Because American Express believes the best vacations happen from Europe to the Orient, Walt Disney® World to Hawaii and everywhere in between.

For dependable service, expert advice, and value wherever your dreams take you, call on American Express. After all, the best traveling companion is a trustworthy friend.

It's easy to recognize a good place when you see one.

American Express Cardmembers have been doing it for years.

The secret? Instead of just relying on what they see in the window, they look at the door. If there's an American Express Blue Box on it, they know they've found an establishment that cares about high standards.

Whether it's a place to eat, to sleep, to shop, or simply meet, they know they will be warmly welcomed.

So much so, they're rarely taken in by anything else.

Always a good sign.

Retrace your steps to place André-Malraux, with its exuberant fountains. The Opéra building is visible down
the avenue of the same name, while, on one corner of the
square, at rue de Richelieu, is the **Comédie Française.**
This theater is the time-honored setting for performances of classical French drama, with tragedies by Racine and Corneille and comedies by Molière regularly on
the bill. The building itself dates from 1790, but the Comédie Française company was created by that most theatrical of French monarchs, Louis XIV, back in 1680.
Those who understand French and who have a taste for
the mannered, declamatory style of French acting—it's
a far cry from method acting—will appreciate an evening here.

To the right of the theater is the unobtrusive entrance to
the gardens of the **Palais-Royal.** The buildings of this
former palace—royal only in that all-powerful Cardinal
Richelieu (1585–1642) magnanimously bequeathed
them to Louis XIII—date from the 1630s. In his early
days as king, Louis XIV preferred the relative intimacy
of the Palais-Royal to the intimidating splendor of the
Louvre. He soon decided, though, that his own intimidating splendor warranted a more majestic setting;
hence, of course, that final word in un-intimacy, Versailles.

Today, the Palais-Royal is home to the French Ministry
of Culture and is not open to the public. But don't miss
the **Jardin du Palais-Royal,** gardens bordered by arcades
harboring discreet boutiques and divided by rows of
perfectly trimmed little trees. They are a surprisingly
little-known oasis in the gray heart of the city. It's hard
to imagine anywhere more delightful for dozing in the
afternoon sun. As you walk into the gardens, there's not
much chance that you'll miss the black-and-white
striped columns in the courtyard or the revolving silver
spheres that slither around in the two fountains at
either end, the controversial work of architect Daniel
Buren. Here, again, you see the same improbable
combination of brash modernism and august architecture as at the Louvre. Why were these curious, stunted
columns, put up in the early 1980s, ever built? Are they
the enigmatic work of a designer of genius, or a point-
less, too-clever-by-half joke? Traditionalists should con-
sole themselves by admiring the restrained facades of
the buildings bordering the gardens. Everyone will
muse on the days when this dignified spot was the haunt
of prostitutes and gamblers, a veritable sink of vice, in
fact. It's hard to imagine anywhere much more respect-

able these days. Walk up to the end, away from the main palace, and peek into the opulent, Belle-Epoque, glass-lined interior of **Le Grand Véfour.** This is more than just one of the swankiest restaurants in the city; it's probably the most sumptuously appointed, too.

Around the corner from here, on rue de Richelieu, stands France's national library, the **Bibliothèque Nationale.** It contains over 7 million printed volumes. A copy of every book and periodical printed in France must, by law, be sent here. Visitors can admire Robert de Cotte's 18th-century courtyard and peep into the 19th-century reading room. The library galleries stage exhibits from time to time from the collections. *58 rue de Richelieu. Open daily noon–6.*

Time Out Wine bars sprang to prominence in London long ago, but they have caught on less quickly in Paris. A splendid trendsetter is English-run **Willi's** at 13 rue des Petits-Champs, behind the Palais-Royal. You can either sample a glass of wine on a stool at the bar or take a sit-down meal in the cute restaurant at the back (the inexpensive menu changes daily).

From the library, walk southeast along rue des Petits-Champs to the circular **place des Victoires.** It was laid out in 1685 by Mansart, a leading proponent of 17th-century French classicism, in honor of the military victories of Louis XIV, that indefatigible warrior whose near-continuous battles may have brought much prestige to his country but came perilously close to bringing it to bankruptcy, too. Louis is shown prancing on a plunging steed in the center of the square; it's a copy, put up in 1822 to replace the original one destroyed in the Revolution. You'll find some of the city's most upscale fashion shops here and on the surrounding streets.

Head south down rue Croix des Petits-Champs. You'll pass the undistinguished bulk of the Banque de France on your right. The second street on the left leads to the circular, 18th-century **Bourse du Commerce,** or Commercial Exchange. Alongside it is a 30-meter- (100-foot-) high fluted column, all that remains of a mansion built here in 1572 for Catherine de Médicis. The column is said to have been used as a platform for stargazing by Catherine's astrologer, Ruggieri.

You don't need to scale Ruggieri's column to be able to spot the bulky outline of the church of **St-Eustache,** away to the left. Since the demolition of the 19th-centu-

ry iron and glass market halls at the beginning of the
'70s, an act that has since come to be seen as little short
of vandalism, St-Eustache has re-emerged as a domi-
nant element on the central Paris skyline. It is a huge
church, the "cathedral" of Les Halles, built, as it were,
as the market people's Right Bank reply to Notre Dame
on the Ile de la Cité. St-Eustache dates from a couple of
hundred years later than Notre Dame. With the exception of the feeble west front, added between 1754 and
1788, construction lasted from 1532 to 1637, spanning
the twilight of Gothic and the rise of the Renaissance.
As a consequence, the church is a curious architectural
hybrid. Its exterior flying buttresses, for example, are
solidly Gothic. Its column orders, rounded arches, and
comparatively simple and thick window tracery are un-
mistakably classical. Few buildings bear such eloquent
witness to stylistic transition.

Nothing now remains of either the market halls or the
rumbustious atmosphere that led 19th-century novelist
Emile Zola to dub Les Halles *le ventre de Paris* ("the bel-
ly of Paris"). Today, the vast site is part shopping mall
and part garden. The latter, which starts by the provoc-
ative, king-size sculpture *Hand* in front of St-Eustache,
is geared for children. They'll also love the bush shaped
like a rhinoceros.

The once-grimy facades of the buildings facing Les
Halles have been expensively spruced up to reflect the
20 mood of the shiny new **Forum des Halles,** the multilevel
mall. Just how long the plastic, concrete, glass, and
mock-marble of this gaudy mall will stay shiny is anyone's guess. Much of the complex is already showing
signs of wear and tear, a state of affairs not much helped
by the hordes of down-and-outs who invade it toward
dusk. Nonetheless, the multitude of shops gathered at
the Forum makes it somewhere no serious shopper will
want to miss. The sweeping white staircase and glass re-
flections of the central courtyard have a certain photo-
genic appeal.

Leave by square des Innocents to the southeast; its
16th-century Renaissance fountain has recently been
restored. As you make your way toward boulevard de
Sébastopol, you can see the futuristic funnels of the
Beaubourg jutting above the surrounding buildings (*see*
The Marais and Ile St-Louis, *below*). Head right, toward
the Seine. Just before you reach place du Châtelet on the
21 river, you'll see the **Tour St-Jacques** to your left. This
richly worked, 170-foot stump, now used for meteoro-

logical purposes and not open to the public, is all that remains of a 16th-century church destroyed in 1797.

Time Out Just north of place du Châtelet, at 4 rue St-Denis, is **Le Trappiste.** Twenty different international beers are available on draft here, as well as more than 180 in bottles. Mussels and french fries are the traditional accompaniment, although various other snacks (hot dogs, sandwiches) are also available. There are tables upstairs and on the pavement.

The Ile de la Cité

From place du Châtelet, cross back over the Seine on the Pont au Change to the Ile de la Cité. To your right looms (22) the imposing **Palais de Justice,** the Law Courts, built by Baron Haussmann in his characteristically weighty classical style about 1860. You can wander around the building, watching the bustle of the lawyers, or attend a court hearing. But the real interest here is the medieval part of the complex, spared by Haussmann in his otherwise wholesale destruction of the lesser medieval buildings of the Ile de la Cité. There are two buildings you'll want to see: the Conciergerie and the Sainte-Chapelle.

(23) The **Conciergerie,** the northernmost part of the complex, was originally part of the royal palace on the island. Most people know it, however, as a prison, the grim place of confinement for Danton, Robespierre, and, most famously, Marie Antoinette during the French Revolution. From here, all three, and countless others who fell foul of the Revolutionary leaders, were taken off to place de la Concorde and the guillotine. The name of the building is derived from the governor, or *concierge,* of the palace, whose considerable income was swollen by the privilege he enjoyed of renting out shops and workshops. Inside, you'll see the guardroom, complete with hefty Gothic vaulting and intricately carved columns, and the Salle des Gens d'Armes, an even more striking example of Gothic monumentality. From there, a short corridor leads to the kitchen, with its four vast fireplaces. Those with a yen to throw a really memorable party can rent the room. The cells, including that in which Marie Antoinette was held, and the chapel, where objects connected with the ill-fated queen are displayed, complete the tour. *Admission: 24 frs adults, 13 frs students and senior citizens. Joint ticket with Sainte-Chapelle: 40 frs. Open daily 9–6, 10–5 in winter.*

The other perennial crowd puller in the Palais de Justice is the **Sainte-Chapelle,** the Holy Chapel. It was built by the genial and pious Louis IX (1226–1270), whose good works ensured his subsequent canonization. He constructed it to house what he took to be the Crown of Thorns from Christ's crucifixion and fragments of the True Cross, all of which he had bought from the impoverished Emperor Baldwin of Constantinople at phenomenal expense. Architecturally, for all its delicate and ornate exterior decoration—notice the open latticework of the pencil-like *flèche,* or spire, on the roof—the design of the building is simplicity itself. In essence, it's no more than a thin, rectangular box, much taller than it is wide. But think of it first and foremost as an oversize reliquary, an ornate medieval casket designed to house holy relics. The trade in relics in the Middle Ages was big business, as was, consequently, the construction of suitable containers, or reliquaries, in which to house them. The more valuable the relics, the more lavish was the reliquary in which they would be reverently placed. If you were the king of France—and a saint in the making, to boot—and you'd just gotten your hands on about the holiest relics of all, you'd naturally want someplace spectacular to keep them: hence, the Sainte-Chapelle.

The building is actually two chapels in one. The plainer, first-floor chapel, made gloomy by insensitive mid-19th-century restorations (which could do with restoration themselves), was for servants and lowly members of the court. The upper chapel, infinitely more spectacular, was for the king and more important members of the court. This is what you come to see. You reach it up a dark spiral staircase. Here, again, some clumsy 19th-century work has added a deadening touch, but the glory of the chapel—the stained glass—is spectacularly intact. The chapel is airy and diaphanous, the walls glowing and sparkling as light plays on the windows. Notice how the walls, in fact, consist of at least twice as much glass as masonry: The entire aim of the architects was to provide the maximum amount of window space. The Sainte-Chapelle is one of the supreme achievements of the Middle Ages and will be a highlight of your visit to Paris. Come early in the day to avoid the dutiful crowds that trudge around it. Better still, try to attend one of the regular, candle-lit concerts given here. *Admission: 24 frs adults, 13 frs students and senior citizens. Joint ticket with Conciergerie: 40 frs. Open daily 9–6; winter, daily 10–5.*

Take rue de Lutèce opposite the Palais de Justice down
25 to place Louis-Lépine and the bustling **Marché aux
Fleurs,** the flower market. There's an astoundingly wide
range of flowers on sale and, on Sundays, there are
birds, too—everything from sparrows to swans. *Open
daily 8–7.*

Notre Dame

Around the corner, looming above the large, traffic-free
place du Parvis (*kilometre zéro* to the French, the spot
from which all distances to and from the city are officially measured), is the most enduring symbol of Paris, its
26 historic and geographic heart, the **Cathédrale Notre
Dame.** The building was started in 1163, with an army of
stonemasons, carpenters, and sculptors working on a
site that had previously seen a Roman temple, an early
Christian basilica, and a Romanesque church. The chancel and altar were consecrated in 1182, but the magnificent sculptures surrounding the main doors were not
put into position until 1240. The north tower was finished 10 years later. Full-scale restoration started in the
middle of the century, the most conspicuous result of
which was the construction of the spire, the *flèche*, over
the roof. It was then, too, that Haussmann demolished
the warren of little buildings in front of the cathedral,
27 creating the place du Parvis. The **Crypte Archéologique,**
the archaeological museum under the square, contains
remains unearthed during excavations here in the
1960s. Slides and models detail the history of the Ile de
la Cité. The foundations of the 3rd-century Gallo-Roman
rampart and of the 6th-century Merovingian church can
also be seen. *Place du Parvis. Admission: 24 frs adults
(36 frs including tour of Notre Dame), 13 frs age 18–24,
5 frs age 7–18. Open daily 10–6:30, 10–5 in winter.*

Visit the place du Parvis early in the morning, when the
cathedral is at its lightest and least crowded. You come
first to the massive, 12th-century columns supporting
the twin towers. Look down the nave to the transepts—
the arms of the church—where, at the south (right) entrance to the chancel, you'll glimpse the haunting, 12th-
century statue of Notre Dame de Paris, Our Lady of
Paris. The chancel itself owes parts of its decoration to a
vow taken by Louis XIII in 1638. Still without an heir
after 23 years of marriage, he promised to dedicate the
entire country to the Virgin Mary if his queen produced
a son. When the longed-for event came to pass, Louis set
about redecorating the chancel and choir.

On the south side of the chancel is the **Treasury,** with a collection of garments, reliquaries, and silver and gold plate. *Admission: 15 frs adults, 10 frs students and senior citizens, 5 frs children. Open Mon.–Sat. 9:30–6, Sun. 2–6.*

The 387-step climb to the top of the **towers** is worth the effort for the close-up view of the famous gargoyles—most of them added in the 19th century—and the expansive view over the city. *Entrance via north tower. Admission: 30 frs adults, 16 frs students and senior citizens. Open daily 9:30–12:30 and 1:45–5.*

On the subject of views, no visit to Notre Dame is complete without a walk behind the cathedral to **Square Jean XXIII,** located between the river and the building. It offers a breathtaking sight of the east end of the cathedral, ringed by flying buttresses, surmounted by the spire. From here, the building seems almost to float above the Seine like some vast, stone ship.

If your interest in the cathedral is not yet sated, duck into the **Musée Notre Dame.** It displays paintings, engravings, medallions, and other objects and documents, all of which trace the cathedral's history. *10 rue du Cloître-Notre-Dame. Admission: 10 frs. Open Wed. and weekends only, 2:30–6.*

There's a final pilgrimage you may like to make on the Ile de la Cité to the **Mémorial de la Déportation,** located at square de l'Ile-de-France, at the eastern tip of the island. Here, in what was once the city morgue, you'll find the modern crypt, dedicated to those French men and women who died in Nazi concentration camps. You may find a visit to the quiet garden above it a good place to rest and to muse on the mysterious dichotomy that enables the human race to construct buildings of infinite beauty and to treat its fellow men with infinite cruelty. *Admission free. Open daily 9–6, 9–dusk in winter.*

The Marais and Ile St-Louis

Numbers in the margin correspond to points of interest on the Marais and Ile St-Louis map.

This tour includes two of the oldest and most historic neighborhoods in Paris: the Marais—once a marshy area north of the Seine, today about the most sought-after residential and business district of the city—and the

Ile St-Louis, the smaller of the two islands in the Seine. It also includes a side trip to the Bastille, site of the infamous prison stormed on July 14, 1789, an event that came to symbolize the beginning of the French Revolution. Largely in commemoration of the bicentennial of the Revolution in 1989, the Bastille area has been renovated.

Renovation is one of the key notes of this tour, especially around the Marais; the word *marais*, incidentally, means marsh or swamp. Well into the '70s, this was one of the city's poorest areas, filled with dilapidated tenement buildings and squalid courtyards. Today, the grubby streets of the Jewish quarter, around the rue des Rosiers, is about the only area to remain undeveloped. The area's regeneration was sparked by the building of the Beaubourg, arguably Europe's most vibrant—and architecturally whimsical—cultural center. The gracious architecture of the 17th and early 18th centuries, however, sets the tone for the rest of the Marais. Try to visit during the Festival du Marais, held every June and July, when concerts, theater, and ballet are performed.

Hôtel de Ville to Beaubourg

❶ Begin your tour at the **Hôtel de Ville,** the city hall, overlooking the Seine. In the Commune of 1871, the Hôtel de Ville was burned to the ground. Today's exuberant building, based closely on the Renaissance original, went up between 1874 and 1884. In 1944, following the liberation of Paris from Nazi rule, General de Gaulle took over the leadership of France here.

From the Hôtel de Ville, head north across rue de Rivoli and up rue du Temple. On your right, you'll pass one of ❷ the city's most popular department stores, the **Bazar de l'Hôtel de Ville,** or BHV, as it's known. The first street on your left, rue de la Verrerie, will take you down to ❸ rue St-Martin and the church of **St-Merri,** an ornate mid-16th-century structure. Its dark interior can be fun to explore, though it contains nothing of outstanding interest. You may find the upscale stores, restaurants, and galleries of rue St-Martin more diverting.

❹ The **Beaubourg,** or, to give it its full name, the Centre National d'Art et de Culture Georges-Pompidou, beckons now. Georges Pompidou (1911–1974) was the president of France who inaugurated the project. If nothing else, the Beaubourg is an exuberant melting pot of culture, which casts its net far and wide: Anything goes here. The center hosts an innovative and challenging series of exhibits, in addition to housing the largest collection of modern art in the world. Unveiled in 1977, the Beaubourg is by far the most popular museum in the world, attracting upward of 8 million visitors a year; but it has begun to show its age in no uncertain terms.

⑤ You'll approach the center across **plateau Beaubourg,** a substantial square that slopes gently down toward the main entrance. In summer, it's thronged with musicians, mime artists, dancers, fire-eaters, acrobats, and other performers. Probably the single most popular thing to do at the Beaubourg is to ride the escalator up to the roof, with the Parisian skyline unfolding as you are carried through its clear plastic piping. There is a sizable restaurant and café on the roof. The major highlight inside is the modern art collection on the fourth floor. The emphasis is largely on French artists; American painters and sculptors are conspicuous by their absence. Movie buffs will want to take in the cinémathèque, a movie theater showing near-continuous programs of classic films from the world over. There are also magnificent reference facilities, among them a language laboratory, an extensive collection of tapes, videos, and slides, an industrial design center, and an acoustics and musical research center. The bookshop on the first floor stocks a wide range of art books, many in English, plus postcards and posters. *Beaubourg, plateau Beaubourg, tel. 42–77–12–33. Admission free. Admission to art museum: 27 frs. Open Wed.–Mon. noon–10 PM, weekends 10 AM–10 PM; closed Tues. Guided tours weekdays 3:30, weekends 11.*

Time Out Don't leave the plateau without stopping for coffee at the **Café Beaubourg** on the corner of rue St-Merri. Architect Christian Porzenparc's conversion of a traditional Paris café is perhaps the most successful attempt in a current series of café renovations. A staircase takes you up from the first floor to a *passerelle*, or footbridge, linking the two sides of a mezzanine. The severe high-tech design is lightened by the little glass-top tables, which are gradually being covered with artists' etchings. The overall effect is one of space and light.

Take rue Rambuteau, which runs along the north side of the center (to your left as you face the building). The **⑥ Quartier de l'Horloge,** the Clock Quarter, opens off the plateau here. An entire city block has been rebuilt, and,

90

The Marais and Ile St-Louis

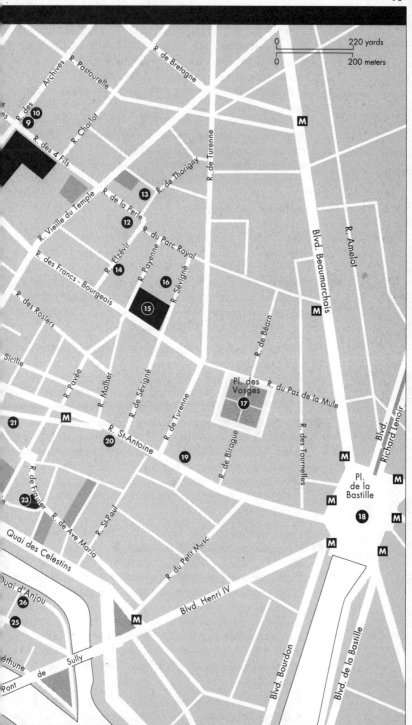

R. Pastourelle
Archives
R. de Bretagne
R. des
R. Charlot
10
9
R. des 4 Fils
R. de Turenne
R. Vieille du Temple
R. de Thorigny
13
R. de la Perle
12
R. du Parc Royal
R. Elzévir
R. des Francs - Bourgeois
14
R. Payenne
16
R. Sévigné
R. des Rosiers
15
Sicilie
R. Pavée
R. Malher
R. de Sévigné
R. de Turenne
R. de Béarn
Pl. des Vosges
R. du Pas de la Mule
17
21
M
R. St-Antoine
20
R. de Birague
R. des Tournelles
19
R. de Fauu
23
R. de Ave Maria
R. St-Paul
M
Pl. de la Bastille
Quai des Celestins
R. du Petit Musc
18
M
M
Quai d'Anjou
26
25
Blvd. Henri IV
M
éthune
de
Sully
Pont
Blvd. Bourdon
Blvd. de la Bastille

Blvd. Beaumarchais
R. Amelot
Blvd. Richard Lenoir

0   220 yards
0   200 meters

though its shops and cafés make a brave attempt to bring it to life, it retains a resolutely artificial quality. The mechanical clock around the corner on rue Clairvaux will amuse kids, however. Saint George defends Time against a dragon, an eagle-beaked bird, or a monstrous crab (symbolizing earth, air, and water, respectively) every hour, on the hour. At noon, 6 PM, and 10 PM, he takes on all three at once. On the other side of the Quartier de l'Horloge, at 11 rue Brantôme, is **AS-ECO**, the only all-night supermarket in the city; note that it's closed on Sundays. However, it's more fun shopping in the little market at the beginning of rue Rambuteau.

Around the Marais

You are now poised to plunge into the elegant heart of the Marais. You won't be able to get into many of the historic homes here—the private *hôtels particuliers*—but this won't stop you from admiring their stately facades. And don't be afraid to push through the heavy formal doors—or *porte-cochères*—to glimpse the discreet courtyards that lurk behind them.

From the Clock Quarter, continue down rue Rambuteau
❼ and take the first left, up rue du Temple, to the **Hôtel d'Avaux** at no. 71, built in 1640. The immense entrance is decorated with the sculpted heads of what, in 17th-century France, passed for savages. A few doors up, at
❽ no. 79, is the **Hôtel de Montmor,** dating from the same period. It was once the scene of an influential literary salon—a part-social and part-literary group—that met here on an impromptu basis and included the philosopher Descartes (1596–1650) and the playwright Molière (1622–1673). Note the intricate ironwork on the second-floor balcony.

Head east on rue des Haudriettes to the little-known
❾ **Musée de la Chasse et de la Nature,** housed in one of the Marais's most stately mansions, the Hôtel de Guénégaud. The collections include a series of immense 17th- and 18th-century pictures of dead animals, artfully arranged, as well as a wide variety of guns and stuffed animals (you might want to pass this by if you are a vegetarian or an opponent of blood sports). *60 rue des Archives, tel. 42–72–86–43. Admission: 20 frs adults, 10 frs children and students. Open Wed.–Mon. 10–12:30 and 1:30–5:30.*

Next door, at 58 rue des Archives, two fairytale towers stand on either side of the Gothic entrance (1380) to the

⑩ **Hôtel de Clisson.** In the mid-15th century this was the Paris base of the Duke of Bedford, regent of France after Henry V's demise, during the English occupation of Paris, a phase of the Hundred Years War that lasted from 1420 to 1435. At the end of the 17th century, it was bought by the glamorous princess of Soubise, a grande dame of Parisian literary society. She later moved into the neighboring Hôtel de Soubise, now the **Archives** ⑪ **Nationales.** Its collections today form part of the **Musée de l'Histoire de France,** whose entrance is at the southern end of the Archives Nationales. You can also visit the apartments of the prince and princess de Soubise; don't miss them if you have any interest in the lifestyles of 18th-century French aristocrats. *60 rue des Francs-Bourgeois, tel. 40–27–62–18. Admission: 12 frs adults, 8 frs children. Open Wed.–Mon. 1:45–5:45.*

Continue east on rue des Francs-Burgeois, turning left onto rue Vielle du Temple and passing the Hôtel de Rohan (on your left, on the corner), built for the archbishop of Strasbourg in 1705. Turn right onto rue de la ⑫ Perle and walk down to the **Musée de la Serrure,** the Lock Museum. It's sometimes also called the **Musée Bricard,** a name you'll recognize on many French locks and keys. The sumptuous building in which the collections are housed is perhaps more interesting than the assembled locks and keys within; it was built in 1685 by Bruand, the architect of Les Invalides *(see* From Orsay to Trocadéro, *below).* But those with a taste for fine craftsmanship will appreciate the intricacy and ingenuity of many of the older locks. One represents an early security system—it would shoot anyone who tried to open it with the wrong key. Another was made in the 17th century by a master locksmith who was himself held under lock and key while he labored over it—the task took him four years. *1 rue de la Perle, tel. 42–77–79–62. Admission: 10 frs. Open Tues.–Sat. 10–noon and 2–5; closed Sun., Mon., Aug., and last week of Dec.*

From here it is but a step to the Hôtel Salé, today the ⑬ **Musée Picasso,** opened in the fall of 1985 and so far showing no signs of losing its immense popularity. Be prepared for long lines at any time of year. What's notable about the collection—other than the fact that it's the largest collection of works by Picasso in the world—is that these were works that Picasso himself owned; works, in other words, that he especially valued. There are pictures from every period of his life, adding up to a grand total of 230 paintings, 1,500 drawings, and nearly 1,700 prints, as well as works by Cézanne, Miró, Renoir,

Braque, Degas, Matisse, and others. If you have any serious interest in Picasso, this is not a place you'd want to miss. The positively palatial surroundings of the Hôtel Salé add greatly to the pleasures of a visit. *5 rue de Thorigny, tel. 42–71–25–21. Admission: 21 frs. Open Wed. 9:45 AM–10 PM, Thurs.–Mon. 9:15–5:15.*

Head back down rue de Thorigny and cross to rue
⑭ Elzévir, opposite. Halfway down on the left is the **Musée Cognacq-Jay,** opened here in 1990 after being transferred from its original home on boulevard des Capucines near the Opéra. The museum is devoted to the arts of the 18th century and contains outstanding furniture, porcelain, and paintings (notably by Watteau, Boucher, and Tiepolo). *8 rue Elzévir, tel. 40–27–07–21. Admission: 12 frs. Open Tues.–Sun. 10–5:30.*

Continue down rue Elzévir to **rue des Francs-Bourgeois.** Its name—Street of the Free Citizens—comes from the homes for the poor, or almshouses, built here in the 14th century, whose inhabitants were so impoverished that they were allowed to be "free" of taxes. In marked contrast to the street's earlier poverty, the substantial
⑮ **Hôtel Carnavalet** became the scene, in the late 17th century, of the most brilliant salon in Paris, presided over by Madame de Sévigné. She is best known for the hundreds of letters she wrote to her daughter during her life; they've become one of the most enduring chronicles of French high society in the 17th century, and the Carnavalet was her home for the last 20 years of her life. In 1880, the hotel was transformed into the **Musée Carnavalet,** or Musée Historique de la Ville de Paris. As part of the mammoth celebrations for the bicentennial of the French Revolution, in July 1989, Madame de Sévigné's letters and the print collection were trans-
⑯ ferred to the neighboring **Hôtel Peletier St-Fargeau,** but the Carnavalet's collections have been added to and now cover the history of Paris from the mid-19th century through to the present. You may find parts of the older collections repetitive. There are large numbers of maps and plans, quantities of furniture, and a substantial assemblage of busts and portraits of Parisian worthies down the ages. The sections on the Revolution, on the other hand, are extraordinary and include some riveting models of guillotines. *23 rue de Sévigné, tel. 42–72–21–13. Admission: 30 frs adults, 20 frs students and senior citizens. Open Tues.–Sun. 10–5:30; closed Mon.*

Now walk a minute or two farther along rue des Francs-
⑰ Bourgeois to **place des Vosges.** Place des Vosges, or place

Royale as it was originally known, is the oldest square in Paris. Laid out by Henri IV at the beginning of the 17th century, it is the model on which all later city squares, that most French urban developments, are based. The combination of symmetrical town houses and the trim green square, bisected in the center by gravel paths and edged with plane trees, makes place des Vosges one of the more pleasant places to spend a hot summer's afternoon in the city. On these days, it will usually be filled with children playing in shafts of sunlight, with the roar of the traffic a distant hum.

You can tour the **Maison de Victor Hugo** at no. 6 (admission 12 frs; open Tues.–Sun. 10–5:40), where the French author lived between 1832 and 1848. The collections here may appeal only to those with a specialized knowledge of the workaholic French writer.

Around the Bastille

From place des Vosges, follow rue de Pas de la Mule and turn right down boulevard Beaumarchais until you ⑱ reach **place de la Bastille,** site of the infamous prison destroyed at the beginning of the French Revolution. Until 1988, there was little more to see at place de la Bastille than a huge traffic circle and the **Colonne de Juillet,** the July Column. As part of the country-wide celebrations for July 1989, the bicentennial of the French Revolution, an **opera house** (Opéra de la Bastille) was put up on the south side of the square. Designed by Argentinian-born Carlos Ott, it seats more than 3,000 and boasts five moving stages. This ambitious project has inspired substantial redevelopment on the surrounding streets, especially along rue de Lappe—once a haunt of Edith Piaf—and rue de la Roquette.

The Bastille, or, more properly, the Bastille St-Antoine, was a massive building, protected by eight immense towers and a wide moat (its ground plan is marked by paving stones set into the modern square). It was built by Charles V in the late 14th century. He intended it not as a prison but as a fortress to guard the eastern entrance to the city. By the reign of Louis XIII (1610–1643), however, the Bastille was used almost exclusively to house political prisoners. Voltaire, the Marquis de Sade, and the mysterious Man in the Iron Mask were all incarcerated here, along with many other unfortunates. It was this obviously political role—specifically, the fact that the prisoners were nearly always held by order of the king—that led to the formation of the "furious mob" (in all probability no more than a largely unarmed rabble) to break into the prison on July 14, 1789, to kill the governor, steal what firearms they could find, and set free the seven remaining prisoners.

Toward the Ile St-Louis

There's more of the Marais to be visited between place de la Bastille and the Ile St-Louis, the last leg of this tour. Take wide rue St-Antoine to the **Hôtel de Sully,** site of the Caisse Nationale des Monuments Historiques, the principal office for the administration of French historic monuments. Guided visits to sites and buildings all across the city begin here, though all of them are for French-speakers only. Still, it's worth stopping here to look at the stately, 17th-century courtyard with its richly carved windows and lavish ornamentation. The bookshop just inside the gate has a wide range of publications on Paris, many of them in English (open daily 10–12:45 and 1:45–6). You can also wander around the gardens.

Those with a fondness for the Baroque should duck into the early 17th-century church of **St-Paul-St-Louis,** a few blocks west on rue St-Antoine. Its abundant decoration, which would be easier to appreciate if the church were cleaned, is typical of the Baroque taste for opulent detail.

The **Hôtel de Beauvais,** located on rue François Miron, is a Renaissance-era *hôtel particulier* dating from 1655. It was built for one Pierre de Beauvais and financed largely by a series of discreet payments from the king, Louis XIV. These surprisingly generous payments—the Sun King was normally parsimonious toward courtiers— were de Beauvais's reward for having turned a blind eye to the activities of his wife, Catherine-Henriette Bellier, in educating the young monarch in matters sexual. Louis, who came to the throne in 1643 at the age of 4, was 14 at the time Catherine-Henriette gave him the benefit of her wide experience; she was 40.

Continue down rue François Miron. Just before the Hôtel de Ville is the site of one of the first churches in Paris, **St-Gervais- St-Protais,** named after two Roman soldiers martyred by the Emperor Nero in the 1st century AD. The original church—no trace remains of it now—was built in the 7th century. The present church, a riot of Flamboyant-style decoration, went up between 1494 and 1598, making it one of the last Gothic constructions in the country. Some find this sort of late Gothic architecture a poor, almost degraded, relation of the pure styles of the 12th and 13th centuries. Does it carry off a certain exuberance, or is it simply a mass of unnecessary decoration? You'll want to decide for yourself. Pause before you go in, to look at the facade, put up between 1616 and 1621. Where the interior is late Gothic, the exterior is one of the earliest examples of classical, or Renaissance, style in France. It's also the earliest example of French architects' use of the classical orders of decoration on the capitals (topmost sections) of the columns. Those on the first floor are plain and sturdy Doric; the more elaborate Ionic is used on the second floor; while the most ornate of all—Corinthian—is used on the third floor.

Don't cross the Seine to Ile St-Louis yet: Take rue de l'Hôtel de Ville to where it meets rue de Figuier. The **23** painstakingly restored **Hôtel de Sens** (1474) on the corner is one of a handful of Parisian homes to have survived since the Middle Ages. With its pointed corner towers, Gothic porch, and richly carved decorative details, it is a strange mixture, half defensive stronghold, half fairytale château. It was built at the end of the 15th century for the archbishop of Sens. Later, its best-known occupants were Henri IV and his queen, Marguerite, philanderers both. While Henri dallied with his mistresses—he is said to have had 56—at a series of royal palaces, Marguérite entertained her almost equally large number of lovers here. Today the building houses a fine arts library, the **Bibliothéque Forney** (admission free; open Tues.–Sat. 1:30–8:30).

The Ile St-Louis

24 Cross pont Marie to the **Ile St-Louis,** the smaller of the two islands in the heart of Paris, linked to the Ile de la Cité by pont St-Louis. The contrast between the islands is striking, considering how close they are. Whereas the Ile de la Cité, the oldest continuously inhabited part of the city, is steeped in history and dotted with dignified, old buildings, the Ile St-Louis is a discreet residential district, something of an extension of the Marais. Once thought to be an unimportant backwater and an area curiously out-of-sync with the rest of the city, Ile St-Louis is now a highly desirable address; a little old-fashioned perhaps, certainly rather stuffy, but with its own touch of class.

The most striking feature of the island is its architectural unity, which stems from the efforts of a group of early 17th-century property speculators. At that time, there were two islands here, the Ile Notre Dame and Ile aux Vaches—the cows' island, a reference to its use as grazing land. The speculators, led by an energetic engineer named Christophe Marie (after whom the pont Marie was named), bought the two islands, joined them together, and divided the newly formed Ile St-Louis into building plots. Louis Le Vau (1612–1670), the leading Baroque architect in France, was commissioned to put up a series of imposing town houses, and by 1664 the project was largely complete.

There are three things you'll want to do here. One is to
㉕ walk along **rue St-Louis en l'Ile,** which runs the length of the island. People still talk about its quaint, village-street feel, although this village street is now lined with a high-powered array of designer boutiques and a constant throng of tourists patroling its length.

Time Out **Berthillon** has become a byword for amazing ice cream. Cafés all over Ile St-Louis sell its glamorous products, but the place to come is still the little shop on rue St-Louis en l'Ile. Expect to wait in line. *31 rue St-Louis en l'Ile. Closed Mon. and Tues.*

㉖ The second place to visit is the **Hôtel de Lauzun.** It was built in about 1650 for Charles Gruyn, who accumulated an immense fortune as a supplier of goods to the French army, but who landed in jail before the house was even completed. In the 19th century, the revolutionary critic and visionary poet Charles Baudelaire (1821–1867) had an apartment here, where he kept a personal cache of stuffed snakes and crocodiles. In 1848, the poet Théophile Gautier (1811–1872) moved in, making it the meeting place of the Club des Haschischines, the Hashish-Eaters' Club. Now the building is used for receptions by the mayor of Paris. *17 quai d'Anjou, tel. 43–54–27–14. Admission: 22 frs. Open Easter–Oct., weekends only 10–5:30.*

The third and most popular attraction is a walk along
㉗ the quays. The most lively, **quai de Bourbon,** is at the western end, facing the Ile de la Cité. There are views of Notre Dame from here and of the Hôtel de Ville and church of St-Gervais-St-Protais on the Right Bank. It can be an almost eerie spot in the winter, when it becomes deserted. In the summer, rows of baking bodies

attest to its enduring popularity as the city's favorite sunbathing spot. •

Time Out   The **Brasserie de l'Ile** remains the most noisy and bustling of the little island's eating spots. Food from the French Alsace district, on the German border, with beer to wash it down, is the draw. Scores of tourists can nearly always be found on the terrace, but good value is guaranteed. *55 quai de Bourbon, tel. 43–54–02–59. Closed Wed. and Thurs. lunch and Aug.*

From the Arc de Triomphe to the Opéra

Numbers in the margin correspond to points of interest on the Arc de Triomphe to the Opéra map.

This tour takes in grand, opulent Paris: the Paris of imposing vistas, long, arrow-straight streets, and plush hotels and jewelers. It begins at the Arc de Triomphe, standing foursquare at the top of the most famous street in the city, the Champs-Elysées. You'll want to explore both its commercial upper half and its verdant lower section. The hinterland of the Champs-Elysées, made up of the imposing streets leading off it, is equally stylish. You're within striking distance of the Seine here (and a ride on a Bateau Mouche) to the south, and the cheerful, crowded Faubourg St-Honoré to the north. This is not so much an area for museums as for window-shopping and monument-gazing. Dazzling vistas open up from place de la Concorde, place de la Madeleine, and L'Etoile. Fashion shops, jewelers, art galleries, and deluxe hotels proliferate. This is also where the French president resides in his "palace" (not a very Republican term, but then French presidents enjoy regal lifestyles) just off the Champs-Elysées.

Local charm is not, however, a feature of this exclusive sector of western Paris, occupying principally the 8th Arrondissement. It's beautiful and rich—and a little impersonal. Frenchmen moan that it's losing its character, and, as you notice the number of fast-food joints along the Champs-Elysées, you'll know what they mean. In short: Visit during the day, and head elsewhere in search of Parisian *ambience* and an affordable meal in the evening.

The Arc de Triomphe and Champs-Elysées

Place Charles de Gaulle is known by Parisians as **L'Etoile,** the star—a reference to the streets that fan out from it. It is one of Europe's most chaotic traffic circles, and short of a death-defying dash, your only way of getting to the Arc de Triomphe in the middle is to take an underground passage from the Champs-Elysées or avenue de la Grande Armée.

❶ The colossal, 164-foot **Arc de Triomphe** was planned by Napoleon—who believed himself to be the direct heir to the Roman emperors—to celebrate his military successes. Unfortunately, Napoleon's strategic and architectural visions were not entirely on the same plane, and the Arc de Triomphe proved something of a white elephant. When it was required for the triumphal entry of his new empress, Marie-Louise, into Paris in 1810, it was still only a few feet high. To save face, a dummy arch of painted canvas was put up.

Empires come and go, and Napoleon's had been gone for over 20 years before the Arc de Triomphe was finally finished in 1836. It boasts some magnificent sculpture by François Rude, such as the *Departure of the Volunteers*, better known as *La Marseillaise*, situated to the right of the arch when viewed from the Champs-Elysées. After showing alarming signs of decay, the structure received a thorough overhaul in 1989 and is now back to its original neo-Napoleonic splendor. The view from the top illustrates the star effect of Etoile's 12 radiating avenues and enables you to admire the vista down the Champs-Elysées toward place de la Concorde and the distant Louvre. In the other direction, you can see down avenue de la Grande Armée toward La Tête Défense and its severe modern arch, surrounded by imposing glass and concrete towers. There is a small museum halfway up the arch devoted to its history. France's Unknown Soldier is buried beneath the archway; the flame is rekindled every evening at 6:30. *Place Charles-de-Gaulle. Admission: 30 frs adults, 16 frs students and senior citizens, 7 frs children. Open daily 10–6, 10–5:30 in winter. Closed public holidays.*

The cosmopolitan pulse of Paris beats strongest on the gracefully sloping, 2-kilometer- (1¼-mile-) long **Champs-Elysées.** It was originally laid out in the 1660s by the landscape gardener Le Nôtre as a garden sweeping away from the Tuileries, but you will see few signs of these pastoral origins as you stroll past the cafés, restaurants, airline offices, car showrooms, movie theaters, and chic arcades that occupy its upper half.

2 Start off by stopping in at the main **Paris Tourist Office** at no. 127. It's at the Arc de Triomphe end of the Champs-Elysées, on the right-hand side as you arrive from Etoile. It is an invaluable source of information on accommodations, places to visit, and entertainment—both in Paris and in the surrounding Ile-de-France region. *Open daily 9–8, 9–9 on weekdays in summer, 9–6 on Sun. out of season.*

The Champs-Elysées occupies a central role in French national celebrations. It witnesses the finish of the Tour de France bicycle race on the last Sunday of July. It is also the site of vast ceremonies on July 14, France's national, or Bastille, day, and November 11, Armistice Day. Its trees are often decked with the French *tricolore* and foreign flags to mark visits from heads of state.

Three hundred yards down on the left, at 116b, is the fa-
3 mous **Lido** nightclub: Foot-stomping melodies in French and English and champagne-soaked, topless razzmatazz pack in the crowds every night. In contrast are the red-
4 awninged **Prince de Galles** (Prince of Wales) and the
5 blue-awninged **George V,** two of the city's top hotels on avenue George-V, a right-hand turn off Champs-Elysées. Continue down avenue George-V, and turn
6 right down Pierre Ier-de-Serbie to the church of **St-Pierre de Chaillot** on avenue Marceau. The monumental frieze above the entrance, depicting scenes from the life of St. Peter, is the work of Henri Bouchard and dates from 1937.

Returning to avenue George-V, continue toward the
7 slender spire of the **American Cathedral of the Holy Trinity,** built by G. S. Street between 1885 and 1888. *Open weekdays 9–12:30 and 2–5, Sat. 9–noon. Services: weekdays noon, Sun. 9 AM and 11 AM; Sun. school and nursery.*

Continue down to the bottom of the avenue, passing the
8 **Crazy Horse Saloon** at no. 12, one of Paris's most enduring and spectacular nightspots, to place de l'Alma and the Seine.

9 The **pont de l'Alma** (Alma bridge) is best known for the chunky stone "Zouave" statue carved into one of the pillars. Zouaves were Algerian infantrymen recruited into the French army who were famous for their bravura and colorful uniforms. (The term came to be used for volun-

The Arc de Triomphe to the Opéra

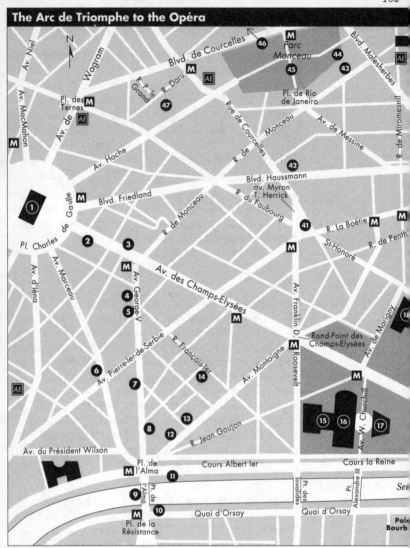

teers in the Union Army during the American Civil War.) There is nothing quite so glamorous, or colorful, about the Alma Zouave, however, whose hour of glory comes in times of watery distress: Parisians use him to judge the level of the Seine during heavy rains. As recently as the spring of 1988, the Zouave was submerged up to his chest, and the roads running along the riverbanks were under several feet of water.

Just across the Alma bridge, on the left, is the entrance ➓ to **Les Egouts,** the Paris sewers (admission: 22 frs adults, 17 frs students and senior citizens; open Sat.–Wed. 11–5). If you prefer a less malodorous tour of the city, stay on the Right Bank and head down the sloping side road to the left of the bridge, for the embarkation ⑪ point of the **Bateaux Mouches.** These popular motorboats set off every half hour, heading east to the Ile St-Louis and then back west, past the Eiffel Tower, as far as the Allée des Cygnes and its miniature version of the Statue of Liberty. *Bateau Mouche* translates, misleadingly, as "fly boat"; but the name Mouche actually refers to a district of Lyon where the boats were originally manufactured.

Stylish avenue Montaigne leads from the Seine back toward the Champs-Elysées. The newly cleaned facade of ⑫ the **Théâtre des Champs-Elysées** is a forerunner of the Art Deco style. The theater dates from 1913 and was the first major building in France to be constructed in reinforced concrete. *15 av. Montaigne.*

Time Out Although power brokers and fashion models make up half the clientele at the **Bar des Théâtres** (opposite the Théâtre des Champs-Elysées at 6 avenue Montaigne), its blasé waiters refuse to bat an eyelid. This is a fine place for an aperitif or a swift, more affordable lunch than around the corner at the luxury restaurants on place de l'Alma.

---

⑬ A few buildings along is the **Plaza Athénée** hotel (the "Plaza"), a favorite hangout for the *beau monde* who frequent the neighboring haute couture houses. Around ⑭ the corner on the rue François-Ier is the **Maison de la Vigne et du Vin de France.** This is the classy central headquarters of the French wine industry and a useful source of information about wine regions. Bottles and maps are on display. *21 rue François-Ier, tel. 47–20–20–76. Admission free. Open weekdays 9–6.*

Double back on rue François-Ier as far as Place François-Ier, then turn left onto rue Jean-Goujon, which
leads to avenue Franklin D. Roosevelt, another spacious
boulevard between Champs-Elysées and the river.
⑮ Halfway down it is the entrance to the **Palais de la
Découverte** (Palace of Discovery), whose scientific and
technological exhibits include working models and a
planetarium. *Av. Franklin-D-Roosevelt. Admission: 20
frs adults, 10 frs children under 18 (13 frs/9 frs extra for
planetarium). Open Tues.–Sat. 9:30–6, Sun. 10–7.*

This "Palace of Discovery" occupies the rear half of the
⑯ **Grand Palais.** With its curved glass roof, the Grand Palais is unmistakable when approached from either the
Seine or the Champs-Elysées and forms an attractive
duo with the **Petit Palais** on the other side of avenue
Winston Churchill. Both these stone buildings, adorned
with mosaics and sculpted friezes, seem robust and venerable. In fact, they were erected with indecent haste
prior to the Paris World Fair of 1900. As with the Eiffel
Tower, there was never any intention that they would be
anything other than temporary additions to the city.
But once they were up, no one seemed inclined to take
them down. Together with the exuberant, lamp-lit
Alexandre III bridge nearby, they recapture the opu-
lence and frivolity of the Belle Epoque—the *fin de siècle*
overripeness with which Paris is still so strongly associated. Today, the atmospheric iron and glass interior of
the Grand Palais plays regular host to major exhibitions. Admire the view from the palaces across the Alexandre III bridge toward the Hôtel des Invalides. *Av.
Winston Churchill. Admission varies according to exhibition. Usually open daily 10:30–6:30, and often until
10 PM Wed.*

⑰ The **Petit Palais** has a beautifully presented permanent
collection of French painting and furniture, with splendid canvases by Courbet and Bouguereau. Temporary
exhibits are often held here, too. The sprawling entrance gallery contains several enormous turn-of-the-
century paintings on its walls and ceilings. *Av. Winston
Churchill. Admission: 12 frs adults, 6 frs children.
Open Tues.–Sun. 10–5:30.*

Time Out One of the more enticing features of the chic, bland
Champs-Elysées arcades is the **Grillapolis** restaurant/
piano bar on the Galérie du Rond-Point (entrance 12
Rond-Point des Champs-Elysées, 300 yards up from av-
enue Winston Churchill on the other side of the Champs-
Elysées). A giant waterwheel makes a soothing accom-

paniment to the different-flavored teas, milk shakes, or meals.

From the Rond-Point des Champs-Elysées, head down avenue de Marigny to rue du Faubourg St-Honoré, a prestigious address in the world of luxury fashion and art galleries. You'll soon spot plenty of both, but may be perplexed at the presence of crash barriers and stern policemen. Their mission: to protect the French president in the **Palais de l'Elysée.** This "palace," where the head of state lives, works, and receives official visitors, was originally constructed as a private mansion in 1718. Although you catch a glimpse of the palace forecourt and facade through the Faubourg St-Honoré gateway, it is difficult to get much idea of the building's size or of the extensive gardens that stretch back to the Champs-Elysées. (Incidentally, when Parisians talk about "l'Elysée," they mean the President's palace; the Champs-Elysées is known simply as "les Champs," the fields.) The Elysée has known presidential occupants only since 1873; before then, Madame de Pompadour (Louis XV's influential mistress), Napoleon, Josephine, the Duke of Wellington, and Queen Victoria all stayed here. President Félix Faure died here in 1899 in the arms of his mistress. The French government—the Conseil des Ministres—attends to more public affairs when it meets here each Wednesday morning. *Not open to the public.*

Toward place de la Concorde

St. Michael's English Church, close to the British Embassy on rue du Faubourg St-Honoré, is a modern building whose ugliness is redeemed by the warmth of the welcome afforded to all visitors, English-speaking ones in particular. *5 rue d'Aguesseau, tel. 47–42–70–88. Services Thurs. 12:45 and Sun. 10:30 (with Sunday school) and 6:30 (with supervised nursery for younger children).*

Continue down rue du Faubourg St-Honoré to rue Royale. This classy street, lined with jewelry stores, links place de la Concorde to the **Eglise de la Madeleine,** a sturdy neo-Classical edifice that was nearly selected as Paris's first train station (the site of what is now the Gare St-Lazare, just up the road, was eventually chosen). With its rows of uncompromising columns, the Madeleine looks more like a Greek temple than a Christian church. Inside, the only natural light comes from three shallow domes. The walls are richly and harmoniously decorated, and gold glints through the murk. The church was designed in 1814 but not consecrated until 1842. The portico's majestic Corinthian colonnade supports a gigantic pediment with a sculptured frieze of the Last Judgment. From the top of the steps, you can admire the view down rue Royale across place de la Concorde to the Palais Bourbon. From the bottom of the steps, another view leads up boulevard Malesherbes to the dome of the church of St-Augustin.

Time Out **L'Ecluse,** on the square to the west of the church, is a cozy wine bar that specializes in stylish snacks, such as foie gras and carpaccio, and offers a range of Bordeaux wines served by the glass. *15 pl. de la Madeleine. Open daily noon–2 AM.*

Alongside the Madeleine, between the church and ㉑ L'Ecluse, is a **ticket kiosk** selling tickets for same-day theater performances at greatly reduced prices. Behind ㉒ ㉓ the church are **Fauchon** and **Hédiard,** two stylish delicatessens that are the ultimate in posh nosh. At the end of the rue Royale, just before place de la Concorde, is the ㉔ legendary **Maxim's** restaurant. Unless you choose to eat here—an expensive and not always rewarding experience—you won't be able to see the interior decor, a riot of crimson velvets and florid Art Nouveau furniture.

There is a striking contrast between the sunless, locked-in feel of the high-walled rue Royale and the ㉕ broad, airy **place de la Concorde.** This huge square is best approached from the Champs-Elysées: The flower beds, chestnut trees, and sandy sidewalks of the avenue's lower section are reminders of its original leafy elegance. Place de la Concorde was built in the 1770s, but there was nothing in the way of peace or concord about its early years. Between 1793 and 1795, it was the scene of over a thousand deaths by guillotine; victims included Louis XVI, Marie Antoinette, Danton, and Robespierre. The obelisk, a present from the viceroy of Egypt, was erected in 1833. The handsome, symmetrical, 18th-century buildings facing the square include the ㉖ deluxe **Hôtel Crillon,** though there's nothing so vulgar as a sign to identify it—just an inscribed marble plaque above the doorway.

Facing one side of place de la Concorde are the **Tuileries Gardens.** Two smallish buildings stand sentinel here. To ㉗ the left, nearer rue de Rivoli, is the **Musée du Jeu de Paume,** fondly known to many as the former home of the

Impressionists (now in the Musée d'Orsay). After extensive renovation, the Jeu de Paume reopened in 1991 as a home to brash temporary exhibits of contemporary art. *Admission: 30 frs adults, 20 frs students and senior citizens. Open Tues.–Fri. 12–7, weekends 10–7.* The other, identical building, nearer the Seine, is the recently restored **Musée de l'Orangerie,** containing some early 20th-century paintings by Monet and Renoir, among others. *Place de la Concorde. Admission: 25 frs adults, 13 frs students and senior citizens. Open Wed.–Mon. 9:45–5:15; closed Tues.*

㉙ As gardens go, the **Jardin des Tuileries** is typically French: formal and neatly patterned, with statues, rows of trees, gravel paths, and occasional patches of grass trying to look like lawns. These may benefit from the overhaul ordered by Culture Minister Jack Lang for the early '90s. It is a charming place to stroll and survey the surrounding cityscape. To the north is the disciplined, arcaded rue de Rivoli; to the south, the Seine and the gold-hued Musée d'Orsay with its enormous clocks; to the west, the Champs-Elysées and Arc de Triomphe; to the east, the Arc du Carrousel and the Louvre, with its glass pyramid.

Place Vendôme and the Opéra

㉚ **Place Vendôme,** north of the Jardin des Tuileries, is one of the world's most opulent squares. Mansart's rhythmic, perfectly proportioned example of 17th-century urban architecture has shone in all its golden-stoned splendor since being cleaned a few years ago. Many other things shine here, too—in jewelers' display windows and on the dresses of guests of the top-ranking **Ritz** hotel. Napoleon had the square's central column made from the melted bronze of 1,200 cannon captured at the battle of Austerlitz in 1805. That's him standing vigilantly at the top. Painter Gustave Courbet headed the Revolutionary hooligans who, in 1871, toppled the column and shattered it into thousands of metallic pieces.

㉛ Cross the square and take rue des Capucines on your left to boulevard des Capucines. The **Olympia** music hall is still going strong, though it has lost some of the luster it acquired as the stage for such great postwar singers as Edith Piaf and Jacques Brel.

Time Out There are few grander cafés in Paris than the **Café de la Paix,** on the corner of place de l'Opéra. This is a good place to people-watch, or just to slow down; but expect the prices to be as grand as the setting.

㉜ The **Opéra,** begun in 1862 by Charles Garnier at the behest of Napoleon III, was not completed until 1875, five years after the emperor's political demise. It is often said to typify the Second Empire style of architecture, which is to say that it is a pompous hodgepodge of styles, imbued with as much subtlety as a Wagnerian cymbal crash. After paying the entry fee, you can stroll around at leisure. The monumental foyer and staircase are boisterously impressive, a stage in their own right, where, on first nights, celebrities preen and prance. If the lavishly upholstered auditorium (ceiling painted by Marc Chagall in 1964) seems small, it is only because the stage is the largest in the world—over 11,000 square yards, with room for up to 450 performers. The **Musée de l'Opéra** (Opéra museum), containing a few paintings and theatrical mementos, is unremarkable. *Admission: 17 frs. Open daily 11–4:30, but closed occasionally for rehearsals; call 47–42–57–50 to check.*

Around the Opéra

Behind the Opéra are the *Grands Magasins*, Paris's most renowned department stores. The nearer of the **㉝** two, the **Galeries Lafayette,** is the most outstanding, if only because of its vast, shimmering, turn-of-the-century glass dome. The domes at the corners of **㉞** **Printemps,** farther along boulevard Haussmann, to the left, can be best appreciated from the outside; there is a **㉟** splendid view from the store's rooftop cafeteria. **Marks & Spencer,** across the road, provides a brave outpost for British goods, such as ginger biscuits, bacon rashers, and Cheddar cheese.

Time Out On the top floor of the **Printemps** department store is a cafeteria offering morning coffee, adequate inexpensive lunches, and, above all, magnificent rooftop views of central Paris.

㊱ The **Trinité** church, several blocks north of the Opéra, is not an unworthy 19th-century effort at neo-Renaissance style. Its central tower is of dubious aesthetic merit but is a recognizable feature in the Paris skyline (especially since its cleaning in 1986). The church was built in the 1860s and is fronted by a pleasant garden.

37 The nearby **Atelier de Gustave Moreau** was the town house and studio of painter Gustave Moreau (1826–1898), doyen of the Symbolist movement, which strove to convey ideas through images. Many of the ideas Moreau was trying to express remain obscure to the general public, even though the artist provided explanatory texts. But most onlookers will be content admiring his extravagant colors and flights of fantasy, which reveal the influence of Persian and Indian miniatures. Fantastic details cover every inch of his canvases, and his canvases cover every inch of wall space, making a trip to the museum one of the strangest artistic experiences in Paris. Go on a sunny day, if possible; the low lighting can strain the eyes even more than Moreau's paintings can. *14 rue de la Rochefoucauld. Admission: 17 frs adults, 9 frs children and senior citizens. Open Thurs.–Mon. 10–12:45 and 2–5:15, Wed. 11–5:15. Guided tours Wed.–Sat. at 2 and 3:30 only.*

38 Rue St-Lazare leads from Trinité to the **Gare St-Lazare,** whose imposing 19th-century facade has been restored. In the days of steam and smoke, the station was an inspiration to several Impressionist painters, notably Monet. Note an eccentric sculpture to the right of the facade—a higgledy-piggledy accumulation of clocks.

39 The leafy, intimate **Square Louis XVI,** off boulevard Haussmann between St-Lazare and St-Augustin, is perhaps the nearest Paris gets to a verdant, London-style square—if you discount the bombastic mausoleum in the middle. The unkempt chapel marks the initial burial site of Louis XVI and Marie Antoinette after their turns at the guillotine on place de la Concorde. Two stone tablets are inscribed with the last missives of the doomed royals—touching pleas for their Revolutionary enemies to be forgiven. When compared to the pomp and glory of Napoleon's memorial at the Invalides, this tribute to royalty (France was ruled by kings until 1792 and again from 1815 to 1848) seems trite and cursory. *Admission to the chapel: 10 frs. Open daily 10–noon and 2–6, 10–4 in winter.*

Before leaving the square, take a look at the gleaming 1930s-style facade of the bank at the lower corner of rue Pasquier. It has some amusing stone carvings halfway up, representing various exotic animals.

40 A mighty dome is the most striking feature of the innovative iron-and-stone church of **St-Augustin,** dexterously constructed in the 1860s within the confines of an awkward, V-shaped site. The use of metal girders obviated the need for exterior buttressing. The dome is bulky but well-proportioned and contains some grimy but competent frescoes by the popular 19th-century French artist William Bouguereau.

㊶ Rue La Boétie leads to another church, **St-Philippe du Roule,** built by Chalgrin between 1769 and 1784. Its austere classical portico dominates a busy square. The best thing inside this dimly lit church is the 19th-century fresco above the altar by Théodore Chassériau, featuring the Descent from the Cross.

㊷ Make your way back to boulevard Haussmann via avenue Myron T. Herrick. The **Musée Jacquemart-André** features Italian Renaissance and 18th-century art in a dazzlingly furnished, late 19th-century mansion. *158 blvd. Haussmann, tel. 42–89–04–91. Admission: 18 frs. Open Wed.–Sun. 1–6.*

㊸ Rue de Courcelles and a right on rue de Monceau will lead to place de Rio de Janeiro. Before venturing into the Parc Monceau at the far end of avenue Ruysdaël, saunter along rue de Monceau to the **Musée Nissim de Camondo.** Inside, you will find the stylish interior of an aristocratic Parisian mansion in the style of Louis XVI, dating from the last days of the regal Ancien Régime. *63 rue de Monceau. Admission: 15 frs adults, 10 frs students and senior citizens. Open Wed.–Sun. 10–noon and 2–5.*

㊹ Rue de Monceau and boulevard Malesherbes lead to the **Musée Cernuschi,** whose collection of Chinese art ranges from neolithic pottery (3rd century BC) to funeral statuary, painted 8th-century silks, and contemporary paintings. *7 av. Velasquez. Admission: 9 frs. Open Tues.–Sun. 10–5:40.*

㊺ The **Parc Monceau,** which can be entered from avenue Velasquez, was laid out as a private park in 1778 and retains some of the fanciful elements then in vogue, including mock ruins and a phony pyramid. In 1797, Garnerin, the world's first-recorded parachutist, staged a landing in the park. The rotunda, known as the Chartres Pavilion, was originally a tollhouse and has well-worked iron gates.

㊻ Leave the Parc Monceau by these gates and follow rue Phalsbourg and avenue de Villiers to the **Musée Jean-Jacques Henner.** Henner (1829–1905), a nearly forgotten Alsatian artist, here receives a sumptuous tribute. His obsessive fondness for milky-skinned, auburn-haired female nudes is displayed in hundreds of drawings and paintings on the three floors of this gracious museum. *43 av. de Villiers, tel. 47–63–42–73. Admission by appointment only.*

Boulevard de Courcelles, which runs along the north side of the Parc Monceau, leads west to rue Pierre-le-Grand (Peter the Great Street). At the far end of that street, at 12 rue Daru, loom the unlikely gilt onion domes of the Russian Orthodox cathedral of **St-Alexandre Nevsky,** erected in neo-Byzantine style in 1860. Inside, the wall of icons that divides the church in two creates an atmosphere seldom found in Roman Catholic or Protestant churches.

From Orsay to Trocadéro

Numbers in the margin correspond to points of interest on the Orsay to Trocadéro map.

The Left Bank has two faces: the cozy, ramshackle Latin Quarter (*see* The Left Bank, *below*) and the spacious, stately 7th Arrondissement. This tour covers the latter. The latest addition to the area is already the most popular: the Musée d'Orsay. Crowds flock to this stylishly converted train station to see the Impressionists, but also discover important examples of other schools of 19th- and early 20th-century art.

The atmosphere of the 7th Arrondissement is set by the National Assembly, down the river from Orsay, opposite place de la Concorde. French deputies meet here to hammer out laws and insult each other. They resume more civilized attitudes when they return to the luxurious ministries that dot the nearby streets. The most famous is the Hôtel Matignon, official residence of the French prime minister.

The majestic scale of many of the area's buildings is totally in character with the daddy of them all, the Invalides. Like the Champ de Mars nearby, the esplanade in front of the Invalides was once used as a parade ground for Napoleon's troops. In a coffin beneath the Invalides dome, M. Bonaparte dreams on.

Musée d'Orsay

The **Musée d'Orsay** opened in December 1986. It is devoted to the arts (mainly French) produced between 1848 and 1914, and its collections are intended to form a bridge between the classical collections of the Louvre and the modern collections of the Beaubourg. The build-

PACK WISELY.

Given a choice, the seasoned traveler always carries less.
Case in point: Sony Handycam® camcorders, America's most
popular. They record up to 2½ hours on a single tape.
VHS-C tapes record only 30 minutes.* And why carry five tapes
when you can record everything on one? Which brings us
to the first rule of traveling: pack a Sony Handycam camcorder.

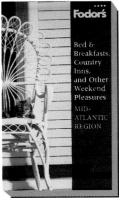

ing began in 1900 as a train station for routes between Paris and the southwest of France. By 1939, the Gare d'Orsay had become too small for mainline travel, and intercity trains were transferred to the Gare d'Auster-litz. Gare d'Orsay became a suburban terminus until, in the 1960s, it closed for good. After various temporary uses (a theater and auction house among them), the building was set for demolition. However, the destruc-tion of the 19th-century Halles (market halls) across the Seine provoked a furor among conservationists, and in the late 1970s, President Giscard d'Estaing, with an eye firmly on establishing his place in the annals of French culture, ordered Orsay to be transformed into a mu-seum.

Exhibits take up three floors, but the visitor's immedi-ate impression is of a single, vast, stationlike hall. The use of an aggressively modern interior design in a build-ing almost a century old has provoked much controver-sy, which you'll want to resolve for yourself.

The chief artistic attraction is the Impressionists, whose works are displayed on the top floor, next to the museum café. Renoir, Sisley, Pissarro, and Monet are all well-represented. Highlights for many visitors are Monet's *Water Lilies* and his *Poppy Field*. Another fa-vorite is Renoir's *Le Moulin de la Galette*. The Post-Impressionists—Cézanne, van Gogh, Gauguin, and Toulouse-Lautrec—are all also represented on this floor.

On the first floor, you'll find the work of Manet and the delicate nuances of Degas. Pride of place, at least in art historical terms, goes to Manet's *Déjeuner sur l'Herbe*, the painting that scandalized Paris in 1863. Another re-working by Manet of a classical motif is his reclining nude, *Olympia*. Gazing provocatively out from the can-vas, she was more than respectable 19th-century Pari-sian proprieties could stand.

Those who prefer more correct academic paintings should look at Puvis de Chavannes's larger-than-life, classical canvases. The pale, limpid beauty of his figures is enjoying considerable attention after years of ne-glect. Those who are excited by more modern develop-ments will make for the early 20th-century Fauves (meaning wild beasts, the name given them by an out-raged critic in 1905)—particularly Matisse, Derain, and Vlaminck.

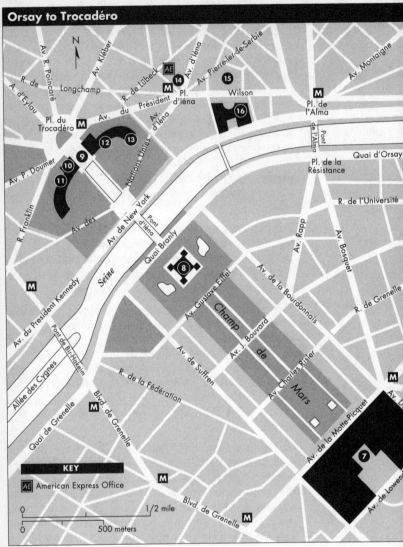

Orsay to Trocadéro

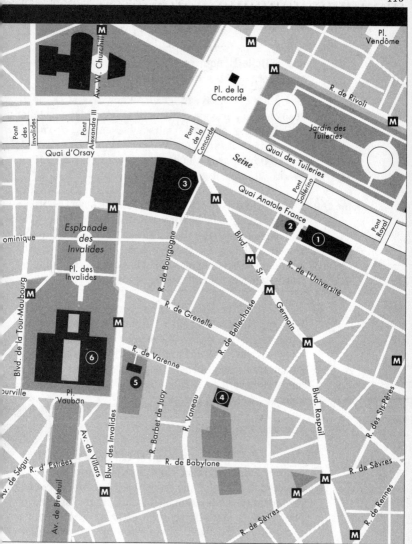

Pl. Vendôme

Pl. de la Concorde

R. de Rivoli

Jardin des Tuileries

Pont des Invalides

Pont Alexandre III

Pont de la Concorde

Quai d'Orsay

Seine

Quai des Tuileries

Pont Solférino

Quai Anatole France

Pont Royal

③

②

①

Esplanade des Invalides

ominique

Pl. des Invalides

R. de Bourgogne

Blvd

St-

R. de l'Université

Germain

R. de Grenelle

R. de Bellechasse

Blvd. de la Tour-Maubourg

R. de Varenne

⑤

R. Barbet de Juoy

R. Vaneau

④

Blvd. Raspail

R. des Sts-Pères

⑥

ourville

Pl. Vauban

Av. de Ségur

R. d' Estrées

Av. de Villars

Blvd. des Invalides

R. de Babylone

R. de Sèvres

Av. de Breteuil

R. de Sèvres

R. de Rennes

Sculpture at the Orsay means, first and foremost, Rodin (though there's more to enjoy at the Musée Rodin, *see below*). Two further highlights are the faithfully restored Belle-Epoque restaurant and the model of the entire Opéra quarter, displayed beneath a glass floor.

The Musée d'Orsay, otherwise known as M.O., is already one of Paris's star attractions. Crowds are smaller at lunchtime and on Thursday evenings. *1 rue de Bellechasse. Admission: 31 frs adults, 16 frs students and senior citizens and on Sun. Open Tues.–Sat. 10–6, Thurs. 10–9:45, and Sun. 9–6.*

Time Out There is no better place to take a break than the **Musée d'Orsay café** itself, handily but discreetly situated behind one of the giant station clocks close to the Impressionist galleries on the top floor. From the rooftop terrace, there is a panoramic view across the Seine toward Montmartre and the Sacré-Coeur.

② Across from the Musée d'Orsay stands the **Musée de la Légion d'Honneur.** French and foreign decorations are displayed in this stylish mansion by the Seine (officially known as the Hôtel de Salm). The original building, constructed in 1786, burned during the Commune in 1871 and was rebuilt in 1878. *2 rue de Bellechasse. Admission: 10 frs. Open Tues.–Sun. 2–5.*

Toward the Invalides

③ Continue along the left bank of the Seine to the 18th-century **Palais Bourbon** (directly across from place de la Concorde), home of the Assemblée Nationale (French Parliament). The colonnaded facade, commissioned by Napoleon, is a sparkling sight after a recent cleaning program (jeopardized at one stage by political squabbles as to whether cleaning should begin from the left or the right). There is a fine view from the steps across to place de la Concorde and the church of the Madeleine. *Not open to the public.*

The quiet, distinguished 18th-century streets behind the Palais Bourbon are filled with embassies and ministries. The most famous, reached via rue de Bourgogne
④ and rue de Varenne, is the **Hôtel Matignon,** residence of the French Prime Minister, and Left Bank counterpart to the President's Elysée Palace. "Matignon" was built in 1721 but has housed heads of government only since 1958. From 1888 to 1914, it was the embassy of the

Austro-Hungarian Empire. *57 rue de Varenne. Neither house nor garden is open to the public.*

Another glorious town house along rue de Varenne is ❺ the Hôtel Biron, better known as the **Musée Rodin.** The splendid house, with its spacious vestibule, broad staircase, and light, airy rooms, retains much of its 18th-century atmosphere and makes a handsome setting for the sculpture of Auguste Rodin (1840–1917). You'll doubtless recognize the seated *Thinker (Le Penseur)*, with his elbow resting on his knee, and the passionate *Kiss.* There is also an outstanding white marble bust of Austrian composer *Gustav Mahler,* as well as numerous examples of Rodin's obsession with hands and erotic subjects.

The second-floor rooms, which contain some fine paintings by Rodin's friend Eugène Carrière (1849–1906), afford views of the large garden behind the house. Don't go without visiting the garden: It is exceptional both for its rosebushes (over 2,000 of them, representing 100 varieties) and for its sculpture, including a powerful statue of the novelist *Balzac* and the despairing group of medieval city fathers known as the *Burghers of Calais. 77 rue de Varenne. Admission: 20 frs, 10 frs Sun. Open Easter–Oct., Tues.–Sun. 10–6; Nov.–Easter, Tues.–Sun. 10–5.*

❻ From the Rodin Museum, you can see the **Hôtel des Invalides,** along rue de Varenne. It was founded by Louis XIV in 1674 to house wounded (or "invalid") veterans. Although no more than a handful of old soldiers live at the Invalides today, the military link remains in the form of the **Musée de l'Armée**—one of the world's foremost military museums—with a vast collection of arms, armor, uniforms, banners, and military pictures down through the ages.

The **Musée des Plans-Reliefs,** housed on the fifth floor of the right-hand wing, contains a fascinating collection of scale models of French towns made to illustrate the fortifications planned by Vauban in the 17th century. (Vauban was a superb military engineer who worked under Louis XIV.) The largest and most impressive is Strasbourg, which takes up an entire room. Not all of Vauban's models are here, however. As part of a cultural decentralization program, France's socialist government of the early 1980s decided to pack the models (which had languished for years in dusty neglect) off to Lille in northern France. Only half the models had been shifted when a conservative government returned to office in 1986 and called for their return. Ex-Prime Minister Pierre Mauroy, the socialist mayor of Lille, refused, however, and the impasse seems set to continue.

The museums are not the only reason for visiting the Invalides. The building itself is an outstanding monumental ensemble in late-17th-century Baroque, designed by Bruand and Mansart. The main, cobbled courtyard is a fitting scene for the parades and ceremonies still occasionally held here. The most impressive dome in Paris towers over the **Eglise du Dôme** (church of the Dome). Before stopping here, however, visit the 17th-century **Eglise St-Louis des Invalides,** the Invalides's original church, and the site of the first performance of Berlioz's *Requiem* in 1837.

The Dôme church was built onto the end of Eglise St-Louis but was blocked off from it in 1793—no great pity perhaps, as the two buildings are vastly different in style and scale. It was designed by Mansart and built between 1677 and 1735. The remains of Napoleon are here, in a series of no fewer than six coffins, one inside the next, within a bombastic tomb of red porphyry, ringed by low reliefs and a dozen statues symbolizing Napoleon's campaigns. Among others commemorated in the church are French World War I hero Marshal Foch; Napoleon's brother Joseph, erstwhile king of Spain; and fortification-builder Vauban, whose heart was brought to the Invalides at Napoleon's behest. *Hôtel des Invalides. Admission: 30 frs adults, 20 frs children. Open daily 10–6. A son-et-lumière (sound-and-light) show in English is held in the main courtyard on evenings throughout the summer.*

Time Out The 7th Arrondissement is one of the most expensive areas in Paris—so you may want to lunch at the **Invalides cafeteria,** situated to the west of the Dôme church behind the souvenir shop. The decor may be uninspired, but the place is clean and boasts an imaginative and wide choice of hot and cold dishes.

Cross the pleasant lawns outside the Dôme church to place Vauban. Follow avenue de Tourville to the right, and turn left onto avenue de La Motte-Picquet.

The Eiffel Tower and the Trocadéro

A few minutes' walk will bring you face-to-face with the Eiffel Tower. Spare a thought for the **Ecole Militaire** on your left; it is 18th-century architecture at its most harmonious. It is still in use as a military academy and therefore not open to the public.

The pleasant expanse of the **Champ de Mars** makes an
8 ideal approach to the **Eiffel Tower,** whose colossal bulk (it's far bigger and sturdier than pictures suggest) becomes increasingly evident the nearer you get. It was built by Gustave Eiffel for the World Exhibition of 1889, the centennial of the French Revolution, and was still in good shape to celebrate its own 100th birthday. Recent restoration hasn't made the elevators any faster (lines are inevitable), but the new nocturnal illumination is fantastic—every girder highlighted in glorious detail.

Such was Eiffel's engineering wizardry that even in the strongest winds his tower never sways more than 4½ inches. Today, it is Paris's best-known landmark and exudes a feeling of permanence. As you stand beneath its huge legs, you may have trouble believing that it nearly became 7,000 tons of scrap-iron when its concession expired in 1909. Only its potential use as a radio antenna saved the day; it now bristles with a forest of radio and television transmitters. If you're full of energy, stride up the stairs as far as the third deck. If you want to go to the top, you'll have to take the elevator. The view at 305 meters (1,000 feet) may not beat that from the Tour Montparnasse, but the setting makes it considerably more romantic. *Pont d'Iéna. Cost by elevator: 2nd floor, 17 frs; 3rd floor, 34 frs; 4th floor, 51 frs. Cost by foot: 8 frs (2nd and 3rd floors only). Open July–Aug., daily 9 AM–midnight; Sept.–June, daily 9:30 AM–11 PM.*

Visible just across the Seine from the Eiffel Tower, on the heights of Trocadéro, is the muscular, sandy-colored
9 **Palais de Chaillot**—a cultural center built in the 1930s to replace a Moorish-style building constructed for the World Exhibition of 1878. The gardens between the Palais de Chaillot and the Seine contain an aquarium and some dramatic fountains. The terrace between the two wings of the palace offers a wonderful view of the Eiffel Tower.

The Palais de Chaillot contains four large museums, two in each wing. In the left wing (as you approach from the Seine) are the Musée de l'Homme and the Musée de la
10 Marine. The **Musée de l'Homme,** on the second and third floors, is an earnest anthropological museum with primitive and prehistoric artifacts from throughout the world. *Admission: 25 frs adults, 15 frs children. Open*
11 *Wed.–Mon. 9:45–5.* The **Musée de la Marine,** on the first floor, is a maritime museum with a salty collection of

ship models and seafaring paraphernalia, illustrating French naval history right up to the age of the nuclear submarine. *Admission: 40 frs adults, 20 frs senior citizens, 10 frs children. Open Wed.–Mon. 10–6.*

⑫ The other wing is dominated by the **Musée des Monuments Français,** without question the best introduction to French medieval architecture. This extraordinary museum was founded in 1879 by architect-restorer Viollet-le-Duc (the man who more than anyone was responsible for the extensive renovation of Notre Dame). It pays tribute to French buildings, mainly of the Romanesque and Gothic periods (roughly 1000–1500), in the form of painstaking copies of statues, columns, archways, and frescoes. It is easy to imagine yourself strolling among ruins as you pass through the first-floor gallery. Substantial sections of a number of French churches and cathedrals are represented here, notably Chartres and Vézelay. Mural and ceiling paintings—copies of works in churches around the country—dominate the other three floors. The value of these paintings has become increasingly evident as many of the originals continue to deteriorate. On the ceiling of a circular room is a reproduction of the painted dome of Cahors cathedral, giving the visitor a more vivid sense of the skills of the original medieval painter than the cathedral itself. *Admission: 16 frs, 8 frs on Sun. Open Wed.–Mon. 9:45–5:15.*

⑬ The **Musée du Cinéma,** located in the basement of this wing, traces the history of motion pictures since the 1880s. *Admission: 22 frs. Open Wed.–Mon. Guided tours only, at 10, 11, 2, 3, and 4.*

Time Out The giant place du Trocadéro is so hideously expensive that none of its many cafés can be recommended. But, if you have the time, head left from the Palais de Chaillot (down rue Franklin) to rue de Passy, a long, lively, narrow street full of shops and restaurants. **Pastavino,** at 30 rue de Passy, has excellent pasta and Italian wine in a room with gleaming modernistic decor. Around the corner, at 4 rue Nicolo, the intimate **Au Régal** has been serving up Russian specialties since 1934, abetted by a comradely welcome and ready supply of vodka.

The area around the Palais de Chaillot offers a feast for **⑭** museum lovers. The **Musée Guimet** (down avenue du Président Wilson, at place d'Iéna) has three floors of Indo-Chinese and Far Eastern art, initially amassed by 19th-century collector Emile Guimet. Among the museum's bewildering variety of exhibits are stone Buddhas, Chinese bronzes, ceramics, and painted screens. *6 pl. d'Iéna. Admission: 25 frs adults, 15 frs students and senior citizens. Open Wed.–Mon. 9:45–5:10.*

Some 200 yards down avenue Pierre-Ier-de-Serbie is **⑮** the **Palais Galliera,** home of the small and some would say overpriced Museum of Fashion and Costume. This stylish, late-19th-century town house hosts revolving exhibits of costume, design, and accessories, usually based on a single theme. *10 av. Pierre-Ier-de-Serbie. Admission: 25 frs adults, 15 frs students and senior citizens. Open Tues.–Sun. 10–5:40.*

⑯ The **Musée d'Art Moderne de la Ville de Paris** has both temporary exhibits and a permanent collection of modern art, continuing where the Musée d'Orsay leaves off. Among the earliest works are Fauvist paintings by Vlaminck and Derain, followed by Picasso's early experiments in Cubism. No other Paris museum exudes such a feeling of space and light. Its vast, unobtrusive, white-walled galleries provide an ideal background for the bold statements of 20th-century art. Loudest and largest are the canvases of Robert Delaunay. Other highlights include works by Braque, Rouault, Gleizes, Da Silva, Gromaire, and Modigliani. There is also a large room devoted to Art Deco furniture and screens, where Jean Dunand's gilt and lacquered panels consume oceans of wall space. There is a pleasant, if expensive, museum café, and an excellent bookshop specializing in 19th- and 20th-century art and architecture, with many books in English. *11 av. du Président Wilson. Admission: 15 frs, free on Sun. for permanent exhibitions only. Open Tues.–Sun. 10–5:40, Wed. 10–8:30.*

The Left Bank

Numbers in the margin correspond to points of interest on the Left Bank map.

References to the Left Bank have never lost their power to evoke the most piquant of all images of Paris. Although the bohemian strain the area once nurtured has lost much of its vigor, people who choose it today as a place to live or work are, in effect, turning their backs on the formality and staidness of the Right Bank.

The Latin Quarter is the geographic and cerebral hub of the Left Bank, populated mainly by Sorbonne students and academics who fill the air of the cafés with their ideas—and their tobacco smoke. (The university began as a theological school in the Middle Ages and later became the headquarters of the University of Paris; in 1968, the student revolution here had an explosive effect on French politics, resulting in major reforms in the education system.) The name Latin Quarter comes from the university tradition of studying and speaking in Latin, a tradition that disappeared during the Revolution.

Most of the St-Germain cafés, where the likes of Sartre, Picasso, Hemingway, and de Beauvoir spent their days and nights, are patronized largely by tourists now, and anyone expecting to capture the feeling of this quarter when it was the epicenter of intellectual and artistic life in Paris will be disappointed. Yet the Left Bank is far from dead. It is a lively and colorful district, rich in history and character, with a wealth of bookshops, art stores, museums, and restaurants.

St-Michel to St-Germain

1 **Place St-Michel** is a good starting point for exploring the rich slice of Parisian life, from its most ancient to its most modern, that the Left Bank offers. Leave your itineraries at home, and wander along the neighboring streets lined with restaurants, cafés, galleries, old bookshops, and all sorts of clothing stores, from tiny boutiques to haute couture showrooms.

For a route crowded more with humanity and less with car and bus traffic, pick up the pedestrian rue St-André des Arts at the southwest corner of place St-Michel. **2** **Studio St-André des Arts,** at no. 30, is one of Paris's most popular experimental cinemas. Just before you reach the Carrefour de Buci crossroads at the end of the **3** street, turn onto the **Cour du Commerce St-André.** Jean-Paul Marat printed his revolutionary newspaper, *L'Ami du Peuple,* at no. 8; and it was here that Dr. Guillotin conceived the idea for a new, "humane" method of execution that was used during the Revolution—it was rumored that he practiced it on sheep first—and that remained the means of executing convicted criminals in France until President Mitterrand abolished it in 1981.

Down a small passageway on the left stands one of the few remaining towers of the 12th-century fortress wall built by Philippe-Auguste. The passage leads you to the **4** **Cour de Rohan,** a series of three cloistered courtyards that were part of the hôtel of the Archbishops of Rouen, established in the 15th century; the name has been corrupted over the years to Rohan.

Rejoin the Cour du Commerce St-André and continue to
5 the **Carrefour de Buci,** once a notorious Left Bank landmark. By the 18th century, it contained a gallows, an execution stake, and an iron collar for punishing trouble-
makers. In September 1792, the Revolutionary army
used this daunting site to enroll its first volunteers, and
many Royalists and priests lost their heads here during
the bloody course of the Revolution. There's nothing
sinister, however, about the Carrefour today. Brightly
colored flowers spill onto the sidewalk at the **Grange à
Buci** flower shop, on the corner of rue Grégoire-de-
6 Tours. **Rue de Buci** has one of the best markets in Paris.
Open Tues.–Sun. till 1 PM.

Time Out If you happen to arrive when the market is closed, **La
Vieille France** patisserie at 14 rue de Buci may help fill
the gap.

Several interesting, smaller streets of some historical
7 significance radiate from the Carrefour. **Rue de
l'Ancienne-Comédie,** which cuts through to the busy
place de l'Odéon, is so named because it was the first
home of the now legendary French theater company,
the Comédie Française. The street was named in 1770,
the very year the Comédie left for the Tuileries palace.
The company moved again later to the Odéon, before
heading to its present home by the Palais-Royal (*see* The
Historic Heart, *above*).

Across the street from the company's first home (no. 14)
8 is the oldest café in Paris, **Le Procope.** Opened in 1686 by
an Italian named Francesco Procopio (only three years
before the Odéon itself opened), it has been a watering
hole for many of Paris's most famous literary sons and
daughters over the centuries; Diderot, Voltaire, Balzac,
George Sand, Victor Hugo, and Oscar Wilde were some
of its more famous and infamous regulars. Ben Franklin
is said to have stopped in whenever business brought
him to Paris.

Stretching north from the Carrefour de Buci toward the
9 Seine is the **rue Dauphine,** the street that singer Juliet
Greco put on the map when she opened the Tabou jazz
club here in the '50s. It attracted a group of young intellectuals who were to become known as the Zazous, a St-
Germain movement promoting the jazz culture,
complete with all-night parties and free love. The cult
author Boris Vian liked to play his trumpet through the
night, an activity that did little to endear him to the

The Left Bank

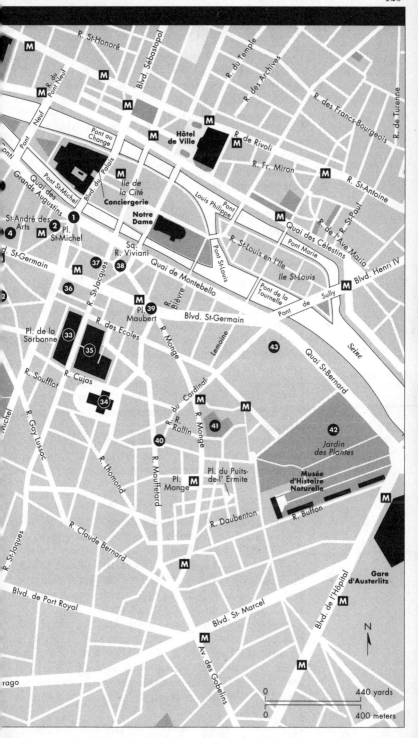

R. St-Honoré

Blvd. Sébastopol

R. du Temple

R. des Archives

R. des Francs-Bourgeois

R. de Turenne

R. du Pont Neuf

R. Neuf

Pont

Pont Neuf

onti

Pont St-Michel

Quai des Grands Augustins

Pont au Change

Pont du Palais

Blvd. du Palais

Hôtel de Ville

R. de Rivoli

R. Fr. Miron

R. St-Antoine

R. St-Paul

Ile de la Cité

Conciergerie

Notre Dame

Louis Philippe

Pont

Quai des Célestins

R. de l'Ave Maria

St-André des Arts

Pl. St-Michel

Pont Marie

R. St-Louis en l'Ile

Ile St-Louis

Blvd. Henri IV

St-Germain

Sq. R. Viviani

Quai de Montebello

R. St-Louis

Pont St-Louis

Pont de la Tournelle

Pont de Sully

Seine

R. St-Jacques

Bièvre

Pl. Maubert

Blvd. St-Germain

Quai St-Bernard

Pl. de la Sorbonne

R. des Ecoles

R. Monge

Lemoine

R. Soufflot

R. Cujas

R. du Cardinal-

R. Monge

Jardin des Plantes

Michel

R. Gay Lussac

R. Thomond

R. Rollin

R. Mouffetard

Pl. Monge

Pl. du Puits-de-l'Ermite

Musée d'Histoire Naturelle

R. Daubenton

R. Buffon

R. Claude Bernard

R. St-Jacques

Gare d'Austerlitz

Blvd. de Port Royal

Blvd. St. Marcel

Blvd. de l'Hôpital

rago

Av. des Gobelins

N

0   440 yards

0   400 meters

club's neighbors. You may still find jazz played here, but the club is a shadow of its former self.

The next street that shoots out of the Carrefour (moving counterclockwise) is rue Mazarine. Here stands the **⑩ Hôtel des Monnaies,** the national mint. Louis XVI transferred the Royal Mint to this imposing mansion in the late 18th century. Although the mint was moved to Pessac, near Bordeaux, in 1973, weights and measures, medals, and limited-edition coins are still made here. In June 1988, an enlarged **Musée Monétaire** opened so that the vast collection of coins, documents, engravings, and paintings could be displayed. The workshops are on the second floor. On Tuesday and Friday afternoons you'll catch the coin and medal craftsmen at work; their ateliers overlook the Seine. *11 quai de Conti. Admission: 15 frs adults, 10 frs students and senior citizens. Free Sun. Open Tues., Thurs.–Sun. 1–6, Wed. 1–9.*

⑪ Next door is the **Institut de France.** With its distinctive dome and commanding position over the quai at the foot of the Pont des Arts, it is not only one of France's most revered cultural institutions but also one of the Left Bank's most impressive waterside sights. The **Académie Française,** the oldest of the five academies that comprise the Institut de France, was created by Cardinal Richelieu in 1635. Its first major task was to edit the French dictionary; today, among other functions, it is still charged with safeguarding the purity of the French language. Election to its ranks is the highest literary honor in the land, subject to approval by the French head of state, and there may only be 40 "immortal" members at any one time. *Guided visits are reserved for cultural associations only.*

Just west along the waterfront, on quai Malaquais, **⑫** stands the **Ecole Nationale des Beaux-Arts,** whose students can usually be seen painting and sketching on the nearby quais and bridges. The school was once the site of a convent, founded in 1608 by Marguerite de Valois, the first wife of Henri IV. During the Revolution, the convent was turned into a depot for works of art salvaged from the monuments that were under threat of destruction by impassioned mobs. Only the church and cloister remained, however, when the Beaux-Arts school was established in 1816. Allow yourself time to wander into the courtyard and galleries of the school to see the casts and copies of the statues that were once stored here, or stop in at one of the temporary exhibitions of professors' and students' works. *14 rue Bona-parte. Open daily 1–7.*

⓭ Tiny **rue Visconti,** running east–west off rue Bonaparte (across from the entrance to the Beaux-Arts), has a lot of history packed into its short length. In the 16th century, it was known as Paris's Little Geneva—named after Europe's foremost Protestant city—because of the Protestant ghetto that formed here. Racine, one of France's greatest playwrights and tragic poets, lived at no. 24 until his death in 1699. Balzac set up a printing shop at no. 17 in 1826, and the fiery Romantic artist Eugène Delacroix (1798–1863) worked here from 1836 to 1844.

Time Out The terrace at **La Palette** beckons as soon as you reach the rue de Seine, at the end of rue Visconti. This popular café has long been a favorite haunt of Beaux-Arts students. One of them was allowed to paint an ungainly portrait of the *patron,* François, which presides over the shaggy gathering of clients with mock authority. *43 rue de Seine.*

Swing right at the next corner onto the pretty rue Jacob, where both Wagner and Stendhal once lived. Follow rue Jacob across rue des Saints-Pères, where it changes to rue de l'Université. You are now in the Carré Rive Gauche, the Left Bank's concentrated quarter-mile of art dealers and galleries.

Return on rue Jacob until you are almost back to rue de Seine. Take the rue de Fürstemberg to the quiet place Fürstemberg, bedecked with white globe lamps and ca-

⓮ talpa trees. Here is **Atelier Delacroix,** Delacroix's old studio, containing only a paltry collection of sketches and drawings by the artist; the garden at the rear of the studio is almost as interesting. Nonetheless, those who feel the need to pay homage to France's foremost Romantic painter will want to make the pilgrimage. *Place Fürstemberg. Admission: 11 frs adults, 6 frs ages 18–25 and over 60, 5 frs on Sun. Open Wed.–Mon. 9:45–12:30 and 2–5:15.*

⓯ **St-Germain-des-Prés,** Paris's oldest church, began as a shelter for a relic of the True Cross brought back from Spain in AD 542. Behind it, rue de l'Abbaye runs alongside the former Abbey palace, dating from AD 990 and once part of a powerful Benedictine abbey. The chancel was enlarged and the church then consecrated by Pope Alexander III in 1163. Interesting interior details include the colorful 19th-century frescoes in the nave by Hippolyte Flandrin, a pupil of the classical painter Ingres, depicting vivid scenes from the Old Testament. The church stages superb organ concerts and recitals; programs are displayed outside and in the weekly periodicals *Officiel des Spectacles* and *Pariscope*.

Across the cobbled place St-Germain-des-Prés stands the celebrated **Deux Magots** café, named after the grotesque Chinese figures, or *magots*, inside. It still thrives on its '50s reputation as one of the Left Bank's prime meeting places for the intelligentsia. Though the Deux Magots remains crowded day and night, these days, you're more likely to rub shoulders with tourists than with philosophers.

In the postwar years, Jean-Paul Sartre and Simone de Beauvoir would meet "The Family" two doors down at the **Café de Flore** on boulevard St-Germain. "The Family" was de Beauvoir's name for their close-knit group, which included fellow-graduates from the prestigious Ecole Normale Supérieure and writers from Gaston Gallimard's publishing house in the nearby rue Sébastien-Bottin. Today the Flore has become more of a gay hangout, but, along with the Deux Magots and the pricey **Brasserie Lipp** across the street, where politicians and show-biz types come to wine and dine (after being "passed" by the doorman), it is a scenic spot that never lacks for action.

A large part of the area south of boulevard St-Germain, around rue de Grenelle and rue des Saints-Pères, has undergone enormous change but is still home to publishing houses, bookstores, and galleries.

For contrast, take rue du Vieux-Colombier through the Carrefour de La Croix Rouge to place St-Sulpice. This newly renovated square is ringed with cafés, and Yves St-Laurent's famous Rive Gauche store is at no. 6. Looming over the square is the enormous 17th-century church of **St-Sulpice.** The 18th-century facade was never finished, and its unequal towers add a playful touch to an otherwise sober design. The interior is baldly impersonal, however, despite the magnificent Delacroix frescoes—notably Jacob wrestling with the angel—in the first chapel on your right. If you now pick up the long rue de Rennes and follow it south, you'll soon arrive in the heart of Montparnasse.

Montparnasse

With the growth of Paris as a business and tourist capital, commercialization seems to have filled any area where departing residents and businesses have created a vacuum. Nowhere else is this more true than in and around the vaulting, concrete space and starkly functionalist buildings that have come to rule Montparnasse. Seeing it now, it is difficult to believe that in the years after World War I, Montparnasse replaced Montmartre as *the* place in which Parisian artists came to live.

㉕ The opening of the 59-story **Tour Maine-Montparnasse** in 1973 forever changed the face of this painters' and poets' haunt. (The name Montparnasse itself came from some 17th-century students, who christened the area after Mount Parnassus, the home of Apollo, leader of the Muses.) The tower was part of a vast redevelopment plan that aimed to make the area one of Paris's premier business and shopping districts. Fifty-two floors of the tower are taken up by offices, while a vast commercial complex, including a Galeries Lafayette department store, spreads over the first floor. Although it is uninspiring by day, it becomes a neon-lit beacon for the area at night. As Europe's tallest high rise, it affords stupendous views of Paris; on a clear day, you can see for 48 kilometers (30 miles). (There's a snack bar and cafeteria on the 56th floor; if you go to the top-floor bar for drinks, the ride up is free.) It also claims to have the fastest elevator in Europe! *Admission: 35 frs adults, 21 frs students and senior citizens, 14 frs children 5–14. Open daily 10 AM–11 PM, weekdays 10 AM–10 PM in winter.*

㉑ Immediately north of the tower is **place du 18 Juin 1940,** part of what was once the old Montparnasse train station and a significant spot in Parisian World War II history. It is named for the date of the radio speech Charles de Gaulle made, from London, urging the French to continue resisting the Germans after the fall of the country to Nazi Germany in May 1940. In August 1944, the German military governor, Dietrich von Choltitz, surrendered to the Allies here, ignoring Hitler's orders to destroy the city as he withdrew; the French General Philippe Leclerc subsequently used it as his headquarters.

Behind the older train station, gare Montparnasse, you'll see the huge new train terminal that serves Chartres, Versailles, and the west of France. Since 1990, the high-speed *TGV Atlantique* leaves here for Brittany (Rennes and Nantes) and the southwest (Bordeaux, via Tours, Poitiers, and Angoulême). To the left of this station is one of the oddest residential complexes to appear in this era of architectural experimentation. The **22** **Amphithéâtre,** built by Ricardo Boffil, is eye-catching but stark and lacking in human dimension.

23 The **Cimetière de Montparnasse** (Montparnasse cemetery) contains many of the quarter's most illustrious residents, buried only a stone's throw away from where they worked and played. It is not at all a picturesque cemetery (with the exception of the old windmill in the corner, which used to be a student tavern) but seeing the names of some of its inhabitants—Baudelaire, Maupassant, Saint-Saëns, and the industrialist André Citroën—may make the visit worthwhile. Nearby, at place Denfert-Rochereau, is the entrance to an extensive complex of **catacombs** (*denfert* is a corruption of the **24** word for hell, *enfer*). The catacombs are stocked with the bones of millions of corpses that were moved here in 1785 from the areas's charnel houses. *Admission: 15 frs adults, 8.50 frs students and senior citizens. Open Tues.–Fri. 2–4, weekends 9–11 and 2–4.*

Montparnasse's bohemian aura has dwindled to almost nothing, yet the area hops at night as *the* place in Paris to find movies of every description, many of them shown in their original language. Theaters and theater-cafés **25** abound, too, especially along seedy **rue de la Gaîté.** The Gaîté-Montparnasse, Le Théâtre Montparnasse, and Le Grand Edgar are among the most popular. Up boulevard du Montparnasse and across from the Vavin Métro station are two of the better-known gathering places of **26** Montparnasse's heyday, the **Dôme** and **La Coupole** brasseries. La Coupole opened in 1927 as a bar/restaurant/dance hall and soon became a home away from home for some of the area's most famous residents, such as Apollinaire, Max Jacob, Cocteau, Satie, Stravinsky, and the ubiquitous Hemingway. It may not be quite the same mecca these days, but it still pulls in a classy crowd.

Across the boulevard, rue Vavin leads past two more celebrated Montparnasse cafés, the **Sélect** and the **Rotonde,** to the Jardin du Luxembourg. But stay on boulevard du Montparnasse for the intersection with **27** boulevard St-Michel, where the verdant **avenue de l'Observatoire** begins its long sweep up to the Luxembourg gardens. Here you'll find perhaps the most fa-

28 mous bastion of the Left Bank café culture, the **Closerie des Lilas.** Now a pricey bar/restaurant, the Closerie remains a staple on all literary tours of Paris not least because of the commemorative plaques fastened onto the bar, marking the places where renowned personages sat. Baudelaire, Verlaine, Hemingway, and Apollinaire are just a few of the names. Although the lilacs *(lilas)* have gone from the terrace, it is still a pretty place, opening onto the luxuriant green of the surrounding parkland, and as crowded in the summer as it ever was in the '30s. *(See* Dining, *below.)*

29 The vista from the Closerie includes the **Paris Observatory** (to the right), built in 1667 by Louis XIV. Its four facades were built to align with the four cardinal points—north, south, east, and west—and its southern wall is the determining point for Paris's official latitude, 48° 50′11″N. French time was based on this Paris meridian until 1911, when the country decided to adopt the international Greenwich Meridian.

A tree-lined alley leads along the avenue de l'Observatoire to the gardens, but before the entrance, you'll pass Davioud's **Fontaine de l'Observatoire** (Observatory Fountain), built in 1873 and decked with four statues representing the four quarters of the globe. Look north from here and you'll have a captivating view of Montmartre and Sacré-Coeur, with the gardens in the foreground.

Palais du Luxembourg

30 From avenue de l'Observatoire walk up to the **Jardin du Luxembourg** (the Luxembourg Gardens), one of the city's few large parks. Its fountains, ponds, trim hedges, precisely planted rows of trees, and gravel walks are typical of the French fondness for formal gar-
31 dens. At the far end is the **Palais du Luxembourg** itself, gray and imposing, built, like the park, for Maria de' Medici, widow of Henri IV, at the beginning of the 17th century. The palace remained royal property until the Revolution, when the state took it over and used it as a prison. Danton, the painter David, and Thomas Paine were all detained here. Today, it is the site of the French Senate and is not open to the public.

32 The **Théâtre National de l'Odéon,** set at the north end of the Luxembourg Gardens, was established in 1792 to house the Comédiens Français troupe. The massive structure you see today replaced the original theater, which was destroyed by fire in 1807. Since World War II, it has specialized in 20th-century productions. It was the base for Jean-Louis Barrault's and Madeleine Renaud's theater company, the Théâtre de France, until they fell out of favor with the authorities for their alleged role in spurring on the student revolutionaries in May 1968. Today, the Théâtre de l'Odéon is the French home of the Theater of Europe and stages some excellent productions by major foreign companies.

The Sorbonne and the Maubert Quarter

If you follow rue Vaugirard (the longest street in Paris) one block east to boulevard St-Michel, you will soon be at the **place de la Sorbonne,** nerve center of the student population that has always held such sway over Left Bank life. The square is dominated by the Eglise de la Sorbonne, whose outstanding exterior features are its 10 Corinthian columns and cupola. Inside is the white marble tomb of Cardinal Richelieu. (The church is open to the public only during exhibitions and cultural events.) The university buildings of La Sorbonne spread out around the church from rue Cujas down to the visitor's entrance on rue des Ecoles.

33 The **Sorbonne** is the oldest university in Paris—indeed, one of the oldest in Europe—and has for centuries been one of France's principal institutions of higher learning. It is named after Robert de Sorbon, a medieval canon who founded a theological college here in 1253 for 16 students. By the 17th century, the church and university buildings were becoming dilapidated, so Cardinal Richelieu undertook to have them restored; the present-day Sorbonne campus is largely a result of that restoration. Despite changes in the neighborhood, the maze of amphitheaters, lecture rooms, and laboratories, and the surrounding courtyards and narrow streets, still have a hallowed air. For a glimpse of a more recent relic of Sorbonne history, look for Puvis de Chavannes's painting of the *Sacred Wood* in the main lecture hall, a major meeting point during the tumultuous student upheavals of 1968 and now a university landmark.

Behind the Sorbonne, bordering its eastern reach, is the rue St-Jacques. The street climbs toward the rue Soufflot, named to honor the man who built the vast, **34** domed **Panthéon,** set atop place du Panthéon. One of Paris's most physically overwhelming sites—it was commissioned by Louis XV as a mark of gratitude for his recovery from a grave illness in 1744—the Panthéon is now a seldom-used church, with little of interest except for Puvis de Chavannes's monumental frescoes and the crypt, which holds the remains of Voltaire, Zola, and Rousseau. In 1789—the year the church was completed—its windows were blocked by order of the Revolutionary Constituent Assembly, and they have remained that way ever since, adding to its sepulchral gloom. *Admission: 24 frs, 13 frs ages 18–24, 5 frs children 7–17. Open daily 10–12 and 2–5.*

Up rue St-Jacques again and across from the Sorbonne are the **Lycée Louis-le-Grand** (Molière, Voltaire, and Robespierre studied here) and the elite **Collège de France,** whose grounds continue around the corner onto rue des Ecoles. In 1530, François I created this school as the College of Three Languages, which taught High Latin, Greek, and Hebrew, and any other subjects eschewed by academics at the Sorbonne. Diagonally across from the college, on the other side of rue des Ecoles, is the **square Paul-Painlevé;** behind it lies the entrance to the inimitable Hôtel et Musée de Cluny.

Built on the site of the city's enormous old Roman baths, the **Musée de Cluny** is housed in a 15th-century mansion that originally belonged to monks of Cluny Abbey in Burgundy. The remains of the baths that can still be seen are what survived a sacking by Barbarians in the 4th century. But the real reason people come to the Cluny is for its tapestry collection. Skeptics in the crowd will be converted, for the fantastic detail of the tapestries gives them an enchanted quality, and the diversity of the themes depicted is extraordinary. The most famous series of all is the graceful *Lady and the Unicorn, or Dame à la Licorne,* woven in the 15th or 16th century, probably in the southern Netherlands. And if the tapestries themselves aren't enough at which to marvel, there is also an exhibition of decorative arts from the Middle Ages, a vaulted chapel, and a deep, cloistered courtyard with mullioned windows, set off by the *Boatmen's Pillar,* Paris's oldest sculpture, at its center. *Admission: 15 frs, 8 frs on Sun. Open Wed.–Mon. 9:30–5:15.*

Above boulevard St-Germain, rue St-Jacques reaches toward the Seine, bringing you past the elegant proportions of the church of **St-Séverin.** Rebuilt in the 16th century and noted for its width and its Flamboyant Gothic style, the church dominates a close-knit Left Bank neighborhood filled with quiet squares and pedestrian streets. Note the splendidly deviant spiraling column in the forest of pillars behind the altar. *Open weekdays 11–5:30, Sat. 11–10.*

Running riot around the relative quiet of St-Séverin are streets filled with restaurants of every description, serving everything from souvlaki-to-go to five-course haute cuisine. There is definitely something for every budget here. Rue de la Huchette is the most heavily trafficked of the restaurant streets and especially good for its selection of cheaper Greek food houses and Tunisian patisseries.

Time Out   If you end up in this area in the evening and are in the mood for entertainment with your supper, duck into **Le Cloître** (19 rue St-Jacques). It's an old, heavily wood-beamed bar with a one- and sometimes two-woman re-vue in the *cave*, or cellar, performing songs of old Paris from the '20s, '30s, and '40s. For a quieter diversion, stop at **Pub St-Jacques** (11 rue St-Jacques).

Cross to the other side of rue St-Jacques. In Square
38 René Viviani, which surrounds the church of **St-Julien-le-Pauvre,** stands an acacia tree that is supposed to be the oldest tree in Paris (although it has a rival claim from another acacia at the Jardin des Plantes). This tree-filled square also gives you one of the more spectacular views of Notre Dame. The tiny church here was built at the same time as Notre Dame (1165–1220), on a site where a whole succession of chapels once stood. The church belongs to a Greek Orthodox order today, but was originally named for St. Julian, bishop of Le Mans, who was nicknamed "Le Pauvre" after he gave all his money away.

Behind the church, to the east, are the tiny, elegant streets of the recently renovated **Maubert** district, bordered by quai de Montebello and boulevard St-Germain. Rue de Bièvre, once filled with tanneries, is now guarded at both ends to protect President Mitterrand's private residence.

Public meetings and demonstrations have been held in place Maubert ever since the Middle Ages. Nowadays, most gatherings are held inside or in front of the ele-
39 gantly art-deco **Palais de la Mutualité,** on the corner of the square, also a venue for jazz, pop, and rock concerts. On Tuesdays, Thursdays, and Saturdays, it is transformed into a colorful outdoor food market.

Head up rue Monge, turn right onto rue du Cardinal-
40 Lemoine, and you'll find yourself at the minute **place de**

la Contrescarpe. It doesn't start to swing until after dusk, when its cafés and bars fill up. During the day, the square looks almost provincial, as Parisians flock to the daily market on rue Mouffetard. There are restaurants and cafés of every description on rue Mouffetard, and if you get here at lunchtime, you may want to buy yourself the makings for an alfresco lunch and take it to the unconventional picnic spot provided by the nearby Gallo-

41 Roman ruin of the **Arènes de Lutèce;** it begins on rue Monge, just past the end of rue Rollin. The ancient arena was discovered only in 1869 and has since been excavated and landscaped to reveal parts of the original Roman amphitheater. This site and the remains of the baths at the Cluny constitute the only extant evidence of the powerful Roman city of Lutetia that flourished here in the 3rd century. It is also one of the lesser-known delights of the Left Bank, so you are not likely to find it crowded.

42 The **Jardin des Plantes** is an enormous swath of greenery containing spacious botanical gardens and a number of natural history museums. It is stocked with plants dating back to the first collections here in the 17th century, and has been enhanced ever since by subsequent generations of devoted French botanists. It claims to shelter Paris's oldest tree, an *acacia robinia*, planted in 1636. There is also a small, old-fashioned zoo here; an alpine garden; an aquarium; a maze; and a number of hothouses. The **Musée Entomologique** is devoted to insects; the **Musée Paléontologique** exhibits fossils and prehistoric animals; the **Musée Minéralogique** houses a stupendous collection of rocks and minerals. *Admission: 12–25 frs. Museums open Wed.–Mon. 2–5.*

Time Out At the back of the gardens, in place du Puits-de-l'Hermite, you can drink a restorative cup of sweet mint tea in **La Mosquée,** a beautiful white mosque, complete with minaret. Once inside, you'll be convinced that you must be elsewhere than the Left Bank of Paris. The students from the nearby Jussieu and Censier universities pack themselves into the Moslem restaurant here, which serves copious quantities of couscous. The sunken garden and tiled patios are open to the public—the prayer rooms are not—and so are the *hammams,* or Turkish baths. *Baths open daily 11 AM–7 PM; Fri. and Sat. men only; Mon., Wed., and Thurs. women only. Admission: 15 frs, 80 frs for Turkish baths. Guided tours of mosque Sat.–Thurs. 9–noon and 2–5.*

In 1988, Paris's large Arab population gained another
⑬ base: the huge **Institut du Monde Arabe,** which overlooks
the Seine on quai St-Bernard, just beyond Université
Jussieu. Jean Nouvel's harmonious mixture of Arabic
and European styles was greeted with enthusiasm
when the center first opened. It contains a sound and
image center, a wall of televisions, with Arab program-
ming, a vast library, a documentation center, and fast
glass elevators that will take you to the ninth floor for
(yet another) memorable view over the Seine and Notre
Dame. *23 quai St-Bernard. Admission free. Open
Tues.–Sun. 1–8.*

Montmartre

*Numbers in the margin correspond to points of interest
on the Montmartre map.*

On a dramatic rise above the city is Montmartre, site of
the Sacré-Coeur basilica and home to a once-thriving artistic community, a heritage recalled today chiefly by
the gangs of third-rate painters clustered in the area's
most famous square, the place du Tertre. Despite their
presence, and the fact that the fabled nightlife of old
Montmartre has fizzled down to some glitzy nightclubs
and porn shows, Montmartre still exudes a sense of history, a timeless quality infused with that hard-to-define
Gallic charm.

Seeing Montmartre means negotiating a lot of steep
streets and flights of steps. If the prospect of trudging
up and down them is daunting, you can tour parts of
Montmartre by public transportation, aboard the
Promotrain or the Montmartrobus. The Promotrain offers daily 40-minute guided tours of Montmartre between 10 AM and midnight. The cost is 25 francs for adults,
10 francs for children under 12, and departures are from
outside the Moulin Rouge on place Blanche. The Montmartrobus is a regular city bus that runs around Montmartre for the price of a Métro ticket. It departs from
place Pigalle. If you're visiting only Sacré-Coeur, take the
funicular that runs up the hill to the church near Anvers
Métro station.

Exploring Montmartre

❶ Begin your tour at **place Blanche,** site of the Moulin
Rouge. Place Blanche—White Square—takes its name
from the clouds of chalky dust churned up by the windmills that once dotted Montmartre (or *La Butte,* mean-

Montmartre

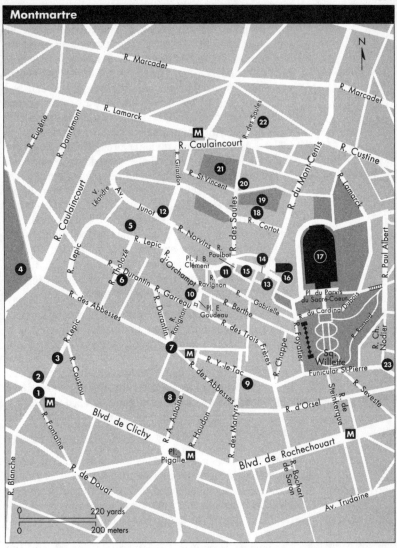

ing "mound" or "hillock"). They were set up here not just because the hill was a good place to catch the wind—at over 300 feet, it's the highest point in the city—but because Montmartre was covered with wheat fields and quarries right up to the end of the 19th century. The carts carrying away the wheat and crushed stone trundled across place Blanche, turning the square white as they passed. Today, only two of the original 20 windmills are intact. A number have been converted to

2 other uses, none more famous than the **Moulin Rouge,** or Red Windmill, built in 1885 and turned into a dance hall in 1900. It was a genuinely wild place in its early days, immortalized by Toulouse-Lautrec in his boldly simple posters and paintings. The place is still trading shamelessly on the notion of Paris as a city of sin: If you fancy a Vegas-style night out, with computerized light shows and troupes of bare-breasted girls sporting feather headdresses, this is the place to go. The cancan, by the way—still a regular feature here—was considerably more raunchy when Lautrec was around.

For a taste of something more authentically French,

3 walk past the Moulin Rouge, up **rue Lepic,** site of one of the most colorful and tempting food markets in Paris (closed Mon.).

Time Out | Stop in at the tiny **Lux Bar** (12 rue Lepic) for coffee and a sandwich. The wall behind the bar is covered with a 1910 mosaic showing place Blanche at the beginning of the century.

Turn left onto rue des Abbesses and walk along to

4 **Cimetière de Montmartre** (Montmartre cemetery). It's by no means as romantic or as large as the better known Père Lachaise cemetery in the east of the city, but it contains the graves of many prominent French men and women, including the 18th-century painters Greuze and Fragonard; Degas; and Adolphe Sax, inventor of the saxophone. The Russian ballet dancer Nijinsky is also buried here.

Walk back along rue des Abbesses. Rue Tholozé, the second street on the left, was once a path over the hill,

5 the oldest in Montmartre. It leads to the **Moulin de la Galette,** one of the two remaining windmills in Montmartre, which has been unromantically rebuilt. To

6 reach it, you pass **Studio 28.** This seems to be no more than a scruffy little movie theater, but when opened in 1928, it was the first purposely built *art et essai,* or experimental theater, in the world. Over the years, the movies of directors like Jean Cocteau, François Truffaut, and Orson Welles have often been shown here before their official premieres.

❼ Return to rue des Abbesses, turn left, and walk to **place des Abbesses.** The little square is typical of the kind of picturesque and slightly countrified style that has made Montmartre famous. The entrance to the Métro station, a curving, sensuous mass of delicate iron, is one of a handful of original Art Nouveau stations left in Paris. The austere, red brick **church of St-Jean l'Evangéliste** (1904) is worth a look, too. It was one of the first concrete buildings in France; the brick had to be added later to soothe offended locals. The **café St-Jean,** next to it, is a popular local meeting place, crowded on weekends.

There are two competing attractions just off the square. Theater buffs should head down the tiny rue André Antoine. At no. 37, you'll see what was originally the ❽ **Théâtre Libre,** or Free Theater, founded in 1887 by André Antoine and immensely influential in popularizing the work of iconoclastic young playwrights such as Ibsen and Strindberg. The other attraction is **rue Yvonne-le-Tac,** scene of a vital event in Montmartre's early history and linked to the disputed story of how this quarter got its name. Some say the name Montmartre comes from the Roman temple to Mercury that was once here, called the Mound of Mercury or *Mons Mercurii*. Others contend that it was an adaptation of *Mons Martyrum*, a name inspired by the burial here of Paris's first bishop, St-Denis. The popular version of his martyrdom is that he was beheaded by the Romans in AD 250, but arose to carry his severed head from rue Yvonne-le-Tac to a place 4 miles to the north, an area now known as St-Denis. He is commemorated by the 19th- ❾ century **Chapelle du Martyre** at no. 9, built over the spot where he is said to have been executed. It was in the crypt of the original chapel here that St. Ignatius of Loyola founded the Jesuit order in 1540, a decisive step in the efforts of the Catholic Church to reassert its authority in the face of the Protestant Reformation. A final twist on the name controversy is that Montmartre briefly came to be known as Mont-Marat during the French Revolution. Marat was a leading Revolutionary figure who was obliged to spend most of the day in the tub, the result of a disfiguring and severe skin condition. It was in his bath that Charlotte Corday, a fanatical opponent of the Revolutionary government, stabbed him to death.

From rue Yvonne-le-Tac, retrace your steps through place des Abbesses. Take rue Ravignan on the right, climbing to the summit via place Emile-Goudeau, an enchanting little cobbled square. Your goal is the ❿ **Bateau-Lavoir,** or Boat Wash House, at its northern edge. Montmartre poet Max Jacob coined the name for the old building on this site, which burned down in 1970. First of all, he said, it resembled a boat. Second, the warren of artists' studios within was always cluttered and paint-splattered, and looked to be in perpetual need of a good hosing down. The new building also contains art studios, but, if you didn't know its history, you'd probably walk right past it; it is the epitome of poured concrete drabness.

It was in the original Bateau-Lavoir that painters Picasso and Braque, early this century, made their first bold stabs at the concept of Cubism—a move that paved the way for abstract painting.

Continue up the hill to place Jean-Baptiste Clément. The Italian painter and sculptor Modigliani (1884–1920) had a studio here at no. 7. Some have claimed he was the greatest Italian artist of the 20th century, the man who fused the genius of the Italian Renaissance with the modernity of Cézanne and Picasso. He claimed that he would drink himself to death—he eventually did—and chose the right part of town to do it in. This was one of the wildest areas of Montmartre. Its bistros and cabarets have mostly gone now, though, and only the **Moulin de Paris** still reflects a glimmer of the old atmosphere. Look for the octagonal tower at the north end of the square; it's all that's left of Montmartre's first water tower, built around 1840 to boost the area's feeble water supply.

Rue Norvins, formerly rue des Moulins, runs behind and parallel to the north end of the square. Turn left ⓬ along it to reach stylish avenue Junot, site of the **Cité Internationale des Arts** (International Residence of the Arts), where the city authorities rent out studios to artists from all over the world. Retrace your steps back to rue Norvins and continue east past the bars and tourist shops, until you reach place du Tertre.

⓭ **Place du Tertre** *(tertre* means hillock) regains its village atmosphere only in the winter, when the somber buildings gather in the grays of the Parisian light and the plane tree branches sketch traceries against the sky. At any other time of year, you'll have to fight your way through the crowds to the southern end of the square and the breathtaking view over the city. The real draw-back is the swarm of artists clamoring to dash off your portrait. If you're in the mood, however. . . . Most are licensed to be there, and, like taxi drivers, their prices are officially fixed. But there is no shortage of con men, sketch pads in hand, who will charge whatever they think they can get away with. If one produces a picture of you without having first asked, you're under no obligation to buy it, though that's not to say you won't have to argue your case. It's best just to walk away.

⑭ La Mère Catherine, the restaurant at the northern end of the square, has an honored place in French culinary history. It was a favorite with the Russian cossacks who occupied Paris in 1814 after Napoleon had been exiled to the island of Elba. Little did they know that when they banged on the tables and shouted *"bistro,"* the Russian word for "quick," they were inventing a new breed of French restaurant. For a restaurant catering almost entirely to the tourist trade, La Mère Catherine is surprisingly good, though prices are high for what's offered.

Time Out Patachou, opened in 1987, sounds the one classy note on place du Tertre (at n° 9). It offers exquisite, if expensive, cakes and teas.

A crash course in Montmartre history is offered by **⑮ L'Historial,** the wax museum around the corner on rue Poulbot. No one can pretend that these figures are among the world's best, but they do at least sketch in the main events and personalities that have shaped Montmartre. *11 rue Poulbot. Admission: 25 frs adults, 20 frs students and senior citizens, 10 frs children. Open daily 10:30–6:30.*

It was in place du Tertre in March 1871 that one of the most destructively violent episodes in French history began, one that colored French political life for generations. Despite popular images of later-19th-century France—and Paris especially—as carefree and prosperous, for much of this period the country was desperately divided into two camps: an ever more vocal and militant underclass, motivated by resentment of what they considered an elitist government, and a reactionary and fearful bourgeoisie and ruling class. It was a conflict that went back at least as far as the French Revolution at the end of the 18th century, and one that twice flared into outbreaks of civil war and rebellion, in 1832 and 1848, as the country oscillated between republican and imperial forms of government. In 1870, France, under the leadership of an opportunistic but feeble Napoleon III (nephew of the great Napoleon), was drawn into a disastrous war with Bismarck's Prussia, which was rapidly growing into one of the most formidable military powers in Europe. (Soon after, Prussia was to dominate a newly united and aggressive Germany.) In September that year, Prussia invaded France, surrounded Paris, and laid siege to it. After four months of appalling suffering—during which time the Louvre became a munitions factory, the Gare de Lyon was converted into a cannon foundry, and the two elephants in the zoo, Castor and Pollux, were eaten by starving Parisians—the new government under French statesman Adolphe Thiers capitulated. Although mass starvation seemed imminent, fears that Thiers would restore an imperial rather than a republican government caused Parisians to refuse to surrender their arms to him. Thiers then ordered that the guns at Montmartre be captured by loyal government forces. Insurgents responded by shooting the two generals ordered to retake the guns. Almost immediately, barricades were thrown up across the city streets, and the fighting began in earnest. The antimonarchists formed the Commune, which for three heady months ruled Paris. In May, from his base at Versailles, Thiers ordered the city retaken. Estimates as to the numbers killed in the fighting vary greatly. Some say 4,000 Communards lost their lives; others claim 20,000. No one, however, doubts that upward of 10,000 Communards were executed by government troops after the collapse of the Commune.

In expiation for this bloodshed, the French government decided, in 1873 (after the downfall of Thiers), to build the basilica of the Sacré-Coeur. It was to be a sort of national guilt offering. Before visiting this landmark, **16** walk to the church of **St-Pierre de Montmartre** at the east side of place du Tertre. It's one of the oldest churches in the city, built in the 12th century as the abbey church of a substantial Benedictine monastery. It's been remodeled on a number of occasions down through the years, and the 18th-century facade, built by Louis XIV, contrasts uncomfortably with the mostly medieval interior. Its setting is awkward, too: The bulk of the Sacré-Coeur looms directly behind it.

17 The **Basilique du Sacré-Coeur,** begun in 1873 and completed in 1910 (though not consecrated until 1919), symbolized the return of relative self-confidence to later-19th-century Paris after the turmoil of the Commune. Even so, the building was to some extent a reflection of political divisions within the country. It was largely financed by French Catholics fearful of an anticlerical backlash and determined to make a grand statement on behalf of the Church. Stylistically, the Sacré-Coeur borrows elements from Romanesque and Byzantine models, fusing them under its distinctive Oriental dome. It was built on a grand scale, but the effect is strangely disjointed and unsettling, rather as if the building had been designed by a gifted but demented designer of railway stations with a pronounced taste for exoticism. (The architect, Abadie, died in 1884, long before the church was finished.) The gloomy, cavernous interior is worth visiting for its golden mosaics; climb to the top of the dome for the view over Paris.

More of Montmartre beckons north and west of the Sacré-Coeur. Take rue du Mont-Cenis down to rue
18 Cortot, site of the **Musée du Vieux Montmartre.** Like the Bateau-Lavoir, the building that is now the museum sheltered an illustrious group of painters, writers, and assorted cabaret artists in its heyday toward the end of the 19th century. Foremost among them were Renoir— he painted the *Moulin de la Galette,* an archetypical Parisian scene of sun-drenched revels, while he lived here—and Maurice Utrillo, Montmartre painter par excellence. Utrillo was the son of Suzanne Valadon, a regular model of Renoir's and a considerable painter in her own right. His life was anything but happy, despite the considerable success his paintings enjoyed. In fact, he painted chiefly as a result of prompting by his mother, who hoped it would prove therapeutic. Utrillo lived a drunkard's life. He was continually in trouble with the police and spent most of his declining years in clinics and hospitals. Having taken the gray, crumbling streets of Montmartre as his subject matter, he discovered that he worked much more effectively from cheap postcards than from the streets themselves. For all that, his best works—almost all produced before 1916; he died in 1955—evoke the atmosphere of old Montmartre hauntingly. Look carefully at the pictures in the museum here and you can see the plaster and sand he mixed with his paints to help convey the decaying buildings of the area. Almost the best thing about the museum, however, is
19 the view over the tiny **vineyard** on neighboring rue des Saules, the only vineyard in Paris, which still produces a symbolic 125 gallons of wine every year. It's hardly vintage stuff, but there are predictably bacchanalian celebrations during the October harvest. *Musée du Vieux Montmartre, 12 rue Cortot. Admission: 25 frs adults,*

*15 frs students and senior citizens. Open Tues.–Sun.
11–6.*

There's an equally famous Montmartre landmark on the
⑳ corner of rue St-Vincent, just down the road: the **Lapin
Agile.** It's a bar-cabaret and originally one of the raun-
chiest haunts in Montmartre. Today, it manages against
all odds to preserve at least something of its earlier fla-
vor, unlike the Moulin Rouge. It got its curious name—
it means the Nimble Rabbit—when the owner, André
Gill, hung a sign outside (you can see it now in the Musée
du Vieux Montmartre) of a laughing rabbit jumping out
of a saucepan clutching a wine bottle. In those days, the
place was still tamely called La Campagne (The Countryside). Once the sign went up, locals rebaptized the
place Lapin à Gill, which, translated, means rabbit, Gill-
style. When in 1886 it was sold to cabaret singer Jules
Jouy, he called it the Lapin Agile, which has the same
pronunciation in French as Lapin à Gill. In 1903, the
premises were bought by the most celebrated cabaret
entrepreneur of them all, Aristide Bruand, portrayed
by Toulouse-Lautrec in a series of famous posters.

㉑ Behind the Lapin Agile is the **St-Vincent Cemetery;** the
entrance is off little rue Lucien-Gaulard. It's a tiny
graveyard, but serious students of Montmartre might
want to visit to see Utrillo's burial place.

Continue north on rue des Saules, across busy rue Caul-
㉒ aincourt, and you come to the **Musée d'Art Juif,** the Museum of Jewish Art. It contains devotional items,
models of synagogues, and works by Pissarro and Marc
Chagall. *42 rue des Saules. Admission: 15 frs adults, 10
frs students and children. Open Sun.–Thurs. 3–6.*

There are several routes you can take back over
Montmartre's hill. Luxurious avenue Junot, from which
you'll see the villa Léandre, one of Montmartre's most
charming side streets, makes for a picturesque return
from the area around the cemetery and the museum. Alternatively, you can turn east onto rue Lamarck, past
several good restaurants, to circle around the quieter
side of the Sacré-Coeur basilica. If you then take the little stairpath named after Utrillo down to rue Paul Al-
㉓ bert, you'll come upon the **Marché St-Pierre** (St. Pierre
Market), the perfect place to rummage for old clothes
and fabrics. Prices are low. *Open Tues.–Sun. 8–1.*

Take rue de Steinkerque, opposite the foot of the Sacré-
Coeur gardens, then turn right onto boulevard de
Rochechouart and continue down to **Place Pigalle** to

519 M.P.H.

190 M.P.H.

75 M.P.H.

0 M.P.H.

WE LET YOU SEE EUROPE AT YOUR OWN PACE.

Regardless of your personal speed limits, Rail Europe offers everything to get you over, around and through anywhere you want in Europe. For more information, call your travel agent or **1-800-4-EURAIL.** *Rail Europe*

MCI brings Europe and America closer together.

Call the U.S. for less with MCI CALL USA®.

It's easy and affordable to call home when you use MCI CALL USA!

- Less expensive than calling through hotel operators
- Available from over 65 countries and locations worldwide
- You're connected to English-speaking MCI® Operators
- Even call 800 numbers in the U.S.

Call the U.S. for less from these European locations.

Dial the toll-free access number for the country you're calling from. Give the U.S. MCI Operator the number you're calling and the method of payment: MCI Card, U.S. local phone company card, Telecom Canada Card or collect. Your call will be completed!

Austria	022-903-012	Hungary	00*800-01411	Poland	0*-01-04-800-222
Belgium	078-11-00-12	Ireland	1800-551-001	Portugal	05-017-1234
Czechoslovakia	00-42-000112	Italy	172-1022	San Marino	172-1022
Denmark	8001-0022	Liechtenstein	155-0222	Spain	900-99-0014
Finland	9800-102-80	Luxembourg	0800-0112	Sweden	020-795-922
France	19*-00-19	Monaco	19*-00-19	Switzerland	155-0222
Germany	0130-0012	Netherlands	06*-022-91-22	United Kingdom	0800-89-0222
Greece	00-800-1211	Norway	050-12912	Vatican City	172-1022

* Wait for 2nd dial tone. Collect calls not accepted on MCI CALL USA calls to 800 numbers

Call 1-800-444-4444 in the U.S. to apply for your MCI Card® now!

complete your tour of the essential Montmartre. There's no question that this is simply a sordid red-light district that's lost a lot of its old bluster. Dim figures lurk in grimy doorways, and gloomy prostitutes and transvestites plod up and down the street; the Moulin Rouge seems downright pasteurized by comparison. Most of the sex shows are expensive and the audiences boisterously lewd.

Other Attractions

The Bois de Boulogne

Class and style have been associated with "Le Bois," as it is known, ever since it was landscaped into an upper-class playground by Baron Haussmann in the 1850s at the request of Napoleon III. This sprawling, 2,200-acre wood, crisscrossed by broad, leafy roads, lies just west of Paris, surrounded by the wealthy residential districts of Neuilly, Auteuil, and Passy.

The manifold attractions of these woods include cafés, restaurants, lakes, gardens, and waterfalls. Rowboats are available at the two largest lakes, the Lac Inférieur and Lac Supérieur. A cheap and frequent ferry crosses to the idyllic island in the middle of the Lac Inférieur.

Besides being a charming place to stroll or picnic, the Bois de Boulogne boasts several individual attractions worth a visit in their own right. Among them is **Parc de Bagatelle,** a beautiful floral park with irises, roses, tulips, and water lilies. The velvet green lawns and majestic 18th-century buildings (often host to art exhibitions) are fronted by a terrace with views toward the Seine. *Entrance: Route de Sèvres à Neuilly, or off Allée de Longchamp (Bus 244 or Métro: Pont de Neuilly). Admission: 5 frs to park, 22 frs to château buildings.*

There is also the **Jardin d'Acclimatation,** a delightful children's amusement park on the northern edge of the Bois de Boulogne, with a zoo, boat trips, and a miniature railway. *Blvd. des Sablons (Métro: Les Sablons). Admission: 8 frs adults, 4 frs children. Open daily 10–6.*

Père Lachaise Cemetery

This largest, most interesting, and most prestigious of Paris cemeteries dates back to the start of the 19th century. It is a veritable necropolis whose tombs compete in grandiosity, originality, and often, alas, dilapidation. Cobbled avenues, steep slopes, and lush vegetation contribute to a powerful atmosphere. Inhabitants include Chopin, Corot, Molière, Proust, Delacroix, Balzac, Oscar Wilde, Sarah Bernhardt, Jim Morrison, Yves Montand, and Edith Piaf. Get hold of a map at the entrance and track them down—and remember that Père Lachaise is an easy place to get lost in. *Rue des Rondeaux (Métro: Gambetta). Open daily 8–6, 8–dusk in winter.*

What to See and Do with Children

Paris has a wealth of attractions for children. Baby-sitting agencies are listed under "Gardes d'Enfants" in *L'Officiel des Spectacles.* The basic rate is about 25 francs per hour.

Aquariums A spell of fish-gazing is a soothing, mesmerizing experience for young and old alike. There are two principal aquariums in Paris, plus the exciting new marine center dreamt up by the famous ocean explorer Captain Cousteau:

Aquarium Tropical, *293 av. Daumesnil, 12e. Admission: 20 frs, 10 frs on Sun. Open Wed.–Mon. 10–noon and 1:30–5:30. Métro: Porte Dorée.*

Centre de la Mer et des Eaux, *195 rue St-Jacques, 5e. Admission: 20 frs adults, 12 frs children. Open Tues.–Fri. 10–12:30 and 1:15–5:30, weekends 10–5:30. RER: Luxembourg.*

Parc Océanique Cousteau, *Forum des Halles, 1er. Admission: 75 frs (children 50 frs). Open Tues.–Sun. 10–5:30. Métro/RER: Les Halles.*

Boating Rowboats can be rented at the **Lac Inférieur** in the Bois de Boulogne and at **Lac des Minimes** and **Lac Daumesnil** in the Bois de Vincennes.

Boat Trips An hour on the Seine on a Bateau Mouche or Vedette is good fun and a great way to get to know the capital. The cost is 30–40 francs for adults, 15–20 francs for children under 10. Departures every half-hour from:

Eiffel Tower, *7e. Métro: Bir-Hakeim.*
Pont de l'Alma, *8e. Métro: Alma-Marceau.*
Square du Vert Galant, *1er. Métro: Pont-Neuf.*

Circus   There's no need to know French to enjoy a circus. Tickets range from 40 to 180 francs. There are evening and weekend matinee performances. Check for details with:

> **Cirque d'Hiver,** *110 rue Amelot, 11e, tel. 47–00–12–25. Métro: Filles-du-Calvaire.*
> **Cirque Grüss,** *145 quai de la Gare, 13e, tel. 45–86–00–52. Métro: quai de la Gare.*
> **Cirque Bormann–Moreno,** *Jardin d'Acclimatation, 16e, tel. 45–01–88–91. Métro: Les Sablons.*

Eiffel Tower   Climb, and then ride the elevator to the top level of the Eiffel Tower for a breathtaking view of Paris and beyond.

Ice Cream   An ice cream is an ice cream, but the city's best (with a choice of some 30 flavors) is sold at **Berthillon's** on the Ile St-Louis. *31 rue St-Louis-en-l'Ile; closed Mon. and Tues. 4e. Métro: Pont-Marie.*

Ice Skating   The only ice rink in Paris is near the Buttes-Chamont park to the northeast. *30 rue Edouard-Pailleron, 19e, tel. 42–08–72–26. Admission: 22 frs (skate hire 15 frs). Open weekdays 11–5, weekends 10–6. Métro: Bolivar.*

Jardin d'Acclimatation   This charming children's play-park in the Bois de Boulogne boasts a miniature train, boat rides, a zoo, and a game area, plus fairground stalls and cafés. *Admission: 8 frs adults, 4 frs children. Open daily 10–6. Métro: Les Sablons.*

Movies   There is no shortage of English movies in Paris, some (often cartoons) geared for children. Consult *Pariscope* or *L'Officiel des Spectacles* for details.

Museums   **Musée de la Femme et Collection d'Automates.** The collection of automata and clockwork dolls bursts into life each afternoon; it's well worth making the short trip to Neuilly, especially since the Jardin d'Acclimatation and Bois de Boulogne (*see above*) are close at hand. *12 rue du Centre, Neuilly. Admission: 12 frs adults, 6 frs children. Open Wed.–Mon. 2:30–5; guided tours at 3. Métro: Pont de Neuilly.*

Musée Grévin. A visit to a waxwork museum is a good way to spend a rainy afternoon. The long-established boulevard Montmartre museum concentrates on imitations of the famous, the newer one in Halles on recapturing the Belle Epoque. *10 blvd. Montmartre, 9e. Admission: 48 frs adults, 34 frs children under 14. Open 1–7, 10–7 during school holidays. Métro: Rue Montmartre.* **Nouveau Musée Grévin.** *Forum des Halles, 1er. Admission: 38 frs adults, 28 frs children under 14.*

*Métro: Les Halles. Open Mon.–Sat. 10:30–6:30, Sun.
1–8.*

Parc Floral This is the east Paris equivalent of the Jardin
de Paris d'Acclimatation, situated in the Bois de Vincennes near
the château. It features a miniature train, a game area,
and miniature golf. *Route de la Pyramide, Vincennes.
Admission: 8 frs adults, 4 frs children, under 6 free.
Open daily 9:30–8 (to 5 in winter). Métro: Château de
Vincennes.*

Parks Paris is not renowned as an open-space city. Its major
parks (Bois de Boulogne and Bois de Vincennes) are on
the outskirts, but there is room to stroll and play at:

Arènes de Lutèce, *5e. Métro: Monge.*
Champs de Mars, *7e. Métro: Ecole Militaire.*
Jardin des Halles, *1er. Métro: Les Halles.*
Jardin des Plantes, *5e. Métro: Jussieu.*
Jardin des Tuileries, *1er. Métro: Tuileries.*
Jardin du Luxembourg, *6e. RER: Luxembourg.*
Jardin du Ranelagh, *16e. Métro: La Muette.*
Parc de la Villette, *19e. Métro: Porte de la Villette.*
Parc de Montsouris, *14e. RER: Cité Universitaire.*
Parc des Buttes-Chaumont, *19e. Métro: Buttes-
Chaumont.*
Parc Monceau, *8e. Métro: Monceau.*

Puppet Shows On most Wednesday, Saturday, and Sunday afternoons,
the Guignol, the French equivalent of Punch and Judy,
can be seen going through their ritualistic battles at the
following spots throughout Paris:

Champs de Mars, *av. du Gén.-Margueritte, 7e. Métro:
Ecole Militaire.*
Chaussée de l'Etang, *St-Mandé (Bois de Vincennes).
Métro: St-Mandé-Tourelle.*
Jardin des Tuileries, *1er. Métro: Concorde.*
Jardin du Luxembourg, *6e. Métro: Vavin. RER-B: Lux-
embourg.*
Jardin du Ranelagh, *av. Ingres, 16e. Métro: La Muette.*
Parc des Buttes-Chaumont, *av. Simon-Bolivar, 19e.
Métro: Buttes-Chaumont.*
Parc Montsouris, *av. Reille, 14e. Métro: Porte
d'Orléans. RER-B: Cité Universitaire.*
Parc de St-Cloud, *Métro: Boulogne–Pont de St-Cloud.*
Rond-Point des Champs-Elysées, *8e. Métro: Champs-
Elysée-Clemenceau.*

Roller Skating Paris's unofficial outdoor roller-skating venue is the
concourse between the two wings of the Palais de
Chaillot at Trocadéro. Or try: **La Main Jaune,** *rue du*

Caporal-Peugeot, 17e, tel. 47–63–26–47. (Métro: Porte de Champerret.) Admission: 40 frs. Open Wed. and weekends 2:30–7.

Zoos Monkeys, deer, birds, and farm animals star at the **Jardin d'Acclimatation** (*see above*), while the **Ménagerie** in the Jardin des Plantes also boasts elephants, lions, and tigers. *57 rue Cuvier, 5e. Admission: 25 frs adults, 13 frs children. Open daily 9–6 (9–5 in winter). Métro: Jussieu, Austerlitz.*

Paris's biggest zoo is in the **Bois de Vincennes,** which in addition to wild beasts includes a museum, films, and exhibitions. *53 av. de St-Maurice, 12e. Admission: 35 frs adults, 20 frs children. Open daily 9–6 (9–5 in winter). Métro: Porte Dorée.*

Dining

Some complain that the French capital is overrated gastronomically; that Parisian restaurateurs exploit gullible tourists who come assuming that all restaurants in Paris are good simply because they're in Paris; that prices are too high and that standards are not what they were. In short, the complaint is that the Parisian restaurateur is resting complacently on his laurels. Of course, not every restaurant offers a gastronomic adventure, and bad meals at unconscionable prices are no more unknown in Paris than at home. The important point to remember, however, is that the city's restaurants exist principally to cater to the demanding needs of the Parisians themselves, and any restaurant that fails to meet their high standards is unlikely to stay in business for long.

It's dangerous to generalize on such a complex subject, but the most expensive and formal restaurants will offer either classical French food (characterized by rich sauces) or nouvelle cuisine (characterized by light, fresh produce artfully arranged on your plate). Many serve a judicious mixture of the two. In less-expensive places—especially the numerous bistros and brasseries—food veers more toward classical styles, though it will almost always be less intimidatingly rich than in the temples of classical cuisine: *cuisine bourgeoise*—straightforward and hearty—just about sums it up.

Almost all restaurants offer two basic types of menu: à la carte and fixed price (*un menu* to the French). The fixed-price menu will almost always offer the best value, though you will have to eat three or sometimes four

Paris Dining

KEY

AE American Express Office

0 — 750 yards
0 — 750 meters

Au Clocher du Village, **1**
Beauvilliers, **14**
Brasserie Lipp, **28**
Chartier, **10**
Chez Papa, **26**
Chez Paul, **19**
Closerie des Lilas, **30**
Coconnas, **16**
Da Graziano, **11**
Dôme, **32**

Drouant, **8**
Fellini, **33**
Jean-Claude Ferrero, **2**
Joël Robuchon, **3**
Jules Verne, **34**
La Colombe, **18**
La Coupole, **31**
La Petite Chaise, **29**
L'Assommoir, **12**

Le Carré des Feuillants, **7**
Le Coupe- Chou, **22**
Le Grand Véfour, **9**
Le Maquis, **13**
Le Procope, **24**
Lucas-Carton, **6**
Mansouria, **15**
Petit St- Benoît, **27**
Polidor, **23**
15 Montaigne, **5**

Saumoneraie, **21**
Taillevent, **4**
Tour d'Argent, **20**
Trumilou, **17**
Vagenende, **25**

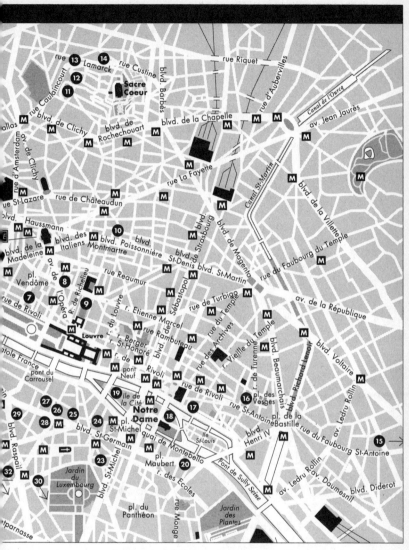

rue Riquet

rue d'Aubervilles

Canal de l'Ourcq

av. Jean Jaurès

rue ⑬ Lamarck ⑭ rue Custine

rue Caulaincourt ⑫

⑪ Sacre Coeur

blvd. Barbès

blvd. de la Chapelle

blvd. de la Villette

blvd. de Clichy

blvd. de Rochechouart

av. de Clichy

rue St-Lazare

rue de Châteaudun

rue La Fayette

Canal St-Martin

blvd. Haussmann

blvd. des Italiens

blvd. de la Madeleine

blvd. ⑩ Poissonnière

blvd. Montmartre

blvd. de Strasbourg

blvd. St-Denis

blvd. St-Martin

blvd. de Magenta

rue du Faubourg du Temple

pl. Vendôme

R. de Richelieu

rue Reaumur

Sébastopol

rue de Turbigo

av. de la République

⑦ rue de Rivoli

⑧ av. de l'Opéra

⑨

r. Etienne Marcel

rue du Louvre

rue du Temple

rue des Archives

Vieille du Temple

r. de Turenne

blvd. Beaumarchais

blvd. Richard Lenoir

blvd. Voltaire

Louvre

r. St-Honoré

r. Berger

r. de Rivoli

rue Rambuteau

Anatole France

pont du Carrousel

pont Neuf

Ile de la Cité

⑲ Notre Dame

rue de Rivoli

pl. des Vosges ⑯

rue St-Antoine

⑰

⑱

Bastille

pl. de la

rue du Faubourg St-Antoine

av. Ledru Rollin

㉗ ㉖ ㉕

㉙ ㉘

blvd. St-Germain ㉔ pl. St-Michel

blvd. St-Michel ㉓

Ile St-Louis

blvd. Henri IV

⑮

Jardin du Luxembourg

㉛ ㉚

quai de Montebello

pl. Maubert

⑳

r. des Ecoles

Pont de Sully Seine

av. Ledru Rollin av. Daumesnil

blvd. Diderot

tparnasse

blvd. Raspail

pl. du Panthéon

rue Monge

Jardin des Plantes

courses, and the choices will be limited. There's nothing to stop you from choosing only one or two dishes from the à la carte menu, but only the most thick-skinned will want to try this in a top restaurant, especially if it's busy. The wilting look of a Parisian waiter is not something that many can happily endure.

All French restaurants must, by law, display their menus outside. Make a point of looking at them carefully before going in. All posted rates include service *(service compris* or *prix nets)*. You are under no obligation to leave an additional tip, but if you feel the service has been exceptional, you may want to leave a few extra francs.

Lunch is usually served from noon to 2. You shouldn't have difficulty getting a table in all but the best restaurants if you arrive by 12:30; after 1, however, you may have problems, especially if you want a full, three-course meal. Dinner is rarely served before 8, and 9:30 or even 10 are not considered unduly late. Almost all restaurants stay open until midnight, some much later, but kitchens usually close around 10:30.

Highly recommended restaurants are indicated by a star ★.

Category	Cost*
Very Expensive	over 500 frs
Expensive	250 frs–500 frs
Moderate	150 frs–250 frs
Inexpensive	50 frs–150 frs

per person, including tax and service but not drinks

1st Arrondissement

Very Expensive **Le Grand Véfour.** Located under the neo-Classical colonnades at the north end of the gardens of the Palais-Royal, Le Grand Véfour can convincingly claim to be the most sumptuously decorated restaurant in the city. The elegantly incised and painted early 19th-century mirrors reflect the crisp white linen of the tablecloths. Haute cuisine is prepared in the traditional manner; new chef Guy Martin has added some *nouvelle* touches (potato terrine with truffles, for instance). The fixed-price menu, available only at lunch, is not cheap but offers good value. *17 rue de Beaujolais, tel. 42–96–56–27. Reservations essential; book 1 week in advance for Fri.*

*and Sat. dinner. Jacket and tie required. AE, DC, MC,
V. Closed Sat. lunch, Sun., and Aug.*

Expensive **Le Carré des Feuillants.** Anyone with pretensions to be
★ numbered among *le beau monde* will already know that
this elegant new restaurant offers one of the city's most
talked-about dining experiences. Try for a table in the
largest of the three dining rooms; it has a memorable
fireplace. The food is predominantly from the southwest
of France, one of the richest gastronomic regions of the
country. Foie gras, truffles, and young pigeon number
among the specialties. The wine list is fabulous. Note
that dinner here can easily move into the very expensive
category. *14 rue de Castiglione, tel. 42–86–82–82. Reservations advised. Dress: casual but elegant. AE, DC,
MC, V. Closed Sat. lunch, Sun., and weekends in July
and Aug.*

Moderate **Chez Paul.** Lovers of the authentic Parisian bistro—and
★ they don't come much more authentic than this—rejoice
at the survival of Chez Paul. It's located on the Ile de la
Cité, between the Pont Neuf and the Palais du Justice,
on one of the prettiest squares in Paris. Dining on the
terrace is an experience to remember. The food is stur-
dily traditional, with snails and calf's head in shallot
sauce as longtime favorites. *15 pl. Dauphine, tel. 43–
54–21–48. Reservations advised. Dress: informal. No
credit cards. Closed Mon., Tues., and Aug.*

2nd Arrondissement

Expensive **Drouant.** This elegant restaurant and café is a Paris in-
stitution, where France's highest literary prize, the
Prix Goncourt, has been awarded since 1914. The glamorous café serves rather traditional bourgeois cuisine,
with the accent on good steaks and seafood. The more
sophisticated restaurant offers excellent nouvelle
dishes. Try the warm oysters with caviar, the rabbit
with fresh spices, or lobster fricassee. *18 rue Gaillon,
tel. 42–65–15–16. Reservations advised. Jacket and tie
required in restaurant only. AE, DC, MC, V.*

4th Arrondissement

Moderate **Coconnas.** With its warm Italian decor and early 18th-
★ century paintings of beautiful place des Vosges, the little Coconnas has won plaudits from restaurant critics
and humble diners alike. Depending on your mood, you
can choose either modern cuisine or cuisine *à l'ancienne*,
solid 19th-century fare with not so much as a hint of nou-

velle innovation. Owned and run by the proprietors of
the Tour d'Argent (*see* 5th Arrondissement, *below*), the
Coconnas has a considerable reputation to live up to. If
the overbooking is anything to go by, it obviously suc-
ceeds. *2 bis pl. des Vosges, tel. 42–78–58–16. Reservations essential. Dress: casual but elegant. AE, DC, MC,
V. Closed mid-Dec.–mid-Jan.*

La Colombe. "The Dove" fulfills its name and serves as
home to 14 white doves. It also offers one of the most
charming dining experiences in Paris. The restaurant is
set in a lovely 13th-century house on the Seine, right
next to Notre Dame. Try to secure a table on the leafy
terrace. The food is predominantly classic, but with
nouvelle touches. The fixed-price lunch menu is also
available for dinner before 9 PM. *4 rue de la Colombe, tel.
46–33–37–08. Reservations advised. Dress: informal.
AE, DC, MC, V. Closed Mon. lunch and Sun.*

Inexpensive **Trumilou.** Overlooking the Seine opposite Ile St-Louis,
★ this very French little bistro is a real find. Despite the
harsh lighting, the mood is boisterous and welcoming,
with many regulars among the diners. Bright and
splashy paintings line the walls. The food is resolutely
traditional, with time-honored favorites like *boeuf
bourguignon* and sweetbreads. *84 quai de l'Hôtel de
Ville, tel. 42–77–63–98. Reservations accepted. Dress:
informal. MC, V. Closed Mon.*

5th Arrondissement

Very Expensive **Tour d'Argent.** The Tour d'Argent is the sort of temple to
★ haute cuisine that has serious gourmets quivering in ex-
pectation. It offers the complete dining experience, and
very much in the grand manner. You come not simply for
the food—though, after some years of noticeably falling
standards, new chef Manuel Martinez has restored this
to its previous high peaks—but for the perfect service,
the discreetly understated decor, the immense wine
list, and the fabled view of Notre Dame. Those who re-
coil at the thought of having to pay for all this—and
make no mistake, the Tour d'Argent is super-
expensive—can take comfort in the knowledge that the
fixed-price lunch menu brings the place within some
sort of reach. *15 quai de la Tournelle, tel. 43–54–23–31.
Reservations required at least 1 week in advance. Jacket and tie required. AE, DC, MC, V. Closed Mon.*

Expensive **Le Coupe-Chou.** Located in an alley at the foot of the
Montagne Ste-Geneviève and the Panthéon, Le Coupe-
Chou has uneven floors, bare stone walls, and candlelit

alcoves. The mood throughout is great for romantic dining. The food is competent rather than memorable, but it's the magical setting that counts. Have your coffee and *digestif* in the small, fire-lit sitting room. *9 rue Lanneau, tel. 46–33–68–69. Reservations advised. Dress: casual but elegant. MC, V. Closed Sun. lunch.*

Moderate **Saumoneraie.** Fish lovers should swim toward rue Descartes, halfway up the Montagne Ste-Geneviève, to the Saumoneraie. The tasteful modern decor is enhanced by wall mosaics and two aquariums—one freshwater, one seawater—where your dinner swims oblivious of its fate. Salmon dominates the wide range of fish and seafood dishes. There's also a fixed-price menu. *8 rue Descartes, tel. 46–34–08–76. Reservations essential. Jacket required. AE, DC, MC, V.*

6th Arrondissement

Expensive **Closerie des Lilas.** Standing on the corner of boulevard St-Michel and boulevard du Montparnasse, the Closerie des Lilas has been an essential part of the Left Bank scene since it opened back in 1907. Hemingway was here so regularly that a plaque commemorates his favorite spot at the bar. Though the lilacs—*les lilas*—may long since have disappeared from the terrace, the place is just as popular as it ever was during its salad days back in the '30s. Straightforward traditional fare is the staple: Try the oysters. The adjoining brasserie offers much the same food at lower prices, but you miss the razzle-dazzle of the terrace. *171 blvd. du Montparnasse, tel. 43–26–70–50. Reservations advised. Dress: casual but elegant. AE, DC, MC, V.*

Moderate **Brasserie Lipp.** The Brasserie Lipp is perhaps *the* Left Bank restaurant. It's been a favorite haunt of politicians, journalists, and assorted intellectuals for longer than most people can remember. Try for a table on the first floor, but don't be surprised to find yourself relegated to the second-floor dining room. Food, service, and atmosphere are polished. *151 blvd. St-Germain, tel. 45–48–53–91. No reservations; expect lines. Dress: jacket required. AE, DC. Closed mid-July–mid-Aug.*

Chez Papa. The refreshing open-plan decor of Chez Papa makes a pleasant change from the bustle and tightly packed tables of most St-Germain restaurants. A shiny, black, baby-grand piano, surrounded by a host of plants, stands out against the white walls and high ceiling. There's soft music from 9 every evening. Cuisine is also surprisingly light, considering that the dishes themselves are usually associated with the sturdiest of French traditional food: snails, cassoulet, and pot-au-feu. A good fixed-price menu makes Chez Papa an ideal lunch or dinner spot. *3 rue St. Benoît, tel. 42–86–99–63. Reservations advised. Dress: informal. AE, DC, MC, V. Closed Sun.*

★ **Le Procope.** Founded in 1686 by an Italian, Francesco Procopio, Le Procope is said to be the oldest café in Paris. It was a meeting place for Voltaire in the 18th century and for Balzac and Victor Hugo in the 19th. In 1987, it was bought by the Blanc brothers, owners of a number of other popular brasseries. Though they gave the Procope something of a face-lift, they haven't changed the busy and bustling mood or tampered with the solid *bourgeoise* cuisine. *13 rue de l'Ancienne Comédie, tel. 43–26–99–20. Reservations advised. Dress: informal. AE, DC, MC, V.*

Vagenende. Dark woods, gleaming mirrors, and superprofessional waiters—perfect in their black jackets and white aprons—take the Vagenende dangerously close to turn-of-the-century pastiche. Nonetheless, the superior brasserie food—seafood and hearty *cuisine bourgeoise*—and the busy atmosphere make this a restaurant to take seriously. The homemade foie gras and the chocolate-based desserts are outstanding. *142 blvd. St-Germain, tel. 43–26–68–18. Reservations advised. Dress: informal. AE, MC, V.*

Inexpensive **Petit St-Benoît.** This is a wonderful place—small, amazingly inexpensive, always crowded, and with decor that's plain to the point of barely existing. The food is correspondingly basic, but quite good for the price. Expect to share a table. *4 rue St-Benoît. No reservations. Dress: informal. No credit cards. Closed weekends.*

Polidor. The Polidor is another of the Left Bank's time-honored bistros, little changed from the days when James Joyce and Hemingway came here to spend long, drunken evenings. The typical bistro fare is offered in generous portions. Try the fixed-price menu for maximum value at lunchtime. *41 rue Monsieur-le-Prince. No reservations. Dress: informal. No credit cards.*

7th Arrondissement

Very Expensive **Jules Verne.** Those who think that the food in a restaurant with a view is bound to take second place to that view should head *tout de suite* for the Jules Verne, located, memorably, on the third floor of the Eiffel Tower. The view, of course, is fantastic, but the food, too, is superb, featuring inventive combinations of classic and nouvelle cuisine. Specialties include baked turbot in vinegar and tarragon, and veal in lemon and vanilla. *Eiffel Tower, tel. 45–55–61–44. Reservations essential; book at least 3 weeks in advance. Jacket and tie required. AE, DC, MC, V.*

Inexpensive **La Petite Chaise.** What was once a coaching inn, opened in 1680, has since become one of the most popular restaurants in the city. While the decor may be on the musty side, the service is charming, and the simple food, with specialties such as seafood pancakes and avocado mousse, is the important factor here. *36 rue de Grenelle, tel. 42–22–13–35. Reservations advised. Dress: informal. MC, V.*

8th Arrondissement

Very Expensive **Lucas-Carton.** Many gastronomes maintain that the
★ Lucas-Carton is absolutely *the* best restaurant in Paris. Are they right? Who can say? What's beyond doubt, however, is that Lucas-Carton offers a gastronomic experience equaled in no more than a handful of restaurants around the world. The decor is strictly Belle Epoque, all glinting mirrors and crimson seats. The food, by contrast, is strictly nouvelle, though nouvelle at its subtle best, which some may find an acquired taste. But duck with honey and spices, or sweetbreads with mixed vegetables prepared by master chef Alain Senderens, will probably be a once-in-a-lifetime experience. *9 pl. de la Madeleine, tel. 42–65–22–90. Reservations essential; book at least 3 weeks in advance. Jacket and tie required. MC, V. Closed weekends, most of Aug., and Christmas–New Year's.*

Taillevent. The exquisite mid-19th-century mansion that houses Taillevent provides the perfect, discreet setting for some of the most refined nouvelle food in the city. Specialties like stuffed baby pigeon on a bed of cabbage à la Taillevent provide the sort of gastronomic memory you'll never forget. The wine list boasts over 500 vintages; it's said to be the most extensive in Paris. *15 rue Lamennais, tel. 45–63–39–94. Reservations at least 1 week in advance. Jacket and tie required. MC, V. Closed weekends and Aug.*

Expensive **15 Montaigne.** Architectural conservationists tried to prevent the construction of this new restaurant (opened 1990), claiming its rooftop site atop the Théâtre des Champs-Elysées blighted the city skyline. Luckily they failed. The view from the restaurant—across the Seine toward the Eiffel Tower and the Invalides—is one of the finest the capital has to offer, and the stylish modern decor has won rave reviews. Well-known throughout Paris, head chef José Lampreia recently passed away, but his former assistant, José Martinez, has taken over the kitchen and remains faithful to his predecessor's repetoire. Ground beef pie with parsley or pigeon with dates are typical examples of the "sophisticated peasant" cuisine. Open daily till midnight. *15 av. Montaigne, tel. 47–23–55–99. Reservations advised. Dress: elegant but casual. MC, V.*

9th Arrondissement

Inexpensive
★
Chartier. Low prices, turn-of-the-century decor, and classic fare have earned Chartier an enviable reputation as one of the best-value places to eat in Paris. The choice isn't wide, but the food is always hearty and filling. Try the steak tartare if it's on the menu and you're feeling adventurous. *7 rue du Fbg. Montmartre, tel. 47–70–86–29. No reservations. Dress: informal. No credit cards.*

11th Arrondissement

Moderate
★
Mansouria. Despite its off-the-beaten-track location to the east of place de la Bastille, Mansouria is worth the trip if you have any interest in Moroccan food—it's in a class of its own. A group of young Moroccan women run the restaurant under the benign leadership of Fatima. The decor is fresh and modern, and the service is friendly and relaxed. Try any of the *tagines*, a range of sophisticated spicy Moroccan "stews," and the pigeon "pie" with sugar. *11 rue Faidherbe, tel. 43–71–00–16. Reservations essential. Dress: informal. MC, V.*

14th Arrondissement

Very Expensive
Dôme. In the heart of Montparnasse, the Dôme still reigns as one of the city's classic brasseries. Have a drink outside on the terrace before venturing into the restored Art Deco interior to enjoy one of the excellent fresh fish platters or the steaming bouillabaisse. *108 blvd. du Montparnasse, tel. 43–35–25–81. Reservations advised. Dress: informal. AE, DC, MC, V. Closed Mon.*

Moderate
★
La Coupole. World-renowned La Coupole is Montparnasse's most prestigious brasserie and certainly worth a visit. The restored Art Deco interior is en-

hanced by 32 pillars painted by the artists of Montparnasse. La Coupole has remained faithful to its traditional brasserie fare—with copious seafood and sauerkraut dishes. Fish lovers will appreciate the sole stuffed with spinach or the monkfish *cassoulet*. A silver-service breakfast and an inexpensive lunchtime menu are favorites with tourists and businessmen alike. *102 blvd. du Montparnesse, tel. 43–20–14–20. Reservations advised for dinner. Dress: informal. AE, DC, MC, V. Open 7:30AM–2AM.*

15th Arrondissement

Fellini. This snug little restaurant in the heart of the bustling 15th Arrondissement serves excellent Italian food: homemade pasta (try the tagliatelli with olive purée) as well as some more daring choices, such as veal in tuna sauce or *insalata di mare*, a variety of seafood cooked in olive oil. *58 rue de la Croix-Nivert, tel. 45–77–40–77. Reservations advised. Dress: informal. MC, V. Closed Sat. lunch and Sun.*

16th Arrondissement

Very Expensive **Joël Robuchon.** Without a doubt, this is one of the very
★ best restaurants in Paris. Joël Robuchon is a chef known for his personalized and exceptionally creative cuisine—*langoustine* (prawn) ravioli with cabbage, potato purée, roasted pig's head, and other dishes are impeccably served in this refined and delightfully decorated restaurant. Reservations must be made months in advance. *32 rue de Longchamp, tel. 47–27–12–27. Reservations essential. Jacket and tie required. MC, V. Closed Sat., Sun., and July.*

Expensive **Jean-Claude Ferrero.** The chic habitués of the 16th Arrondissement feel very much at home in this oh-so-classy restaurant. Nouvelle cuisine reigns supreme. Any of the mushroom dishes is excellent; otherwise, try the beef in crusty pastry. The restaurant is located in a stately town house and boasts a charming, plant-filled courtyard. *38 rue Vital, tel. 45–04–42–42. Reservations essential. Jacket and tie required. AE, DC, MC, V. Closed Sat., Sun., May 1–18, and 3 weeks in Aug.*

Moderate **Au Clocher du Village.** The simple, country-village-like interior of the Clocher du Village, with old posters on the walls, wine presses hanging from the ceiling, lace curtains, and a gleaming brass coffee machine on the bar, provides the perfect complement to simple, well-prepared classic French cuisine. Service is straightforward (some may find it a bit curt). It's a place like this that can make eating out in Paris special. There's nothing very fancy here, yet the whole place exudes that inimitable Gallic culinary flair. *8 bis rue Verderet, tel. 42–88–35–87. Reservations advised. Dress: informal. MC, V. Closed Sat., Sun., and Aug.*

18th Arrondissement

Very Expensive
★ **Beauvilliers.** This is *the* luxury restaurant in Montmartre. Chef Michel Deygat has won lavish praise for his nouvelle-inspired dishes; red mullet in green peppers and veal kidneys in a truffle-based sauce are among his specialties. An excellent fixed-price menu (lunch only) keeps prices, which can otherwise be high, within reach. Vast bouquets of fresh flowers add colorful touches to the formality of the three main dining rooms; there's a tiny terrace for summer evening dining. *52 rue Lamarck, tel. 42–54–54–42. Reservations essential. Jacket and tie required. MC, V. Closed Sun., Mon. lunch, and first 2 weeks in Sept.*

Moderate
★ **Da Graziano.** Located right under one of the neighborhood's remaining windmills, Da Graziano offers an exquisite taste of Italy in the heart of Montmartre. Owner Federighi Graziano is as chic as his restaurant—chandeliers, mirrors, and flowers proliferate—and as Tuscan as the cuisine. His fresh pasta is memorable. He also offers a range of French dishes, some named after stars who have dined here. Try the smoked beef *à la* Jean Marais. The inexpensive fixed-price lunch menu makes the climb up the hill well worthwhile. *83 rue Lepic, tel. 46–06–84–77. Reservations essential. Dress: casual but elegant. MC, V. Closed Feb.*

★ **L'Assommoir.** L'Assommoir is known not just for its subtle cuisine—there's a superb range of sophisticated fish dishes—but for the personality of owner/chef Philippe Larue, who speaks English to perfection and has a tremendous sense of humor. He has covered the walls of his charming little bistro with samples from his vast collection of paintings. L'Assommoir also has the advantage of being on a peaceful little street away from crowded place du Tertre. *12 rue Girardon, tel. 42–64–55–01. Reservations advised. Dress: casual but elegant. MC, V. Closed Sun. evening, Mon., and mid-July–mid-Aug.*

Le Maquis. Visitors often miss this spot on the little-traveled north side of the Montmarte hill, but it's a favorite with locals, who come for the warm, friendly atmosphere and the excellent, traditional French cuisine. The reasonably priced, superb-quality lunchtime fare (the fixed menu changes daily) usually keeps the place packed at midday, so you might want to call ahead for a lunch reservation. In the evenings, try the blanquette of veal, salted pork with lentils, or chicken with garlic. Owner/chef Claude Lesage is a master baker, so be sure to sample the homemade breads accompanying each dish, and try one of his fresh-baked cakes for dessert. *69 rue Caulaincourt, tel. 42–59–76–07. Reservations advised. Dress: casual. MC, V. Closed Sun. and Mon.*

Lodging

At last count, the Paris Tourist Office's official (albeit incomplete) hotel guide listed 1,123 hotels in the 20 central city districts, or *arrondissements*, alone. The range of hotel experiences is as wide as these figures suggest. You will find everything from palatial hotels offering service in the grand manner to small, family-run establishments providing basic but congenial accommodations. In between, there are chain hotels, medium-price hotels—some poor, others excellent—apartments, and even the odd motel. Despite this huge choice, you should always be sure to make reservations well in advance.

Our listings have been compiled with the aim of identifying hotels that offer maximum atmosphere, convenience, and comfort. We do not include many chain hotels for the simple reason that those in Paris are little different from those in other major cities. Except for the largest and most expensive hotels, almost all Parisian lodgings have certain idiosyncrasies. Plumbing can be erratic, though rarely to the point where it becomes a problem. Air-conditioning is the exception rather than the rule, and on stuffy, sultry summer nights, when you have no choice but to open the windows, you may be bothered by street noise. Ask for a room *sur cour*—overlooking the courtyard (almost all hotels have one)—or, even better, if there is one, *sur le jardin*—overlooking the garden. Our reviews indicate the number of rooms with tub (*baignoire*) and the number of rooms with shower (*douche*) only. If you have a preference, make it known to the management. At Parisian hotels there is almost always an extra charge for breakfast; the cost will be anything from about 20 francs per person in the least expensive hotels to 90 francs per person in the

162

Paris Lodging

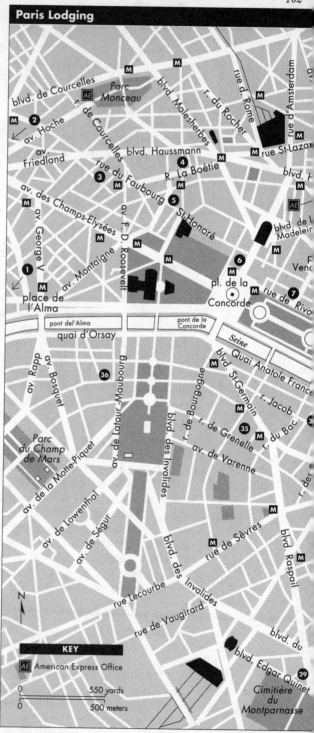

KEY

AE American Express Office

0   550 yards
0   500 meters

most expensive. If you want more than the standard French breakfast of *café au lait* (coffee with milk) and a croissant, the price will almost certainly be increased.

All French hotels are officially graded from four-star deluxe to one star. These grades depend, theoretically, on amenities as well as price. The ratings, however, can be misleading, since many hotels prefer to be under-starred for tax reasons. Our gradings are based on price (*see below*). Bear in mind that prices in any given hotel can vary considerably depending on the time of year and the type of room. Our listings always give the higher grade, so it's worth asking if there are any less expensive rooms. Rates must be posted in all rooms, and all extras must be clearly shown. Double rooms, other than in the cheapest hotels, are nearly always more expensive than single rooms. Note also that you'll be paying per room and not per person.

Highly recommended lodgings are indicated by a star ★.

Category	Cost*
Very Expensive	over 1,000 frs
Expensive	600 frs–1,000 frs
Moderate	300 frs–600 frs
Inexpensive	under 300 frs

* *All prices are for a standard double room, including tax and service.*

1st Arrondissement

Very Expensive
★ **Inter-Continental.** An aura of elegant luxury reigns throughout this exquisite late-19th-century hotel, which was designed by the architect of the Paris Opéra, Garnier. Three of its opulent public rooms are official historic monuments. In summer, breakfast on the patio is a delicious experience. Service is impeccable. There are two year-round indoor restaurants: La Rôtisserie Rivoli and the Café Tuileries; in summer, you can also eat outdoors at the Terrasse Fleurie. *3 rue de Castiglione, tel. 44–77–11–11. 450 fully equipped rooms and suites, many with Jacuzzis. Facilities: 2 restaurants, bar, patio. AE, DC, MC, V.*

Expensive **Normandy.** For a combination of Belle Epoque elegance and an excellent central location near the Palais-Royal, the Normandy is hard to beat. Rooms are individually decorated and vary considerably in size. Some of the least expensive ones have shower only. There's a restaurant and a wood-paneled, English-style bar. *7 rue de l'Echelle, tel. 42–60–30–21. 130 rooms, plus 4 large and 4 small suites, most with bath. Facilities: restaurant (closed weekends). AE, DC, MC, V.*

Moderate **Louvre Forum.** Located on a quiet street close to St-Eustache church, this hotel is convenient for visits to the Louvre, Palais-Royal, and Les Halles. Most of the rooms have no character, but they are equipped with a phone, TV, and minibar. Those on the top floor have sloped ceilings that make them prettier but also smaller. The hotel does have an attractive vaulted breakfast room in its basement, as well as a ground-floor lounge with flagstone floor, rugs, and old-fashioned armchairs. *25 rue du Bouloi, tel. 42–36–54–19. 28 rooms with bath or shower. AE, DC, MC, V.*

★ **Montpensier.** This handsome 17th-century mansion was transformed into a hotel in 1874. It offers the kind of small-hotel charm and character that Paris is known for, as the clientele, many of them regulars, will testify. All the rooms are individually decorated and vary greatly in size. Those on the top floor, for example, are tiny and modern. The location, on an attractive street running parallel to the gardens of the Palais-Royal, is ideal. There's no restaurant or bar. *12 rue de Richelieu, tel. 42–96–28–50. 43 rooms, 37 with bath or shower. MC, V.*

Inexpensive **Lille.** You won't find a less expensive base for exploring the Louvre than this hotel, located just a short distance from the Cour Carrée. The hotel hasn't received a facelift in years, but then neither have the prices. The decor is somewhat shabby, but it's the epitome of Vieux Paris, and the money you save by staying here can come in handy if you indulge in a shopping spree along the nearby rue de Rivoli or Forum des Halles. *8 rue du Pélican, tel. 42–33–33–42. 14 rooms, some with shower. No credit cards.*

2nd Arrondissement

Expensive **Edouard VII.** The double-paned windows keep out the
★ noise of the elegant but busy avenue de l'Opéra. Rooms are soberly decorated in browns, grays, and whites, and the bathrooms are remarkably well-equipped. Try the flower-filled Delmonico restaurant for reasonably priced, traditional cuisine. *39 av. de l'Opéra, tel. 42–61–56–90. 80 rooms and 4 luxury suites, all with bath, 10 rooms with shower only. Facilities: bar, restaurant,*

conference room for up to 35. AE, DC, MC, V. Restaurant closed Sun. and Aug.

★ **Gaillon-Opéra.** The oak beams, stone walls, and marble tiles of the Gaillon-Opéra single it out as one of the most charming hotels in the Opéra neighborhood. To add to the charm, there are plants throughout and a flower-filled patio. There's a small bar but no restaurant. *9 rue Gaillon, tel. 47–42–47–74. 26 rooms and 1 suite, all with bath. Facilities: bar. AE, DC, MC, V.*

3rd Arrondissement

Very Expensive **Pavillon de la Reine.** The Queen's Pavilion on historic place des Vosges is the setting for this hotel, which opened in 1986. Public areas and rooms are discreetly but luxuriously decorated; all the bathrooms are decorated in marble. Ask for a room overlooking the flower-filled patio or with a view onto the square. There's no restaurant, but breakfast is served in a vaulted cellar. *28 pl. des Vosges, tel. 42–77–96–40. 53 rooms and duplexes, all with bath. Facilities: parking. AE, DC, MC, V.*

4th Arrondissement

Expensive **Deux-Iles.** This cleverly converted 17th-century man-
★ sion on the residential Ile St-Louis has long won plaudits for charm and comfort. Flowers and plants are scattered around the stunning hall. The fabric-hung rooms, though small, have exposed beams and are fresh and airy. Ask for a room overlooking the little garden courtyard. There's no restaurant, but drinks are served in the cellar bar until 1 AM. The lounge is dominated by a fine chimneypiece and doubles as a second bar. *59 rue St-Louis-en-l'Ile, tel. 43–26–13–35. 8 rooms with bath, 9 with shower. Facilities: bar (closed Sun.). No credit cards.*

Moderate **Place des Vosges.** A loyal American clientele swears by
★ the small, historic Place des Vosges, which is located on a charming street just off the exquisite square of the same name. The entrance hall is imposingly grand and is decorated in Louis XIII style, but some of the rooms are little more than functional. A number of the smaller ones fall into the inexpensive category. There's no restaurant, but there's a welcoming little breakfast room. *12 rue de Birague, tel. 42–72–60–46. 11 rooms with bath, 5 with shower. MC, V.*

Inexpensive **Sévigné.** Located in the Marais district and convenient to the St-Paul Métro station and the place des Vosges, this hotel remains a good bet for quality low-budget accommodations. The hotel is clean and well-run, and the staff is personable. Extensive renovation a few years back resulted in a mirror-lined lobby, new breakfast room, and a shower or bath in every room. Rooms facing rue Malher are quieter, but those facing busy rue St-Antoine offer a view of the church of St-Paul-St-Louis. *2 rue Malher, tel. 42–72–76–17. 30 rooms with shower or bath. No credit cards.*

5th Arrondissement

Expensive **Elysa.** The Elysa is what the French call an *"hôtel de*
★ *charme."* Though the building is not large, most rooms are surprisingly spacious, and all have been renovated; cream-colored furniture is set against pale blue or pink fabrics. There's no restaurant or bar, but you'll find a minibar in every room and a breakfast lounge serving Continental or buffet breakfasts. Moreover, the Elysa is one of the rare hotels in the city with a sauna. *6 rue Gay Lussac, tel. 43–25–31–74. 25 rooms with bath, 5 with shower. Facilities: sauna. AE, DC, MC, V.*

Moderate **Esméralda.** Lovers of small, charming Parisian hotels
★ will want to stay at this simple lodging, where the rooms are a little dusty but positively exude Gallic charm. Esméralda is set in a fine 17th-century building opposite Notre Dame (request a room with a view), near Square Viviani. All the rooms are small—some are midget-size—but all have the same feel of timeworn clutter and warmth. Many have copies of 17th-century furniture. *4 rue St-Julien-le-Pauvre, tel. 43–54–19–20. 15 rooms with bath, 4 with shower. No credit cards.*

6th Arrondissement

Very Expensive **Relais Christine.** The Relais Christine is one of the most
★ appealing of the Left Bank hotels, impeccably luxurious yet oozing charm. The hotel is located on a quiet street between the Seine and the boulevard St-Germain and occupies some precious 16th-century cloisters. The best rooms look out over the central lawn. All are spacious and comfortable, particularly the duplexes on the upper floors. Air-conditioning and double-glazed windows add to their appeal. There's no restaurant, and only guests may use the bar. *3 rue Christine, tel. 43–26–71–80. 38*

rooms and 13 duplexes, all with bath. Facilities: parking, conference room for 15, bar. AE, DC, MC, V.

Expensive **Hôtel d'Angleterre.** Some claim the Hôtel d'Angleterre
★ is the ultimate Left Bank hotel—a little small and shabby, but elegant and perfectly managed. The 18th-century building was originally the British ambassador's residence; later, Hemingway made it his Paris home. Room sizes and rates vary greatly, though all rooms are individually decorated. Some are imposingly formal, others are homey and plain. Ask for one overlooking the courtyard. There's no restaurant, but a small bar has been installed. *44 rue Jacob, tel. 42-60-34-72. 29 rooms with bath. Facilities: bar. AE, DC, MC, V.*

Moderate **Marronniers.** There are few better places in Paris than
★ the Marronniers for great value and atmosphere. Located on appealing rue Jacob, the hotel is reached through a small courtyard. All rooms are light and full of character. Those on the attic floor have sloping ceilings, uneven floors, and terrific views over the church of St-Germain-des-Prés. The vaulted cellars have been converted into two atmospheric lounges. There's a bar but no restaurant. *21 rue Jacob, tel. 43-25-30-60. 37 rooms with bath. Facilities: bar. No credit cards.*

Inexpensive **Dhély's.** Who would have thought that you could find such a reasonably priced hotel so close to the lively, bohemian place St-Michel? Tucked away behind a portico on the tiny rue de l'Hirondelle, the clean, white facade of this hotel is a pleasure to stumble upon. Few of the rooms have showers. Be sure to reserve well in advance. *22 rue de l'Hirondelle, tel. 43-26-58-25. 14 rooms, some with shower. No credit cards.*

7th Arrondissement

Very Expensive **Saint-Simon.** Set back from a peaceful little street leading to boulevard St-Germain, the Saint-Simon is a favorite with American visitors. Parts of the building date back to the 17th century; others date from the 18th. Try for one of the rooms with a terrace; they look over the courtyard and neighboring gardens. There's no restaurant, but there's a pleasant bar and a cellar lounge for breakfast. The regular doubles are significantly less expensive than the suites. *14 rue St-Simon, tel. 45-48-35-66. 29 rooms and 5 suites, all with bath. Facilities: bar. No credit cards.*

Expensive ★ **Université.** This appealingly converted 18th-century town house is located between boulevard St-Germain and the Seine. Rooms have their original fireplaces and are decorated with English and French antiques. Ask for one of the two rooms with a terrace on the sixth floor. Though there's no restaurant, you can rent the vaulted cellar for parties. Drinks and snacks are served all day in the bar or, in good weather, in the courtyard. *22 rue de l'Université, tel. 42–61–09–39. 21 rooms with bath, 7 with shower. Facilities: bar. No credit cards.*

Moderate ★ **Pavillon.** The entrance to the family-run Pavillon lies behind a garden at the end of an alley off rue St-Dominique, guaranteeing peace and quiet. Although some rooms in this former 19th-century convent are tiny, all have been redecorated and feature Laura Ashley wallpaper and old prints. Breakfast is served in the little courtyard in summer. There's no restaurant or bar, but snacks can be served in your room. *54 rue St-Dominique, tel. 45–51–42–87. 18 rooms, most with shower. MC, V.*

8th Arrondissement

Very Expensive ★ **Crillon.** There can surely be no more sumptuous a luxury hotel than this regal mansion overlooking place de la Concorde. The Crillon was founded in 1909 by the champagne family Taittinger (which still runs it) with the express intention of creating the best hotel in the city. They chose as their setting two adjoining town houses built by order of Louis XV. Renovations in the '80s added comfort—all rooms are air-conditioned—though not at the expense of the original imposing interior. Mirrors, marbles, tapestries, sculptures, great sprays of flowers, and glistening floors are found in all the public rooms. The expansive bedrooms have judicious mixtures of original and reproduction antiques. The bathrooms are, of course, marble. If you want to enjoy the amazing view over place de la Concorde to the National Assembly, you'll have to reserve one of the palatial suites. Of the three restaurants, the best is Les Ambassadeurs, housed in what was originally the Grand Salon and offering the best hotel food in the city. *10 pl. de la Concorde, tel. 42–65–24–24. 189 rooms and suites, all with bath. Facilities: 3 restaurants, bars, private reception rooms. AE, DC, MC, V.*

★ **Le Bristol.** Luxury and discretion are the Bristol's trump cards. The understated facade on rue du Faubourg St-Honoré might mislead the unknowing, but the

Bristol ranks among Paris's top four hotels. The air-conditioned and spaciously elegant rooms all have authentic Louis XV and Louis XVI furniture. Moreover, the management has filled the public room with old-master paintings, sculptures, sumptuous carpets, and tapestries. The marble bathrooms are simply magnificent. Nonguests can take tea in the vast garden or dine in the summer restaurant; later, you can listen to the pianist in the bar, open till 1 AM. There's an enclosed pool on the roof, complete with solarium and sauna for guests only. The service throughout is impeccable. *112 rue du Fbg. St-Honoré, tel. 42–66–91–45. 155 rooms and 45 suites, all with bath. Facilities: restaurant, bar, pool, sauna, solarium, parking, conference facilities for 200. AE, DC, MC, V.*

Expensive **Bradford.** The Bradford prides itself on providing slightly old-fashioned, well-polished service, in an appealing, fusty atmosphere, the kind that has many guests coming back year after year. It's no surprise that this is a family-run hotel. An old wooden elevator takes you up to the rooms from the flower-filled lobby. Some are vast, with brass beds and imposing fireplaces. Hardly any have TV; that's not the Bradford style. Drinks are served in the soothing Louis XVI–style lounge on the first floor; there's no restaurant. *10 rue St-Philippe-du-Roule, tel. 43–59–24–20. 36 rooms with bath, 12 with shower. MC, V.*

Moderate **Ceramic.** These are the lowest rates you'll pay this close to the Arc de Triomphe and Champs-Elysées. The hotel sports an impressive 1904 tiled facade that embodies Belle Epoque ambience, and the reception area, replete with crystal chandeliers and velvet armchairs, is glamorous. Those guest rooms that face the street, such as rooms 412, 422, and 442, have huge bay windows and intricate plaster moldings. Rooms facing the courtyard are quiet and rather average. *34 av. de Wagram, tel. 42–27–20–30. 53 rooms with bath or shower. MC, V.*

Inexpensive **Argenson.** This friendly, family-run hotel provides what
★ may well be the best value in the swanky 8th Arrondissement. Some of the city's greatest sights are just a 10-minute walk away. Old-time charm in the form of period furnishings, molded ceilings, and floral arrangements is not compromised by some modern touches, such as the new bathrooms that were installed in 1988. The best rooms are numbers 23, 33, 42, 43, and 53. *15 rue d'Argenson, tel. 42–65–16–87. 48 rooms with bath or shower. DC, MC, V.*

9th Arrondissement

Very Expensive **Grand.** The restoration of the Grand's reception area and honey-colored facade put the final touches on a lengthy renovation program that has transformed this 19th-century palace by place de l'Opéra. All rooms have been lavishly redecorated in Art Nouveau style and are now air-conditioned. The hotel prides itself on its exemplary business facilities, not the least of which are its three restaurants. The Opéra is the most formal and imposing, while the Relais Capucines offers less intimidatingly grand meals; Le Patio serves buffet lunches and breakfast. *2 rue Scribe, tel. 40–07–32–32. 515 rooms and suites with bath. Facilities: 3 restaurants, 2 bars, 13 conference rooms, secretarial services, travel agency, shops, parking. AE, DC, MC, V.*

Moderate **London Palace.** You'll want to stay here for the location, near the Opéra, and for the straightforward, family-run ambience. The mood throughout is strictly functional but perfectly acceptable for a short stay. There's no restaurant or bar. Public parking lots are nearby. *32 blvd. des Italiens, tel. 48–24–54–64. 19 rooms with bath, 30 with shower. AE, MC, V.*

11th Arrondissement

Inexpensive **Résidence Alhambra.** This hotel is on the edge of the his-
★ torical Marais quarter and is conveniently close to five Métro lines. The Alhambra's gleaming white exterior and flower-filled window boxes provide a bright spot in an otherwise drab neighborhood. The smallish guest rooms are painted in fresh pastel shades and have marble-topped breakfast tables. The lobby is filled with plants and leather armchairs. Most rooms have color TV, unusual for hotels in this price range. *13 rue de Malte, tel. 47–00–35–52. 50 rooms, most with bath or shower. MC, V.*

12th Arrondissement

Moderate **Modern Hôtel-Lyon.** Despite its less than inspiring name, the Modern Hôtel-Lyon, located between place de la Bastille and the Gare de Lyon, has been run by the same family since 1910. They pride themselves on maintaining the hotel's reputation for personal service. As part of a floor-by-floor renovation program new wallpaper and carpets were recently installed. Rooms are decorated in beige and cream shades. There's no restaurant, but there's a good bar. *3 rue Parrot, tel. 43–43–41–52. 51 rooms and 1 suite, 36 with bath, 15 with shower. Facilities: bar. AE, MC, V.*

Inexpensive **Jules-César.** The address may be unfashionable, but the Bastille, Jardin des Plantes, and Ile St-Louis are just a short walk away, and the Gare de Lyon is just around the corner. The hotel, built in 1914, has been restored: The lobby is rather glitzy, but the guest rooms are more subdued. Rooms facing the street are larger than those in the back and have a somewhat better view. The largest is room 17, which can accommodate a third bed. *52 av. Ledru-Rollin, tel. 43–43–15–88. 4 rooms with bath, 44 with shower. MC, V.*

14th Arrondissement

Moderate
★ **Royal.** This small hotel, set in a late-19th-century building on attractive boulevard Raspail, has already won much praise, especially from American guests. The mood throughout is stylish yet simple, with salmon-pink rooms, and a wood-paneled, marble-floored lobby filled with plants. You can sit in the small conservatory, where drinks are served; there's no bar or restaurant. *212 blvd. Raspail, tel. 43–20–69–20. 33 rooms and suites with bath, 15 with shower. AE, MC, V.*

Inexpensive **Midi.** This place is close to both Montparnasse and the Latin Quarter, and there are Métro and RER stations nearby. Don't be put off by the nondescript facade and reception area; most of the rooms are adequately furnished, and those facing the street are both large and quiet. Request room 32, if possible, and avoid the cheapest rooms, which are quite dingy and unattractive. *4 av. Réné-Coty, tel. 43–27–23–25. 50 rooms, 20 with bath, 21 with shower. No credit cards.*

16th Arrondissement

Moderate **Queen's Hotel.** One of only a handful of hotels located in the desirable residential district around rue la Fontaine, Queen's is within walking distance of the Seine and the Bois de Boulogne. The hotel is small and functional, but standards of comfort and service are high. Flowers on the facade add an appealing touch. *4 rue Bastien-Lepage, tel. 42–88–89–85. 7 rooms with bath, 15 with shower. MC, V.*

18th Arrondissement

Moderate **Regyn's Montmartre.** Despite small rooms (all recently renovated), this small, owner-run hotel on Montmartre's place des Abbesses is rapidly gaining an enviable reputation for simple, stylish accommodations. A predominantly young clientele and a correspondingly relaxed atmosphere have made this an attractive choice for some. Try for one of the rooms on the upper floors, with great views over the city. *18 pl. des Abbesses, tel. 42–54–45–21. 14 rooms with bath, 8 with shower. MC, V.*

Utrillo. Newly renovated, the Utrillo is on a quiet side street at the foot of Montmartre. The decor is appealing, with prints in every room and a marble-topped breakfast table. Because the color white is emphasized throughout, the hotel seems light, clean, and more spacious than it actually is. *7 rue Aristide-Bruant, tel. 42–58–13–44. 30 rooms with bath or shower. Facilities: sauna. AE, DC, MC, V.*

19th Arrondissement

Inexpensive **Le Laumière.** Though it's located some ways from downtown, the low rates of this two-star hotel, close to the tumbling Buttes-Chaumont park, are hard to resist. Most rooms are functional only, but some of the larger ones overlook the garden. The staff is exceptionally helpful. There's no restaurant, but breakfast is available until midday. *4 rue Petit, tel. 42–06–10–77. 54 rooms, 39 with bath or shower. AE, DC, MC, V.*

4 Excursions

Chantilly and Senlis

Haughty, spacious Chantilly, with its vast woods, classy racecourse, famous Baroque stables, and elegant lake and château, is only 48 kilometers (30 miles) from Paris, yet it attracts far fewer sightseeing hordes than Versailles or Fontainebleau and is a perfect setting for a day away from the capital. A trip here can easily be combined with a visit to old-world Senlis, 10 kilometers (6 miles) to the east, whose crooked, mazelike streets are dominated by the soaring spire of its Gothic cathedral.

Getting There

By Car **From Paris:** Highway A1 runs just past Senlis; Chantilly is 6 miles west along the pretty D924.

From Euro Disney: Take the A4/E50 toward Reims and turn left to Meaux. Follow the road left, then turn right on the N330 to Senlis. Chantilly is 10 kilometers (6 miles) west along the D924. It's about a 90-minute trip.

By Train **From Paris:** Chantilly is 30 minutes from the Gare du Nord; a shuttle bus links Chantilly to Senlis.

Tourist Information

Office du Tourisme, 23 av. Maréchal-Joffre, 60500 Chantilly, tel. 16/44–57–08–58.

Exploring

While the lavish exterior of the **Château de Chantilly** may be overdone—the style is 19th-century Renaissance pastiche—the building itself contains an outstanding collection of medieval manuscripts and 19th-century French paintings, notably by Ingres. *Admission: 30 frs. Open Wed.–Mon. 10–6, 10:30–12:30 and 2–5 in winter.*

Les Grandes Ecuries (the stables), near the château and adjoining the racecourse, are majestic 18th-century buildings housing the **Musée du Cheval** (Museum of the Horse). The spacious stables were built to accommodate 240 horses and more than 400 hounds for stag and boar hunts. *Admission: 40 frs. Open Wed.–Mon. 10:30–6:30 in summer; 2–4:30 Wed.–Fri., 10:30–5 weekends in winter.*

The **Cathédrale Notre Dame** in Senlis (place du Parvis) dates from the second half of the 12th century. The su-

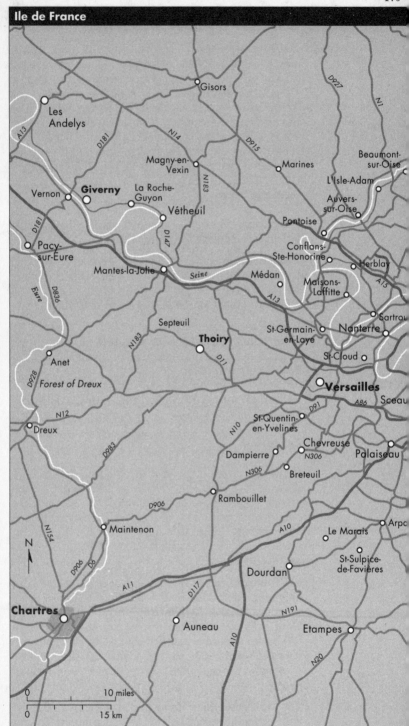

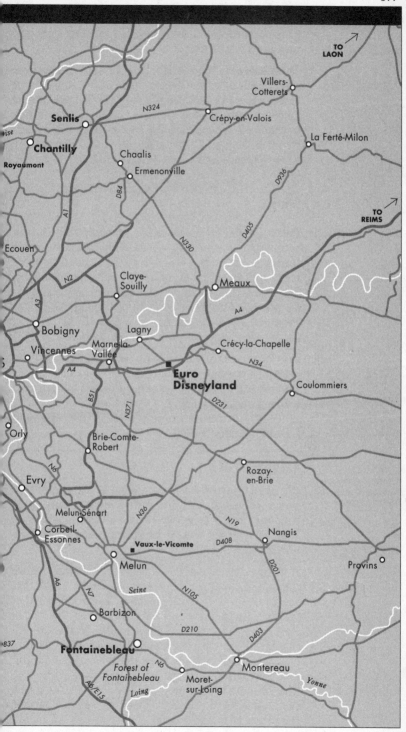

TO
LAON

Villers-
Cotterets

N324

Senlis

Crépy-en-Valois

La Ferté-Milon

Chantilly

Royaumont

Chaalis

Ermenonville

aise

D84

Ecouen

A1

D936

D405

TO
REIMS

N330

N2

A3

Claye-
Souilly

Meaux

Bobigny

Lagny

A4

Vincennes

Marne-la-
Vallée

Euro
Disneyland

Crécy-la-Chapelle

B51

A4

N34

Coulommiers

N371

D231

Orly

Brie-Comte-
Robert

Rozay-
en-Brie

N6

Evry

Melun-Sénart

N36

N19

Nangis

Corbeil-
Essonnes

Vaux-le-Vicomte

D408

D201

Provins

Melun

A6

N7

Seine

N105

Barbizon

D210

D403

•837

Fontainebleau

N6

Forest of
Fontainebleau

Moret-
sur-Loing

Montereau

Yonne

A6/E15

Loing

perb spire—arguably the most elegant in France—was added around 1240. This is one of France's oldest (and narrowest) cathedrals.

The **Musée de la Vénerie** (Hunting Museum), across from the cathedral, within the grounds of the ruined royal castle, claims to be Europe's only full-fledged hunting museum, with related artifacts, prints, and paintings (including excellent works by 18th-century artist Jean-Baptiste Oudry). *Château Royal. Admission: 12 frs. Visits on the hour Thurs.–Sun. 10–5, Mon. 10–3, Wed. noon–5.*

Dining

Chantilly **Relais Condé.** Although this is probably the classiest restaurant in Chantilly—pleasantly situated across from the racecourse—there's a reasonable fixed-price menu (160 francs) that makes it a suitable lunch spot. The food is tasty, straight-forward, and copious. *42 av. du Maréchal-Joffre, Chantilly, tel. 16/44–57–05–75. Reservations essential. Dress: informal. AE, DC, V. Closed Mon., Sun. evening, and Feb. Moderate.*

Senlis **Les Gourmandins.** This is a cozy, two-floor restaurant in old Senlis, serving some interesting dishes and offering a fine wine list. The 100-franc fixed-price menu is a good bet for a weekday lunch. *3 pl. de la Halle, Senlis, tel. 16/ 44–60–94–01. Reservations advised. Dress: informal. AE, MC, V. Moderate.*

Chartres

Although Chartres is chiefly visited for its magnificent Gothic cathedral with its world-famous stained-glass windows, the whole town—one of the prettiest in France, with old houses and picturesque streets—is worth leisurely exploration.

Worship on the site of the cathedral goes back to before the Gallo-Roman period; the crypt contains a well that was the focus of Druid ceremonies. The original cult of the fertility goddess merged into that of the Virgin Mary with the arrival of Christianity. In the late 9th century, King Charles the Bold presented Chartres with what was believed to be the tunic of the Virgin. This precious relic attracted hordes of pilgrims, and Chartres swiftly became—and has remained—a prime destination for the faithful. Pilgrims trek to Chartres from Paris on foot to this day.

The noble, soaring spires of Chartres compose one of the most famous sights in Europe. Try to catch a glimpse of them surging out of the vast golden grainfields of the Beauce as you approach from the northeast, from, say, Rambouillet or Maintenon. (Either spot makes a delightful place to stop on your way to Chartres from Paris. Each has a graceful old château with superb grounds, Rambouillet with its lake and Maintenon with its ruined aqueduct.)

Getting There

By Car **From Paris:** The A11/A10 expressways link Paris to Chartres (55 mi). To get to Rambouillet from Paris, take A13 toward Versailles, then A12 N10 (33 mi). D906 continues to Maintenon (15 mi), then to Chartres (12 mi).

From Euro Disney: Take the A4 into Paris and follow the A11/A10. It's about a two-hour drive.

By Train **From Paris:** There are hourly trains from Paris (Gare Montparnasse) to Chartres (travel time is 50–70 minutes, depending on service), many of which stop at Rambouillet and Maintenon.

Guided Tours

Paris Vision (214 rue de Rivoli, tel. 42–60–31–25) and **Cityrama** (4 pl. des Pyramides, tel. 42–60–30–14) can arrange guided visits to a number of sites in the Paris region. All depart from place des Pyramides (off rue de Rivoli at the Louvre end of the Tuileries Gardens). Both feature half-day trips to Chartres on Tuesday, Thursday, and Saturday afternoons (250 frs); and full-day trips to Chartres and Versailles (395 frs) on the same days.

Tourist Information

Office du Tourisme, pl. de la Cathédrale, 28000 Chartres, tel. 16/37–21–50–00.

Exploring

Today's **Chartres cathedral** is the sixth church to occupy the same spot. It dates mainly from the 12th and 13th centuries, having been erected after the previous, 11th-century building burned down in 1194. A well-chronicled outburst of religious fervor followed the discovery that the Virgin's relic had miraculously survived unsinged. Reconstruction went ahead at a breathtaking pace. Just 25 years were needed for Chartres cathedral to rise again, and it has remained substantially unchanged ever since.

The lower half of the facade is all that survives from the 11th-century Romanesque church. (The Romanesque style is evident in the use of round, rather than pointed, arches.) The main door—the **Portail Royal**—is richly sculpted with scenes from the Life of Christ. The flanking towers are also Romanesque, though the upper part of the taller of the two **spires** (380 feet as against 350 feet) dates from the start of the 16th century, and its fanciful flamboyance contrasts with the stumpy solemnity of its Romanesque counterpart. The **rose window** above the main portal dates from the 13th century. The three windows below it contain some of the finest examples of 12th-century stained glass in France.

The interior is somber, and your eyes will need time to get used to the darkness. Their reward will be a view of the gemlike richness of the stained glass, with the famous deep "Chartres blue" predominating. Window-by-window cleaning, a laborious process, has recently been completed. The oldest window, and perhaps the most stunning, is *Notre Dame de la Belle Verrière* (literally, Our Lady of The Beautiful Window), in the south choir. It is well worth taking a pair of binoculars to pick out the details. If you wish to know more about stained-glass techniques and the motifs used, visit the small exhibit in the gallery opposite the north porch.

The vast black-and-white medieval pattern on the floor of the nave is the only one of its kind to have survived from the Middle Ages. The faithful were expected to travel along its entire length (some 300 yards) on their knees.

Guided tours of the crypt start from the Maison des Clercs opposite the south front. The Romanesque and Gothic chapels running around the crypt have recently been stripped of the 19th-century paintings that used to disfigure them. You will also be shown a 4th-century Gallo-Roman wall and some 12th-century wall paintings.

Just behind the cathedral stands the **Musée des Beaux-Arts,** a handsome 18th-century building that used to serve as the bishop's palace. Its varied collection includes Renaissance enamels, a portrait of Erasmus by Holbein, tapestries, armor, and some fine, mainly

French paintings of the 17th, 18th, and 19th centuries. There is also a room devoted to the forceful 20th-century works of Maurice de Vlaminck, who lived in the region. *29 cloître Notre Dame. Admission: 10 frs adults, 5 frs students. Open Wed.–Sat. and Mon. 10–11:45 and 2–5:45, Sun. 2–4:45.*

The museum gardens overlook the old streets that tumble down to the river Eure. Take rue Chantault down to the river, cross over, and head right, along rue de la Tannerie (which becomes rue de la Foulerie) as far as rue du Pont St-Hilaire. From here, there is a picturesque view of the roofs of old Chartres nestling beneath the cathedral. Then cross the bridge and head up to the **Eglise St-Pierre,** whose own magnificent windows date back to the early 14th century. There is yet more stained glass (17th century) to admire at the **Eglise St-Aignan** nearby, just off rue St-Pierre.

Wander among the steep, narrow streets, with the spires of the cathedral as your guide. Near the station is the striking monument to Jean Moulin, martyred World War II Resistance hero and onetime prefect of Chartres.

The river Eure snakes northeast from Chartres to the town of **Maintenon,** whose Renaissance **château** once belonged to Louis XIV's mistress, Madame de Maintenon (her private apartments are open to visitors). A round brick tower (14th century) and a 12th-century keep remain from previous buildings on the site. The formal gardens stretch behind the château to the ivory-covered arches of the ruined **aqueduct**—one of the Sun King's most outrageous projects. His aim: to provide Versailles (30 miles away) with water from the Eure. In 1684, some 30,000 men were signed up to construct a three-tier, 3-mile aqueduct as part of this project. Many died of fever before the enterprise was called off in 1688. *Admission: 25 frs. Open Wed.–Mon. 2–6, 2–5 in winter.*

Rambouillet, surrounded by a huge forest, is a town once favored by kings and dukes; today it is the occasional home of the French president. When he's not entertaining visiting dignitaries here, the **château** and its extensive **grounds** (lake, islands, and flower beds) are open to the public. Most of the buildings date from the early 18th century, but the bulky **Tour François Ier,** named after the king who breathed his last here in 1547, once belonged to a 14th-century castle. *Admission: 22 frs adults, 12 frs senior citizens. Open Wed.–Mon. 10–11:30 and 2–5:30.*

Dining

Chartres **La Vieille Maison.** Situated close to Chartres cathedral, in the same narrow street as Le Buisson Ardent (*see below*), La Vieille Maison is an intimate spot centered around a flowery patio. The menu changes regularly but invariably includes re gional specialties such as asparagus with chicken, and truffles. Prices, though justified, can be steep; the 160-franc menu is a good bet. *5 rue au Lait, tel. 16/37–34–10–67. Reservations advised. Jacket and tie required. AE, DC, MC, V. Closed Mon., Sun. evening. Moderate–Expensive.*

Le Buisson Ardent. This wood-beamed restaurant offers attentive service, fixed-price menus, imaginative food, and a view of Chartres cathedral. Try the chicken ravioli with leeks or the rolled beef with spinach. *10 rue au Lait, tel. 16/37–34–04–66. Reservations advised. Dress: informal. AE, DC, V. Closed Sun. evening. Inexpensive–Moderate.*

St-Symphorien **Château d'Esclimont.** This is a magnificent restored Renaissance château, 4 miles west of the Ablis exit on expressway A11 and about 15 miles from both Rambouillet and Chartres. Set in luxuriant grounds, with lawns and lake, this member of the Relais et Châteaux chain is a regular target for high-profile Parisian businessmen. The cuisine is sophisticated and varied: Quail, rabbit fricassee, and lobster top the menu. *St-Symphorien-le-Château, tel. 16/37–31–15–15. Reservations essential. Dress: jacket and tie required. MC, V. Expensive.*

Fontainebleau

Fontainebleau, with its historic château, is a favorite place for excursions, especially since a lush forest (containing the painters' village of Barbizon) and the superb château of Vaux-le-Vicomte are close by.

Like Chambord in the Loire Valley or Compiègne to the north of Paris, Fontainebleau earned royal esteem as a hunting base. As at Versailles, a hunting lodge once stood on the site of the current château, along with a chapel built in 1169 and consecrated by exiled (later murdered and canonized) English priest Thomas à Becket. The current building was begun under the flamboyant Renaissance king, François I, the French equivalent, and contemporary, of England's Henry VIII.

Sun King Louis XIV's architectural fancy was concentrated on Versailles (itself inspired by Vaux-le-Vicomte), but he commissioned Mansart to design new pavilions at Fontainebleau and had Le Nôtre replant the gardens. However, it was Napoleon who made a Versailles, as it were, out of Fontainebleau, by spending lavishly to restore it to its former glory. He held Pope Pius VII prisoner here in 1812, signed the second Church-State concordat here in 1813, and, in the cobbled Cour des Adieux, bade farewell to his Old Guard in 1814 as he began his brief exile on the Mediterranean island of Elba.

Another courtyard—the Cour de la Fontaine–was commissioned by Napoleon in 1812 and adjoins the Etang (or lake) des Carpes. Ancient carp are supposed to swim here, although Allied soldiers drained the pond in 1915 and ate all the fish, and, in the event they missed some, Hitler's hordes did likewise in 1940.

Getting There

By Car **From Paris:** Take A6 then N7 to Fontainebleau from the Porte d'Orléans or Porte d'Italie (72 kilometers [45 miles] from Paris). N7 runs close to Barbizon, 8 kilometers (5 miles) northwest of Fontainebleau. Vaux-le-Vicomte, near Melun, is 21 kilometers (13 miles) north of Fontainebleau. Take N6 north to Melun, then N36 (northeast), turning right 3 kilometers (2 miles) out of Melun along D215.

From Euro Disney: Follow the A4/E50 toward Paris and turn left immediately onto the N371 to Melun, then take the N6. The trip is less than an hour's drive.

By Train **From Paris:** Fontainebleau is about 50 minutes from the Gare de Lyon; take a bus to complete the trip from the station to the château. Barbizon and Vaux-le-Vicomte are not accessible by train.

Guided Tours

Paris Vision and **Cityrama** offer half-day trips to Fontainebleau and Barbizon *(see* Guided Tours in Chartres, *above,* for addresses). Cost: 270 frs. Departures 1:30 Wed., Fri., and Sun.

Tourist Information

Office du Tourisme, 31 pl. Napoléon-Bonaparte, Fontainebleau, tel. 16/64–22–25–68.

Exploring

The **château of Fontainebleau** dates from the 16th century, although additions were made by various royal incumbents over the next 300 years. The famous **horseshoe staircase** that dominates the Cour du Cheval Blanc (which later came to be called the Cour des Adieux, or Courtyard of Farewell) was built by du Cerceau for Louis XIII (1610–1643). The **Porte Dauphine,** designed by court architect Primaticcio, is the most beautiful of the various gateways that connect the complex of buildings; its name commemorates the fact that the Dauphin—the male heir to the throne, later Louis XIII—was christened under its archway in 1606.

Napoleon's apartments occupied the first floor. You can see a lock of his hair, his Légion d'Honneur medal, his imperial uniform, the hat he wore on his return from Elba in 1815, and the one bed in which he definitely did sleep (almost every town in France boasts a bed in which the emperor supposedly spent a night). There is also a throne room—one of Napoleon's foibles, as the earlier kings of France had been content with the one at Versailles—and the **Queen's Bedroom,** known as the room of the six Maries (occupants included ill-fated Marie Antoinette and Napoleon's second wife, Marie-Louise). The endless **Galerie de Diane,** built during the reign of Henri IV (1589–1610), was used as a library. Highlights of other salons include 17th-century tapestries, marble reliefs by Jacquet de Grenoble, and paintings and frescoes by the versatile Primaticcio.

The jewel of the interior, though, is the ceremonial ballroom, or **Salle de Bal,** nearly 100 feet long and dazzlingly furnished and gilded. It is luxuriantly wood-paneled, and a gleaming parquetry floor reflects the patterns in the ceiling. Like the château as a whole, the room exudes a sense of elegance and style—but on a more intimate, human scale than at Versailles: This is Renaissance, not Baroque. *Admission: 25 frs adults, 13 frs ages 18–25 and senior citizens; 13 frs Sun. Open Wed.–Mon. 9:30–12:30 and 2–5; gardens open 9–dusk (admission free).*

On the western edge of the 42,000-acre Forest of Fontainebleau lies the village of **Barbizon,** home to a number of mid-19th-century landscape artists, whose innovative outdoor style paved the way for the Impressionists. Corot, Millet, Rousseau, Daubigny, and Diaz, among others, all painted here, repairing to **Père Ganne's Inn** after working hours to brush up on their social life. The inn still stands—it's been converted into an art gallery—and you can soak up the arty mood here and at the houses of Millet and Rousseau farther along the single main street (rue Grande). *Musée Auberge du Père Ganne, 92 rue Grande. Admission free. Open Wed.–Mon. 10–5:30; Wed., Fri., and Sun. only in winter.*

North of Fontainebleau stands the majestic château of **Vaux-le-Vicomte,** started in 1656 by court finance wizard Nicolas Fouquet. The construction process was monstrous: Villages were razed, then 18,000 workmen were called in to execute the plans of designers Le Vau, Le Brun, and Le Nôtre and to prove that Fouquet's aesthetics matched his business acumen. Unfortunately, his political savvy was less apparent. The housewarming party was so lavish that star guest Louis XIV, tetchy at the best of times, threw a fit of jealousy. He hurled Fouquet in the slammer and promptly began building Versailles to prove just who was boss.

Entry to the high-roofed château is from the north. Decoration of the cupola, in the **salon,** was halted at Fouquet's arrest. Le Brun's major contribution is the ceiling of the **Chambre du Roi,** depicting *Time Bearing Truth Heavenwards.* The word "squirrel" in French is *écureuil,* but locals call squirrels—which are portrayed along the frieze—*fouquets.* The kitchens and archive room can be visited in the basement.

Le Nôtre's carefully restored **gardens** contain statues, waterfalls, and fountains, and provide fine views. There is also a **Musée des Equipages**—carriages, saddles, and smithy—on the grounds. *Admission: 42 frs adults, 34 frs students. Grounds only: 20 frs. Château open daily 10–6; 11–5 in winter. Closed Dec./Jan. except Christmas/New Year's. Candlelight visits May–Sept., Sat. evenings 8:30–11.*

Dining

Barbizon **Le Relais.** Solid home-cooked meals are served alfresco. Among the offerings are duckling with cherries and lamb with parsley. Expect crowds in midsummer. The five-course, 145-franc weekday menu is excellent value. *2 av. Charles-de-Gaulle, Barbizon, tel. 60–66–40–28. Reservations advised. Dress: informal. MC, V. Closed Tues. and Wed., last 2 weeks in Aug., and most of Jan. Moderate.*

Fontainebleau **Le Beauharnais.** Conveniently situated in the Aigle Noir hotel opposite Fontainebleau château, this recently restored restaurant offers imaginative nouvelle cuisine dishes, including calf sweetbread with prawns and duck with marjoram, in a grand setting. Set menus are priced at 220 and 300 francs, and there's a tranquil garden for alfresco dining in summer. *27 pl. Napoléon-Bonaparte, Fontainebleau, tel. 64–22–32–65. Reservations recommended. Jacket and tie required. AE, DC, MC, V. Expensive.*

Giverny

This charming village in southern Normandy has become a place of pilgrimage for art lovers. It was here that Claude Monet lived for 43 years, dying in 1926 at the age of 86. After decades of neglect, his pretty pink house with green shutters, his studios, and, above all, his garden with its famous lily pond have been lovingly restored—thanks to gifts from around the world and in particular from the United States. Late spring is perhaps the best time to visit, when the apple trees are in blossom and the garden is a riot of color; however, Giverny is worth a day trip from Paris at least into mid-autumn.

Monet was brought up in Normandy and, like many of the Impressionists, was attracted by the soft light of the Seine Valley, north of Paris. After several years at Argenteuil, just north of Paris, he moved downriver to Giverny in 1883 along with his two sons, his mistress Alice Hoschedé (whom he later married), and her six children. By 1890, a prospering Monet was able to buy the house outright. Three years later, he purchased another plot of land across the road to continue his gardening experiments, diverting the river Epte to make a pond.

The water lilies and Japanese bridges became special features of Monet's garden and now help to conjure up an image of the bearded brushman dabbing cheerfully at his canvases—capturing changes in light and weather in a way that was to have a major influence on 20th-century art. From Giverny, Monet enthusiasts may want to continue up the Seine Valley to the site of another of his celebrated painting series: Rouen cathedral. (The *Water Lilies—Nymphéas* in French—can be seen in Paris at the Orangérie and Marmottan museums, and the cathedral series can be seen at the Musée d'Orsay.)

Getting There

By Car **From Paris:** Take expressway A13 from Paris to the Vernon exit (D181). Cross the Seine in Vernon and follow D5 to Giverny.

From Euro Disney: For the first leg of this two-hour trip take the A4/E50 into Paris, then the A13.

By Train **From Paris:** Take the train from Gare St-Lazare to Vernon (50 min). Giverny is a 6-kilometer (3½-mile) walk or a taxi ride away.

Guided Tours

Guided excursions are organized by **American Express** (11 rue Scribe, tel. 42–66–09–99) and the **RATP** (pl. de la Madeleine), on either a half-day or full-day basis, combined with trips to Rouen.

Exploring

Monet's house has a warm family feeling that may come as a welcome break after visiting formal French châteaux. The rooms have been restored to Monet's original designs: the kitchen with its blue tiles, the buttercup-yellow dining room, and Monet's bedroom on the second floor. You will see the Japanese prints Monet collected so avidly and reproductions of his own works displayed around the house. His studios are also open for viewing. The garden, with flowers spilling out across the paths, is as cheerful and natural as the house—quite unlike formal French gardens. The enchanting water garden, with its lilies, bridges, and rhododendrons, is across the road. *84 rue Claude Monet. Admission: 30 frs. Open Apr.–Oct., Tues–Sun. 10–noon and 2–6.*

Dining

Douains **Château de Brécourt.** This 17th-century brick château, set in extensive grounds, is a member of the stylish Relais & Châteaux chain and lies 11 kilometers (7 miles) west of Giverny (via D181 at Douains, near Pacy-sur-Eure). Creative dishes in an august setting make

Brécourt a popular spot for people who drive to Giverny. The menu includes lamb in basil and turbot with caviar, as well as a dessert of pears in a flakey pastry roasted in honey. *Tel. 16/32–52–40–50. Reservations advised. Dress: informal. AE, DC, MC, V. Expensive.*

Giverny **Les Jardins de Giverny.** This new restaurant is close to Monet's house, and the old-fashioned dining room overlooks a rose garden. Tourists who lunch here are treated to inventive dishes such as scallops with mushrooms or seafood terrine with a mild pepper sauce. *1 rue du Milieu, tel. 16/32–21–60–80. Reservations advised. Dress: casual. AE, MC, V. Closed Sun. evening, Mon., and Feb. Moderate.*

Reims and Laon

Champagne and cathedrals make a trip to the renowned city of Reims and the lesser-known town of Laon an ideal two-day break from the French capital. Reims is the capital of the champagne industry. Several major producers have their headquarters here, and you will not want to miss the chance to visit the chalky, labyrinthine champagne cellars that tunnel beneath the city. Reims cathedral, one of the most historic in France, was the setting for the coronations of French kings (Charles X was the last to be crowned here, back in 1825). Despite some indifferent 20th-century rebuilding, Reims is rich with attractions from Roman times to the modern era. Laon, which occupies a splendid hilltop site 40 kilometers (25 miles) northwest of Reims, is known as the "crowned mountain" on account of the many-towered silhouette of its venerable cathedral. This enchanting old town could easily be turned into one of France's leading tourist traps, were lethargic local authorities not firmly locked into the past: Laon was once, after all, the capital of France—almost 12 centuries ago.

Getting There

By Car **From Paris:** Expressway A4 goes via Reims on its way east from Paris to Strasbourg. The Belgium-bound N2 links Paris to Laon. Expressway A26 links Laon and Reims—a 40-kilometer (25-mile) trip.

From Euro Disney: The A4/E50 goes directly to Reims in less than two hours; from there, take the A26 to Laon.

By Train **From Paris:** Scheduled trains cover the 177 kilometers (110 miles) from Paris (Gare de l'Est) to Reims in 90 minutes. The Paris–Laon route (from the Gare du Nord) takes up to two hours. Trains run daily between Laon and Reims.

Tourist Information

Office du Tourisme, 2 rue Guillaume-de-Machault, 51000 Reims, tel. 16/26–47–25–69; place du Parvis, 02000 Laon, tel. 16/23–20–28–62.

Exploring

The glory of Reims's **Cathédrale Notre Dame** is its facade. Its proportions are curiously deceptive, and the building is actually considerably larger than it appears. Above the north (left) door is the **Laughing Angel,** a delightful statue whose famous smile is threatening to turn into an acid-rain scowl—pollution has succeeded war as the ravager of the building. The postcard shops nearby have views of the cathedral after World War I, and on seeing the destruction, you'll understand why restoration here is an ongoing process. The high, solemn **nave** is at its best in the summer, when the lower walls are adorned with 16th-century tapestries relating the life of the Virgin. The east-end **windows** were designed by Marc Chagall. Stand beneath them, look back toward the west end, and admire the interplay of narrow pointed arches of differing sizes.

With the exception of the 15th-century **towers,** most of the original building was constructed in the hundred years after 1211. A stroll around the outside will reinforce the impression of the harmony and discipline of its lines, which almost belie its decorative richness. The east end presents an idyllic vista across well-tended lawns. There are spectacular light shows both inside (40 frs) and outside (free) the cathedral in July and August.

The **Palais du Tau** next door is the former archbishop's palace and affords excellent views of the cathedral. It contains tapestries, coronation robes, and several outstanding statues removed for safekeeping from the cathedral's facade. *2 pl. du Cardinal-Luçon. Admission: 24 frs adults, 13 frs senior citizens, 6 frs children under 18. Open daily 10–noon and 2–6; 10–noon and 2–5 in winter.*

The nearby **Musée St-Denis,** Reims's fine art museum, has an outstanding painting collection crowned by 27 Corots and David's celebrated portrait of Revolutionary leader Marat dead in his bath. Nine Boudins and Jongkinds are among the finer Impressionist works here. *8 rue Chanzy. Admission: 15 frs. Open Wed.– Mon. 10–noon and 2–6.*

As you leave the museum, turn right and continue along rue Chanzy/rue Gambetta to the 11th-century **Basilique St-Rémi,** devoted to the 5th-century saint who gave his name to the city. The building is nearly as long as the cathedral, and its interior seems to stretch away into the dim distance. The Gothic choir area has much original 12th-century stained glass. *Rue Simon.*

Several champagne producers run tours of their **champagne cellars,** combining video presentations with guided walks through their cavernous, chalk-hewn, underground warehouses. Few producers show much generosity when it comes to pouring out samples of their noble liquid, so we recommend you double back across town to **Mumm,** which does. (*34 rue du Champ-de-Mars. Open weekdays 9:30–noon and 2–5:30; closed in winter*). If you don't mind paying for samples, however, the most spectacular cellars are those of Taittinger. (*9 pl. St-Nicaise. Open daily 9–11 and 2–5; closed weekends in winter*).

Across from the Mumm Cellars is a modern **chapel** decorated by the contemporary Paris-based Japanese artist, Foujita. Head down rue du Champ-de-Mars toward the railroad station, turn right onto avenue de Laon, then left onto rue Franklin D. Roosevelt. A short way along is the **Salle de Guerre,** where Eisenhower established Allied headquarters at the end of World War II. It was here, in a well-preserved, map-covered room, that the German surrender was signed in May 1945. *Open Wed.– Mon. 10–noon and 2–6. Admission: 14 frs, 7 frs children.*

The **Porte Mars** is an impressive Roman arch that looms up just across from the railroad station. It is adorned by faded bas-reliefs depicting Jupiter, Romulus, and—of course—Remus.

Visitors interested in the history of World War I may want to visit the **chemin des Dames,** a section of the road between Reims and Laon. The disastrous French offensive launched here by General Nivelle in April 1917 led to futile slaughter and mutiny. Take N44 from Reims to Corbény, then wind your way for some 27 kilometers (17 miles) along D18/D985 west, past Cerny-en-Laonnois, until it meets N2, which heads north to Laon, 12 miles away.

Laon's **Cathédrale Notre Dame** was constructed from 1160 to 1235 and is a superb example of early Gothic style. The light, recently cleaned interior gives the impression of immense length (120 yards in total). The flat ceiling at the east end—an English-inspired feature—is unusual in France. The second-floor galleries that run around the building are typical of early Gothic; what isn't typical is that you can actually visit them (and the towers) with a guide from the Tourist Office on the cathedral square. The airy elegance of the five remaining towers is audacious by any standard, and rare: French medieval architects preferred to concentrate on soaring interiors and usually allowed for just two towers at the west end. You don't have to be an architectural scholar to appreciate the sense of movement about Laon's west-end facade compared with the more placid, two-dimensional feel of Notre Dame in Paris. Also look for the stone bulls protruding from the towers, a tribute to the stalwart beasts who carted the blocks of stone from quarries far below.

The medieval **ramparts,** the old fortification walls, lie virtually undisturbed by passing traffic and provide a ready-made route for a tour of old Laon. Another notable and well-preserved survivor from medieval times is the **Chapelle des Templiers,** a small octagonal 12th-century chapel on the grounds of the town museum. *Admission: 9 frs. Open Wed.–Mon. 10–noon and 2–6; 10–noon and 2–5 in winter; closed Tues.*

Dining

Laon La Petite Auberge. You can expect some imaginative nouvelle dishes from young chef Marc Zorn in this 18th-century-style restaurant close to the station in Laon's *ville basse* (lower town). Fillet of plaice with champagne vinegar and tuna with horseradish sauce are among the choices. The 150-franc menu is a good lunchtime bet. *45 blvd. Pierre-Brossolette, tel. 16/23–23–02–38. Reservations recommended. Dress: informal. AE, DC, V. Moderate.*

Reims Boyer. Gérard Boyer is one of the most highly rated chefs in France. Duck, foie gras in pastry, and truffles (served in a variety of ways) figure among his specialties. The setting, not far from the Basilique St-Rémi, is magnificent, too: a 19th-century château, built for the champagne firm Pommery, surrounded by an extensive, well-tended park. *Les Crayères, 64 blvd. Henry-Vasnier, tel. 16/26–82–80–80. Reservations essential. Jacket and tie required. AE, DC, MC, V. Closed Mon., Tues. lunch, Christmas, and New Year's. Very Expensive.*

Florence. An old, high-ceilinged mansion is the setting for this elegant and well-run restaurant. Chef Jos Bergman serves wonderfully light versions of classical French dishes—and at fair prices (two set menus for 200 and 280 francs). *43 blvd. Foch, tel. 16/26–47–12–70. Reservations advised. Dress: informal. AE, DC, MC, V. Closed Sun. eves. and most of Aug. Moderate.*

Lodging

Laon **Paix.** The Paix is a modern, central hotel with stylish rooms, a pleasant little garden, and a swimming pool. The Drouet restaurant serves up good but not inexpensive cuisine (closed Sun.). *52 rue St-Jean, 16/23–23–21–95. 15 rooms, all with either bath or shower plus minibar and television. Facilities: restaurant, swimming pool. AE, DC, V. Moderate.*

Bannière de France. This comfortable old hotel, just five minutes' walk from Laon cathedral, is favored by British travelers, perhaps because Madame Lefèvre speaks English well and offers a cheerful welcome. There is a venerable dining room where you can enjoy sturdy cuisine (trout, guinea-fowl) at unbeatable value. *11 rue Franklin-Roosevelt, tel. 16/23–23–21–44. 18 rooms, not all with bath or shower. AE, DC, MC, V. Facilities: restaurant. Closed Christmas and New Year's. Inexpensive.*

Reims **Gambetta.** This hotel near Reims cathedral has small, fairly basic rooms and a decent restaurant, the Vonelly (closed Sun. evening, Mon., and Aug.), which serves such specialties as scallop salad with spinach and fillet of duck with onions. *9 rue Gambetta, tel. 16/26–47–41–64. 14 rooms with shower. Facilities: restaurant. AE, MC, V. Inexpensive.*

Thoiry

Thoiry, 40 kilometers (25 miles) west of Paris, is an ideal day-trip destination, especially for families with children. It offers a splendid combination of history and culture—chiefly in the form of a superbly furnished 16th-century château with its own archives and gastronomy museum—and outdoor adventure. Its safari park boasts over 800 animals and is a great place to picnic; drinks and snacks can be bought here, too.

Getting There

By Car **From Paris:** Take highway A13 then highway A12 from Paris to Bois d'Arcy, then take N12 toward Dreux. Just past Pontchartrain, D11 heads off right toward Thoiry.

From Euro Disney: Follow the A4 to Paris, then follow directions as from there.

By Train **From Paris:** From Gare Montparnasse to Montfort-L'Amaury (35 min), then a 10-minute taxi ride. A special shuttle bus operates to and from the château on Sundays in summer.

Exploring

The **château** was built in 1564. Its handsome Renaissance facade is set off by **gardens** landscaped in the disciplined French fashion by Le Nôtre; there is a less formal Jardin à l'Anglaise (English Garden) for contrast. Owners Vicomte de La Panouse and his American wife, Annabelle, have restored the château and grounds to their former glory and opened both to the public. Highlights of the **interior** include the grand staircase, the 18th-century Gobelins tapestries in the dining room that were inspired by the adventures of Don Quixote, and the Green and White Salon with its old harpsichord, portraits, and tapestries.

The distinguished history of the Panouse family—one member, Comte César, fought in the American Revolution—is retraced in the **Archive Museum,** where papal bulls, Napoleonic letters, and Chopin manuscripts (discovered in the attic in 1973) are displayed side by side with missives from Thomas Jefferson and Benjamin Franklin.

Since 1984, the château pantries have housed a **Museum of Gastronomy,** whose *pièces montées* (banquet showpieces) re-create the designs of the premier 19th-century chef, Antoine Carême (his clients included George IV of England and the emperors of Austria and Russia). One is over 5 meters (15 feet) high and took eight months to confect. Engravings, old copper pots, and early recipe books are also on display.

You can stroll at leisure around the picturesque grounds, stopping off at the Pré Angélique to watch a cricket match (summer weekends) and admiring giraffes, wolves, and—from the safety of a raised footbridge—the world's first *ligrons*, crosses between a lion and a tiger. There is an exploratory play area for children, featuring giant burrows and cobwebs. For obvious reasons, pedestrians are not allowed into the Bear Park or the African Reserve. Keep your car windows closed if you want to remain on peaceful terms with marauding lions, rhinos, elephants, and mega-horned Watutsi cattle. *Château Admission: 23 frs. Château park and game reserve admission: 84 frs adults; first two children 69 frs, thereafter free. Open weekdays 10–6, weekends 10–6:30 in summer; 10–5 in winter.*

Dining

The château's **self-service restaurant** in the converted 16th-century stables (same hours as the safari park) offers a palatable choice of fixed-price meals. Cold starters include salami, tomato salad, and green salad; the main course may be roast chicken, veal with mushrooms, steak and chips, or andouillette. *Inexpensive.*

Etoile. This restaurant, belonging to a three-star hotel, is situated just 300 yards from the château along the main street. There is a special tourist menu as well as a wide choice of à la carte selections. Filling, traditional French dishes are served: steak, chicken, fish, and pâté. *38 rue de la Porte St-Martin, tel. 34–87–40–21. Reservations advised. Dress: informal. AE, DC, MC, V. Closed Mon. and Jan. Inexpensive.*

Versailles

Paris in the 17th century was a rowdy, rabble-ridden city. Louis XIV hated it and lost no time in casting his royal eye over the Ile-de-France in search of a new power base. Marshy, inhospitable Versailles, 24 kilometers (15 miles) to the west, was the site he chose.

Today, the château of Versailles seems monstrously big, but it wasn't large enough for the sycophantic army of 20,000 noblemen, servants, and hangers-on who moved in with Louis. A new city—a new capital, in fact—had to be constructed from scratch to accommodate them. Vast mansions had to be built, along with avenues broader than the Champs-Elysées—all in an extravagant Baroque style.

It was hardly surprising that Louis XIV's successors rapidly felt uncomfortable with their architectural inheritance. Indeed, as the 18th century wore on, and the taste for intimate, private apartments expanded at the expense of the public, would-be heroic lifestyles of 17th-century monarchs, subsequent rulers built themselves small retreats on the grounds, where they could escape the overpowering formality of court life. The two most famous of these structures are the **Petit Trianon,** built by Louis XV and a model of classical harmony and proportion; and the simple, "rustic" **Hameau,** or hamlet, that Marie Antoinette built so that she could indulge her desire to play at being a simple shepherdess.

The contrast between the majestic and the domesticated is an important part of Versailles's appeal, but pomp and bombast dominate the mood here, and you won't need reminding that you're in the world's grandest palace—or one of France's most popular tourist traps. The park outside is the ideal place to get your breath back. Le Nôtre's gardens represent formal landscaping at its most rigid and sophisticated.

Getting There

By Car **From Paris:** Take highway A13 from Porte d'Auteuil then follow the signs to Versailles.

From Euro Disney: Take the A4 and turn left onto the A86 to Creteil/Orly just before you reach Paris, then follow the signs to Versailles.

By Train **From Paris:** There are three train routes from Paris to Versailles (20–30 min). The RER-C to Versailles Rive-Gauche takes you closest to the château (just 549 meters [600 yards] from it via avenue de Sceaux). The other trains run from Gare St-Lazare to Versailles Rive-Droite (1 kilometer [⅔ mile] via rue Foch and avenue de St-Cloud), and from Gare Montparnasse to Versailles-Chantiers (1¼ kilometer [¾ mile] via rue des Etats Généraux and avenue de Paris).

From Euro Disney: Take the RER-A to Châtelet-les-Halles, then the C line to Versailles Rive Gauche or Versailles-Chantiers.

Guided Tours

Paris Vision and **Cityrama** (*see* Guided Tours in Chartres, *above*, for addresses) offer half- and full-day guided bus tours of Versailles, Fontainebleau, Barbizon, and Chartres. Trips cost from 180 francs (half day) to 300 francs (full day).

Tourist Information

Office de Tourisme, 7 rue des Réservoirs, tel. 39–50–36–22.

Exploring

The **château** was built under court architects Le Vau and Mansart between 1662 and 1690; entrance is through the gilt-and-iron gates from the huge place d'Armes. In the center of the building, across the sprawling cobbled forecourt, are the rooms that belonged to the king and queen. The two wings were occupied by the royal children and princes; attendants were housed in the attics.

The highlight of the tour, for many, is the **Galerie des Glaces** (Hall of Mirrors), now fully restored to its original dazzle. It was here that Bismarck proclaimed the unified German Empire in 1871, and here that the controversial Treaty of Versailles, asserting Germany's responsibility for World War I, was signed in 1919.

The royal bedchambers are formal; the **petits appartements,** where royal family and friends lived, are more on a human scale. The miniature **opera house,** set within the first oval room in France, was built by Gabriel for Louis XV in 1770. The chapel, built by Mansart, is a study in white-and-gold solemnity. *Admission to château: 30 frs; Sun. 15 frs. Open Tues.–Sun. 9–7 (5:30 in winter); closed Mon.*

The 250-acre **grounds** include woods, lawns, flower beds, statues, lakes, and fountains. They are at their best in the fall. The fountains play on several Sundays in summer, making a fabulous spectacle. *The grounds are free and open daily.*

At one end of the Petit Canal, about a mile from the château, stands the **Grand Trianon,** built by Mansart in the 1680s. This pink-marble pleasure palace is now used to entertain visiting heads of state; at other times it is open to the public. *Admission: 20 frs joint ticket for Grand and Petit Trianons; 10 frs Sun. Open Tues.–Sun. 11–12:30 and 2–5:30.*

The **Petit Trianon,** close by, is a sumptuously furnished 18th-century mansion containing mementos of Marie Antoinette, its most famous inhabitant. The grounds include the so-called hamlet *(hameau)* with watermill, lake, and pigeon loft—outrageously pretty and too good to be true. *Open Tues.–Sun. 2–5; closed Mon.*

The town of Versailles tends to be underestimated. Visitors are usually exhausted from exploring the palace and park, but the town's spacious, leafy boulevards are also agreeable places to stroll. The **Cathédrale St-Louis** is an austere edifice built from 1743 to 1754 by Mansart's grandson, and it contains fine paintings and an organ loft. The **Eglise Notre Dame** is a sturdy Baroque monument, built from 1684 to 1686 by the elder Mansart as the parish church for the Sun King's new town, for which Louis XIV deigned to lay the foundation stone. The collection of the **Musée Lambinet,** housed nearby in an imposing 18th-century mansion, is wide-ranging, with a maze of cozy, finely furnished rooms full of paintings, weapons, fans, and porcelain. *54 blvd. de la Reine. Admission free. Open Tues.–Sun. 2–6; closed Mon.*

Dining

Les Trois Marches. This is one of the best-known restaurants in the Paris area. It was recently relocated to the sumptuous Trianon Palace Hotel, near the château park. Chef Gérard Vié specializes in nouvelle cuisine dishes such as lobster with tomato. The great style that reigns here can be experienced less expensively by coming for the fixed-price (260 frs) weekday lunch. *1 blvd. de la Reine, tel. 39–50–13–21. Reservations essential. Jacket and tie required. AE, DC, MC, V. Closed Sun. and Mon. Very Expensive.*

Potager du Roi. This restaurant is owned by a former chef of Les Trois Marches, so quality is assured. The novelle menu includes lamb kidneys with cabbage and fresh pasta with cockles and mussels. The enclosed terrace is a friendly setting. Fixed menus are 120 and 165 francs. *1 rue du Maréchal-Joffre, tel. 39–50–35–34. Reservations advised. Dress: informal. MC, V. Closed Sun. and Mon. Moderate.*

Quai No. 1. Barometers, sails, and model boats contribute to the salty decor at this small, charming fish and seafood restaurant. Home-smoked salmon is a specialty here, though any dish on the two set menus will prove to be a good value. *1 av. de St-Cloud, tel. 39–50–42–26. Reservations advised. Dress: casual. MC, V. Closed Sun. evening and Mon. Moderate.*

Index

Personal Itinerary

Departure *Date*

Time

Transportation

Arrival *Date*   *Time*

Departure *Date*   *Time*

Transportation

Accommodations

Arrival *Date*   *Time*

Departure *Date*   *Time*

Transportation

Accommodations

Arrival *Date*   *Time*

Departure *Date*   *Time*

Transportation

Accommodations

Personal Itinerary

Arrival	*Date*	*Time*
Departure	*Date*	*Time*
Transportation		
Accommodations		

Arrival	*Date*	*Time*
Departure	*Date*	*Time*
Transportation		
Accommodations		

Arrival	*Date*	*Time*
Departure	*Date*	*Time*
Transportation		
Accommodations		

Arrival	*Date*	*Time*
Departure	*Date*	*Time*
Transportation		
Accommodations		

Fodor's Travel Guides

U.S. Guides

Alaska

Arizona

Boston

California

Cape Cod, Martha's
Vineyard, Nantucket

The Carolinas & the
Georgia Coast

Chicago

Disney World & the
Orlando Area

Florida

Hawaii

Las Vegas, Reno,
Tahoe

Los Angeles

Maine, Vermont,
New Hampshire

Maui

Miami & the Keys

New England

New Orleans

New York City

Pacific North Coast

Philadelphia & the
Pennsylvania Dutch
Country

San Diego

San Francisco

Santa Fe, Taos,
Albuquerque

Seattle & Vancouver

The South

The U.S. & British
Virgin Islands

The Upper Great
Lakes Region

USA

Vacations in New York
State

Vacations on the
Jersey Shore

Virginia & Maryland

Waikiki

Washington, D.C.

Foreign Guides

Acapulco, Ixtapa,
Zihuatanejo

Australia & New
Zealand

Austria

The Bahamas

Baja & Mexico's
Pacific Coast Resorts

Barbados

Berlin

Bermuda

Brazil

Budapest

Budget Europe

Canada

Cancun, Cozumel,
Yucatan Penisula

Caribbean

Central America

China

Costa Rica, Belize,
Guatemala

Czechoslovakia

Eastern Europe

Egypt

Euro Disney

Europe

Europe's Great Cities

France

Germany

Great Britain

Greece

The Himalayan
Countries

Hong Kong

India

Ireland

Israel

Italy

Italy's Great Cities

Japan

Kenya & Tanzania

Korea

London

Madrid & Barcelona

Mexico

Montreal &
Quebec City

Morocco

The Netherlands
Belgium &
Luxembourg

New Zealand

Norway

Nova Scotia, Prince
Edward Island &
New Brunswick

Paris

Portugal

Rome

Russia & the Baltic
Countries

Scandinavia

Scotland

Singapore

South America

Southeast Asia

South Pacific

Spain

Sweden

Switzerland

Thailand

Tokyo

Toronto

Turkey

Vienna & the Danube
Valley

Yugoslavia

Special Series

Fodor's Affordables

Affordable Europe

Affordable France

Affordable Germany

Affordable Great Britain

Affordable Italy

Fodor's Bed & Breakfast and Country Inns Guides

California

Mid-Atlantic Region

New England

The Pacific Northwest

The South

The West Coast

The Upper Great Lakes Region

Canada's Great Country Inns

Cottages, B&Bs and Country Inns of England and Wales

The Berkeley Guides

On the Loose in California

On the Loose in Eastern Europe

On the Loose in Mexico

On the Loose in the Pacific Northwest & Alaska

Fodor's Exploring Guides

Exploring California

Exploring Florida

Exploring France

Exploring Germany

Exploring Paris

Exploring Rome

Exploring Spain

Exploring Thailand

Fodor's Flashmaps

New York

Washington, D.C.

Fodor's Pocket Guides

Pocket Bahamas

Pocket Jamaica

Pocket London

Pocket New York City

Pocket Paris

Pocket Puerto Rico

Pocket San Francisco

Pocket Washington, D.C.

Fodor's Sports

Cycling

Hiking

Running

Sailing

The Insider's Guide to the Best Canadian Skiing

Fodor's Three-In-Ones (guidebook, language cassette, and phrase book)

France

Germany

Italy

Mexico

Spain

Fodor's Special-Interest Guides

Cruises and Ports of Call

Disney World & the Orlando Area

Euro Disney

Healthy Escapes

London Companion

Skiing in the USA & Canada

Sunday in New York

Fodor's Touring Guides

Touring Europe

Touring USA: Eastern Edition

Touring USA: Western Edition

Fodor's Vacation Planners

Great American Vacations

National Parks of the West

The Wall Street Journal Guides to Business Travel

Europe

International Cities

Pacific Rim

USA & Canada

WHEREVER YOU TRAVEL, *H*ELP IS NEVER FAR AWAY.

From planning your trip to providing travel assistance along the way, American Express® Travel Service Offices* are always there to help.

EURO DISNEY

American Daro Voyages
Disneyland Hotel
Marne La Vallee
1-60-456-520

PARIS

11 Rue Scribe
1-47-777-707

83 Bis, Rue De Courcelles
1-47-66-0300

5 Rue De Chaillot
1-47-23-7215

38 Avenue De Wagram
1-42-27-5880

155 Avenue Victor Hugo
1-47-27-4319